WHAT WILL PEOPLE THINK?

*To Phylis & Doug,
There's a story
in all of us
Love, Judy*

What Will People Think?

A MEMOIR

JUDY OPP HOOFF

LUMINARE PRESS
WWW.LUMINAREPRESS.COM

What Will People Think? A Memoir
Copyright © 2023 by Judy Opp Hooff

All rights reserved. This book or any portion thereof may not be reproduced or used in any manner whatsoever without the express written permission of the publisher, except for the use of brief quotations in a book review.

Printed in the United States of America

Luminare Press
442 Charnelton St.
Eugene, OR 97401
www.luminarepress.com

LCCN: 2023912207
ISBN: 979-8-88679-227-0

*With love to my husband,
children and grandchildren*

*and in memory of my parents,
Edna and Alvin (Ally)*

Contents

Introduction 1

CHAPTER ONE
Ancestral History 3

CHAPTER TWO
Homesteading in America 14

CHAPTER THREE
1930's–40's 23

CHAPTER FOUR
Early Childhood—Eureka 30

CHAPTER FIVE
Life on the Farm 47

CHAPTER SIX
Starting School 77

CHAPTER SEVEN
Winter on the Plains 91

CHAPTER EIGHT
Spring and Summer of 1951 109

CHAPTER NINE
Helfenstein Household 138

CHAPTER TEN
Summer—1952 164

CHAPTER ELEVEN
1953 175

CHAPTER TWELVE
Health Concerns 189

CHAPTER THIRTEEN
Moving to Oregon 198

CHAPTER FOURTEEN
Teenage Years. 220

CHAPTER FIFTEEN
College and Career. 252

CHAPTER SIXTEEN
Marriage 263

CHAPTER SEVENTEEN
Children 277

CHAPTER EIGHTEEN
Reflections. 287

Introduction

What made me decide to write about my childhood and life so far? When I have shared childhood memories with friends throughout the years, they've seemed amused to hear about my experiences growing up in rural South Dakota. Occasionally people have commented, "You were like Laura Ingalls, in *Little House on the Prairie*." There were striking similarities; although I grew up many generations later, I was most definitely on the same Dakota prairie.

As time goes by, it seems I've become more reflective and nostalgic about my early childhood. Sharing significant events in my life, and particularly my formative years, is something I'd thought about, but finding the right time and beginning to write proved to be more challenging. While working through the grieving process after my father's death in 1995 and thinking about my loss, I recalled vivid memories of my childhood. It felt like the right time to share my story, but where would I begin? Having an interest in genealogy and being curious about my ancestors' arrivals in the United States, I decided to begin my writings with a brief background of the Opp and Neuharth lineages. I am fortunate to have documented reference material, and I'm pleased to share a portion of our treasured ancestral history with you.

As I began my memoirs I was surprised to find it easier to write in longhand rather than using my laptop. Initially I

Introduction

wrote for six hours without putting my pen down! I understand this part of the writing process is referred to as "the zone." It felt as though my hand couldn't move across the paper fast enough—being totally absorbed in my writing, I'd lost all awareness of time! There was an initial sense of pride and accomplishment, and I'd discover the process to be very cathartic. However, sometime in the early stages I got writer's block and was unable to continue until I made some difficult decisions. Was I going to recount only the pleasant memories of my childhood, or would I also be able to reveal some troublesome recollections? As a result, my writings were put aside for several years.

So here I am, a bit older and possibly wiser, understanding that if I'm to tell my story it's important to reveal the complete account. Admittedly there are doubts, but I've come to understand that first and foremost, I need to write my story for myself. Becoming a grandparent may have also brought me back to my memoirs, since our grandson appeared interested in the stacks of legal pads filled with cursive writing! After reading several farm stories to Ryder, he seemed curious about my early childhood. Sharing accounts of growing up on the plains of South Dakota is important, but I'm also hoping to convey a sense of ancestry to my children and grandchildren. I now have time to devote to this project and believe my writings may be one of the best gifts I can give them.

CHAPTER ONE

Ancestral History

Ryder was curious at age seven, and I was about the same age when I began to ask questions regarding my ancestral history. Most often my questions were directed to Grandpa Opp, since I thought he might have the answers—he was one of the oldest people I knew! I was curious about family left behind when his parents emigrated from Russia to the United States. There were questions about why they left their homeland, how many family members were left behind, did they write to each other and did he think they would ever see each other again? Being naturally inquisitive, I had many questions, but mostly I recall being a bit dissatisfied with Grandpa's answers. He spoke only German and understood limited English, and he seemed to avoid my questions. Grandpa's standard response was "That was a long time ago," or "We didn't ask our parents all those questions!"

Growing up in this German-Russian community I learned that topics of a particularly delicate nature weren't to be discussed. The Opp family specifically avoided sensitive issues and conflicts, which maybe was not that unusual for earlier generations. Nonetheless, whenever I got too close to uncomfortable subject matter, I instinctively knew when to back off! This behavior was also evident with my parents: conversation moved along comfortably until unpleasant subject matter was raised. I learned to avoid exchanges that might be too confrontational, resulting in some unresolved issues throughout the years.

It's possible Grandpa didn't know about family left behind in Russia because he was only three years old when his family immigrated to America. When old enough to ask the same questions, he too may have realized certain topics weren't to be discussed. Presumably our ancestors had distressing memories of leaving many family members behind as they left their homelands. Ultimately, Grandpa told me this was our home in America and I wasn't to ask so many questions about the past.

We're fortunate to have considerable paternal history of both the Opp and Neuharth families. The early lineage of the Opp ancestry has been traced to the Alsace region of France, dating back to the fifteenth century. Our ancestors inhabited this area for several centuries until Napoleon's armies ravished the Alsace countryside, which was then a German territory. The French government attempted to force the Germans to give up their language and customs. As conditions became intolerable, people feared for their lives, prompting many families to flee in the middle of the night! One such family was an ancestor by the name of Heinrich Opp. He and his family left Alsace for Wurttemburg, Germany in 1784. The descendants of Heinrich Opp included a son by the name of Urban, who would eventually emigrate to Russia in 1803–04.

The following two paragraphs are excerpts from a booklet titled *Neuharth* written by Walter D. Neuharth, my father's first cousin. "The Neuharth family originated in the village of Neuharth, known today as Karlsdorf-Neuthard, a municipality of Germany. Their lineage is traced to the 1100's. Conrad Neuharth's name was found in records dating to 1140. He was an armorer and became very proficient in his art. Emperor Frederick I elevated him to the dignity of a patrician and gave him a coat of arms. He resided in the province of Zweibrüken, Germany. Conrad was elected to the senate of the Holy Roman Empire and married Martha Buck. They had two sons, Ulrich and Casper, who also became armorers. Conrad died in 1191 as chief master of the Armorers Guild. His son Casper received the same honors as his father and purchased an estate in Zweibrüken, and he died in 1236. Casper's son, George, managed the estate of his father and married Martha Dauer. After his death in 1280 the estate was left to his three sons, Andrew, Veit, and Michael. Andrew made an agreement with his brothers and purchased the estate, giving them money for their share. The brothers apparently squandered their portion of the inheritance, and they both died in poverty. Andrew prospered and purchased additional property. He married Anna Frank and died in 1317. His descendants continued to flourish as landlords. The Neuharth years of 1140–1317 have been substantiated by the *Pastor Mizer Report*, which verifies authentic sources taken from "European Armor and Genealogy" in *Biblia Vien, Book VII*, page 209, in Vienna, Austria. Regrettably, records of the Neuharth family are missing from the years 1317 to 1595. All events, births, baptisms, marriages, and deaths between 1595 and 1809 were obtained through a genealogist in Vienna, Austria."

AFTER COMPLETING RESEARCH OF THE NEUHARTH lineage, Walter accumulated additional data which led him to the small village of Rumbach, Germany. He discovered this to be his ancestors' home until they migrated to the Odessa region of Russia, where they lived from 1809 through 1874. Walter established contact with members of the Neuharth family on his first trip to Rumbach in 1973. During his second visit in 1977, additional ancestral information was obtained from distant cousins living in the area. The Neuharth booklet is found in my library detailing comprehensive history, research, sources, photos, and the family tree.

A large number of both Opp and Neuharth ancestors fled Germany after 1809. Catherine the Great had proclaimed a homestead act granting the Germans religious freedom, one hundred acres of land, tax exemption for ten years, and immunity from military service. The requirements were that they be married, be in good health, and have 300 gulden ($120.00). Applications were made by members of both families, but some were refused because of health reasons. The arduous, 1500-mile journey to Russia was made by oxcart. For the next seventy years our ancestors sought a livelihood by cultivating the difficult land referred to as the steppes. Unfortunately, during Czar Alexander II's reign from 1855–1881, all privileges granted by Catherine the Great were revoked. The German colonists of Southern Russia lost all special rights; they were now obliged to become Russianized! The thought of trading their language and cultural identity for that of the Russians was asking too much, so they began searching for a new life. Their destination was America.

Reaching the decision to leave Russia may not have been difficult for my great-grandparents—history tells us the life they'd been subjected to was intolerable. Much like their ancestors who had uprooted their families when they left Germany years earlier, it was now their time to do the same. In making that courageous decision to leave Russia most family members were left behind, which must have been very unsettling. Privileges had been revoked by Alexander II, but there were other reasons our ancestors were motivated to leave Russia. Records indicate they were also fleeing disease, famine, and religious persecution, all well-founded motives for seeking new opportunities in America.

For immigrants willing to pursue a new beginning in the United States, the 1884 Homestead Act was enacted, allowing settlers to claim land consisting of 160 acres. After building a permanent structure and establishing residency, immigrants were able to purchase land for $1.25 per acre. My paternal great-grandparents, Daniel Jr. and Katherine (Gohl) Opp, took advantage of this opportunity. They were part of the massive immigration movement to America which took place in the late 1800's.

Arrival of Russian immigrants to Eureka, South Dakota

When Daniel Jr. and Katherine settled in the Dakota Territory, a wooden-shanty structure measuring twelve by fourteen feet was constructed on the land they'd claimed. This temporary dwelling is where their family of eight lived for six months! Mud-sod homes were typically the first shelters built, and they were common across the plains. Unfortunately, cold winter weather had arrived by the time my ancestors reached their final destination, so constructing a mud-sod shelter wouldn't be possible. Sod shelters were preferable, as they offered better insulation from the elements; instead, a one-room wooden structure provided housing during their first winter on the frigid plains of the Dakota Territory. A cookstove was used for warmth and cooking. Limited firewood, dried reeds, and animal manure were used to fuel the stove. The family survived that first brutal winter, but the close living quarters proved to be very confining!

What Will People Think?

I thought it would be of interest to share a small portion of my great-uncle's memoirs. Daniel was the oldest son of my great-grandparents and Grandpa Opp's oldest brother. His writings began around 1920 and continued through the early fifties until his death. In reading Daniel's composition I was amazed at his command of the English language, and found his writing ability to be impressive despite having had only a few years of formal education. Daniel begins his memoirs with his earliest recollections of immigrating to the United States.

"It was in the year 1884, when the great immigration took place from South Russia to the Dakota Territory and the wholly unknown far North America. In the beginning of September, 27 families from the colony of Gluckstal shook the Russian dust from their feet, and began the journey to free America; among them were our parents. I was a boy of twelve years of age, when we left the place, where my cradle stood, which will always remain dear to my memory. I have had no more education since that time, and any deficiency in writing must be attributed to it.

Our journey progressed nicely, so that after twenty-one days, we arrived at our destination, namely Menno, South Dakota. From there the immigrants scattered in all directions. We, and our neighbor John Nies, were received into the home of my father's cousin at Menno, but for only the short duration of two weeks. It soon developed that there were no more free homesteads to be taken up in that part of the state. For that reason, George G. Neuharth and several other families had come up from Menno in the spring of 1884 and had already settled in which is now McPherson County, in the northern part of South Dakota. In May 1884 Valentine Mettler and George G. Neuharth were the first German-Russians to set foot in McPherson County. When our father and J. Nies heard of this new settlement they could no longer be detained, and they bought a couple of oxen, a cow, a wagon, a breaking plow, and some provisions. All was loaded into a railcar, and we were on the way to Frederick, South Dakota, which at the time was the nearest railroad station to McPherson County. Having arrived there, supplies were unloaded as quickly as possible; the wagon was set up and loaded with the goods. While all this was underway, we boys herded the oxen, and when we looked about, we noticed that not far from us three wagons, to which oxen were hitched, made halt. We also noticed by their language that they were some of our kinsmen, so we reported this to our parents. And what did we discover? They were acquaintances from our old home, who, during the summer, had settled sixty miles west of Frederick. Naturally, we were greatly elated to find acquaintances in a strange land, who could show us the way to the new settlement.

    In the meantime, evening had approached; but regardless of that, we decided to go as far as the Elm River, six miles distant, where the other three teams agreed to overtake us that night, which they did. Having arrived at the Elm River we made camp, and it was the first night that we arranged our night quarters on the wild prairie under the clear heavens. All went well, for it was not cold. The next morning we continued our journey, always toward the unknown west; and since we were heavily loaded, we could cover only twenty-six miles a day. This time we remained overnight at Koto, six miles north from Leola. Here we found a store, a post office, and several other small buildings. Up to this time the weather was nice. The land was level, but all had been taken up. The next morning after breakfast we started out again. But, alas, one of our neighbor's oxen had gone lame, and consequently we could proceed only slowly and some of our acquaintances left us.

Five miles west of Koto the hills began, and we drove all day without seeing any living being. Nothing but dismal hills which were covered with stones and bones. Who would have believed it at the time, that any human beings would live here in a desert that had been forsaken not only by Indians, but also by the wild animals? That they had been here was evidenced by the many and untimely unbleached bones. In the meantime, night had descended again, and the time had arrived to prepare our night quarters on the wild prairie under the stars. We had a little hay left, but we needed that for food for our cattle, so nothing was left for us but the bare ground, which was sufficiently large for us. After we had eaten our evening meal, we were supposed to go to sleep. We, the twelve children of the two families, lay in the middle, and our parents on both sides of us. After the customary evening blessings, which the mothers invoked upon their wards, we soon would have been overcome by sleep; but here on the open prairie, that was quite another matter.

It was a cold, frosty, October night, and we noticed that our mothers, more in a sitting than in a reclining position, watched over us, asking now this, now that child, if it was cold, which we older children constantly denied. We could clearly see by the bright moonlight how the tears, like pearly dewdrops, rolled down the cheeks of our mothers. Yes, those were pioneer days. That we were on our feet early the next morning, the dear reader may imagine, for the black prairie was covered with frost. The lake, near which we camped, was frozen so hard that we could hardly water our cattle. We had neither wood nor any other kind of fuel with which to build a fire to warm ourselves. In all haste we devoured our bread with tears and then continued into the blackened hills. At noon we could look west from Long Lake, South Dakota, into our promised land, which we reached at three o'clock in the afternoon. We had arrived at our destination!"

Daniel's writings have been a treasured gift for his descendants, but I was disappointed to learn there was no mention of his early life, their departure from Russia, or the family's passage to America. It's quite possible that the memory of leaving family behind and their departing voyage was too troubling for Daniel to record. Again, very telling of the family's reluctance to address unpleasant matters. Daniel's recollections of early pioneer days in South Dakota are included in a booklet titled *Origin & History of the Christian D. Opp Family*.

My great-great-grandparents, George and Barbara (Schnabel) Neuharth were born in Kassel, Southern Russia in 1836 and 1839. Their oldest son George, my great-grandfather, was born in 1861. His mother died when he was only three years old. George's father would marry Elizabeth Rosin, and the family began their immigration to America in 1874 with their three children when George was twelve years old. They were the first of the Neuharth ancestry to take up a homestead under the Homestead Act. There'd be six more children born to my great-great-grandparents in the following years.

It was desirable for immigrants to follow families and relatives who'd already settled in various locations of the United States. Familiarity of language, religion, and customs helped them better acclimate to their new surroundings. However, for the first settlers arriving on this barren land, life was far more difficult. While reading several stories of early settlers, one stated, "As we first laid eyes on the Dakota prairie, we thought it seemed only fit for buffalo, jackrabbits, and an occasional lost Indian!" Families that followed had been informed of the harsh living conditions and made aware of challenges they'd likely encounter, but many immigrants were unprepared for what they found when they arrived. For most, there wasn't the option of returning to their homelands—life was far more difficult where they'd come from. I understand some people had very unrealistic expectations of living conditions in America, with a few being so naive as to believe the streets were paved with gold!

CHAPTER TWO

Homesteading in America

Upon their arrival to America, my ancestors were told the Dakota Territory had a similar climate to Russia for farming. Being familiar with working the land in their homeland, the plains of Dakota seemed a promising place to begin their new lives. Of course they knew there were no streets where they were headed, much less streets paved with gold! Instead, what greeted them was brutal cold, illness, and challenging conditions which tested their endurance. Only the very fittest survived those first few years of living off the land. Hard work, determination, and faith in their religious convictions kept them focused on their dreams of a better life in this new country. Homesickness must have been a common occurrence for the first few families that arrived, but the thought of returning to their homeland wasn't an option, even if it was desired. Grandpa was right: they were in America now—this was their new home!

Great-Grandpa George Neuharth married Christine Goerhing in Menno, South Dakota in 1883. Christine had immigrated to America with her parents at the age of sixteen.

The following year they acquired land in McPherson County about fourteen miles northeast of what would become Eureka. During the first few years, supplies were obtained in the settlements of Frederick and Ipswich, South Dakota. The expansive prairie had an abundance of buffalo bones, which were the stock-in-trade. Animal bones were dried and charred, and they produced a substance called bone black. Coarsely crushed, it filtered impurities out of sugarcane juice, leaving a clear liquid that evaporated to pure white sugar. Bone black was also used as a pigment for paints, dyes, cosmetics, and as a lubricant for iron and steel forging. Bones were picked off the vast prairie, loaded on wagons, hauled to the distant towns, and bartered for provisions. A wagonload of Buffalo bones varied from eight to twelve dollars in value.

In 1887, Great-Grandpa was one of several men who founded my hometown of Eureka. Located in north-central South Dakota, this German-Russian community derived its name from a Greek exclamation meaning "I have found it!" Great-Grandpa George was a farmer, and after breaking ground on their homestead his first crop was flax. It's been noted that he had only hand tools to bring in his first harvest. Lack of implements hindered progress and at times cultivating the land was temporarily delayed due to extreme weather conditions. The winters of 1886 and 1889 were particularly severe due to heavy snowfall; he spoke of the challenges caring for his seventy-five head of cattle in those difficult conditions. Massive amounts of snow often covered the entire house, making it necessary to tunnel from the house to the barn. As snowbanks became hard it wasn't unusual for livestock to walk over the tops of buildings! Although hardships were discouraging, each year brought some progress. My great-grandparents' oldest daughter

Christina, my grandmother, was the first baby girl born in McPherson County. They would have fourteen children. Tragically, seven died in infancy and as youngsters, including two sons and a daughter who died within a three-day period during the diphtheria epidemic of 1898.

In the early 1900's my great-grandparents' son George contracted tuberculosis, so the family relocated to Lodi, California in 1905. It was determined that a change in climate might be better for his son's health. While living in Lodi Great-Grandpa developed an interest in the local wine, and after procuring knowledge from several local vintners he began to make his own wine. It was a time when wine making was very much in its infancy in Northern California. Sadly, young George's health declined. He passed away within a year, and the family returned to Eureka. Once back home, Great-Grandpa was actively engaged in the wholesale wine industry with former associates in California, and he continued to have wine transported by rail until prohibition was declared. During the forties and fifties he again attempted to practice his wine-making skills. Not always having California grapes available for wine making, he utilized what little fruit was available on the plains: cherries, chokecherries, and crab apples were often used. I remember tasting some of Great-Grandpa's more "unusual" varieties, such as dandelion, radish, and rhubarb wine! Despite lacking the good grapes, wine making continued to be an interest for the remainder of his life.

What Will People Think?

Great-grandparents, George and Christina Neuharth

During his lifetime Great-Grandpa devoted a great deal of his time to farming and carpentry, as well as numerous civic activities. Serving as the first chairman of the Eureka Hospital Association, he was also a bank director and a city alderman for several terms. After my great-grandmother's death in 1937 he no longer had a permanent home. It was common for elderly family members to spend several weeks or longer with each of their children and many grandchildren. For the last ten years of his life he would travel from one home to the next. It's been noted that his children were given much of their inheritance when he retired—I understand Great-Grandpa regretted that decision! He frequently quoted a German proverb which inferred you shouldn't give away your wealth until death; the English translation implied, "keep your eyes wide open until you fall asleep!"

Great-Grandpa George visited us for a week or so every summer. I recall that he wore a three-piece black suit, white shirt, black tie, and dressy black bowler hat every day! His very small suitcase always contained a bottle of homemade wine. I'd watch him drink a juice glass of his wine each morning. He attributed his longevity to the nectar of the gods, and clearly it worked for him. Reportedly, he'd been ill for only three weeks prior to his death. It was his first time being hospitalized or under doctor's care. Great-Grandpa had reached the age of ninety-six.

My mother's family, the Helfensteins and Wolfs, were also originally from Germany. Presumably both families made the same journey from Germany to Russia as my paternal ancestors, also taking advantage of the Homestead Act offered by Catherine the Great. There are records of my great-grandfather Gottfried Helfenstein's birth in Neusatz, Southern Russia in 1863. We know he lost his parents as a child and often spoke of spending his early years living with strangers. Gottfried married Katherine Heinle on Oct. 22, 1886 in Johannestal, Southern Russia. My grandfather, also named Gottfried, was born in Southern Russia in 1893. He was one of three children born in Russia before the family immigrated to America in 1895. The Helfenstein homestead was established three miles south of the North Dakota border. Five more children were added to their family before my great-grandmother died in 1910; after her death my great-grandfather married Katherina Schock in 1911.

On January 5, 1919 my grandfather Gottfried was married to Eva Wolf, daughter of Christian F. Wolf, Sr. and Christina (Schmidt) Wolf of Long Lake, South Dakota. Eva was born on September 12, 1898 in Russia. My grandparents took over the farm after Gottfried Sr.'s death in 1934, and eight children including my mother were raised there. In 1947 my grandparents retired to Eureka, and their son Walter and his wife Edna continued to farm the Helfenstein homestead.

Regrettably, we lack extensive history of my maternal ancestry, but while researching the Helfenstein name I discovered it to be a German noble family during the High and late Middle Ages. I understand there may have been considerable prosperity, but lacking ancestral history I'm uncertain if there's a relationship with our family. Several castles still bear the Helfenstein name, and one fortified castle remains above the city of Geislingen an der Steige, in the Baden-Württemberg area of Germany.

In my writings I've included the unusual circumstances regarding my maternal great-grandmother Wolf's immigration to America. It's been rumored that she experienced troubling personal situations prior to her arrival in America. Our family can only speculate about the events regarding Great-Grandma's history. Noting the personality difference between my mother's and father's families, it's not surprising we lack information regarding my great-grandmother's immigration, as well as significant details of my maternal ancestors. It seemed the Helfenstein-Wolf families were more practical in their thinking; they appeared to be far more concerned about the present and future, rather than documenting ancestral historical events of their past.

Reflecting on Daniel Opp's memoirs, he wrote of crop failures, prairie fires, and brutally cold winters. He mentioned how their survival skills were tested, recalling illnesses such as diphtheria and the flu epidemic of 1918 which took numerous members of his family. Infant mortality was very high, and he spoke of the many women who died in childbirth. Lives were lost because there weren't doctors in the first few years to care for the sick, and midwives provided care until the turn of the century. I understand my great-grandmother Helfenstein was a midwife and considered a healer. She supposedly had great success helping people with her remedies long before the first doctors began to practice medicine in the region.

My mother recalled that her grandmother's treatments and cures worked surprisingly well, and she often spoke of a remedy to treat sore throats. A dirty sock (it had to be your own sock) containing garlic cloves was worn around one's neck at bedtime. Mom claimed her sore throat usually disappeared by the next morning! It's been noted that the first doctor to establish his practice in the community frequently referred patients to my great-grandmother, because she was apparently successful in treating many of their ailments. A number of traditional beliefs and convincing cures were handed down to family members; a cure for treating warts involved tying off a wart with silk thread. As a child I remember my mother tying a silk thread over a wart on my finger. The thread was then buried in the yard, and as it disintegrated, my wart mysteriously vanished! It's quite possible Mom inherited some of her grandmother's healing abilities! Another treatment involved rubbing a wart with a bleached bone found on the prairie. The bone was tossed behind one's back, making certain they didn't watch where it landed—as if by magic, the wart disappeared!

Our ancestors dealt with distressing hardships, which was never more prevalent than during the flu epidemic of 1918. The dreaded disease of diphtheria also claimed many lives during that period. As a result of the many deaths, families were brought together quickly if there was a death of a spouse. If a woman died from disease or childbirth it wasn't unusual for the widower to promptly remarry, because men typically didn't have the required skills to care for young children or maintain a household. Likewise, women who'd lost their husbands needed to marry for the economic security of their children.

It was common to have large families in that era; an average-sized family might include ten or twelve children. Large families were needed to help work the crops, tend livestock, and of course care for younger children. My great-aunt Katherine Neuharth actually gave birth to nineteen children! I remember her to be small in stature; it's doubtful she weighed more than 120 pounds. Surprisingly, fourteen of her children lived to adulthood, and she lived to be ninety years old! My father stated he never saw his aunt in a non-pregnant state. While raising all those children, families somehow managed to care for one another.

After several decades, farming proved to be profitable for most immigrants who had settled in the rural community of Eureka. Along with bountiful crops came more adequate housing, health care, and better education for their children. Soon, hundreds of small farms dotted the countryside of McPherson County, South Dakota. Eureka began to thrive, primarily because of the rich soil and abundant wheat crops. At the height of prosperity, forty-two grain houses handled four million bushels of wheat a year. Facilities employed over two hundred men during the industrious wheat production. Grain sacks were hauled from grain houses to railroad cars. The new Chicago, Milwaukee, and St. Paul rail system was built to transport bountiful wheat harvests to larger cities. Eureka became a prosperous, bustling community during this period, with earnings of over

$100,000 a month at the profitable grain station. In the late 1800's Eureka had the distinction of being featured in *Life* magazine as being the "Wheat Capital of the World!"

Grain Houses in late 1800's

Clearly, my ancestors and fellow immigrants had brought their knowledge of farming from their homeland. With oxen and hand tools they'd successfully transformed the once-barren land into a rich, vibrant, and productive soil. Sadly, this bustling town once known for its prosperous wheat production began a slow decline. This part of Eureka's history is unclear; references have been made that removal of the railroad accounted for a reduction in wheat production and prosperity. I'm uncertain of what prompted removal of the railroad. Eureka was at the end of the rail line when it was constructed. The railroad disappeared many years ago, as did the distinction of being the "Wheat Capital of the World."

CHAPTER THREE

1930's–40's

In the following decades my great-grandparents' and grandparents' lives were considerably easier, but that changed as the stock market crash of 1929 plunged our country into a deep depression. What closely followed was the severe drought of the thirties, often referred to as the "dust bowl" and the "dirty thirties!" This bleak period tested the endurance of the entire nation. It was particularly devastating for farmers; sustained high temperatures, extreme drought, and poor land-management practices led to a severe economic impact. During the decade-long drought, huge dust storms in the central plains caused rich topsoil on once fertile land to disappear, resulting in the inability to produce crops. My mother would speak of raging wind and choking black dust storms blocking the sun for several days at a time! They made attempts to keep dust from entering their house by placing wet towels around windows and doors, but their efforts were in vain; floors, furniture, and even dishes inside kitchen cupboards were covered with the fine black dust. Throughout the breadbasket of America countless farmers left their land during this dismal period, often migrating west with their families in search of employment.

Our family persevered through those difficult times. Living off the land enabled them to have several cows, a few pigs, chickens, and a small vegetable garden. The need to conserve well water and lack of sufficient grassland for animals limited the amount of livestock, but it was adequate to sustain their family at the onset of the depression. To make matters worse, the meager crops across the plains were decimated by a grasshopper infestation in 1931! As a final insult, prairies in the dust-bowl states were overrun with hundreds of thousands of jackrabbits when pastures dried up. They devoured everything edible, including the bark off trees and fence posts! The devastating outcome deprived farm animals of badly needed grains to survive, so a mixture of sorghum and thistles was fed to the few livestock that remained.

Despite the grim outlook of the economic crisis, our family was able to deal with the resulting hardship. There were shortages of certain foods, but I've been told they never experienced hunger—people in large cities weren't always as fortunate. Bartering during this severe economic period became a practical way of doing business. Highway 45 was being constructed in 1934 and '35; it was one of the many WPA (Works Progress Administration) projects across the country during the decade-long depression. The work crew set up their campsite about a quarter mile from the Helfenstein homestead, which was located next to the highway. My grandmother was hired to cook the evening meal for ten to fifteen workers each day for several weeks. I understand she earned one dollar per plate, which was thought to be a considerable amount of money during the depression. My mother would've been about fourteen years old at the time, so I'm sure she helped grandma with all that cooking.

As the drought ended, farmland became more productive through soil conservation programs and proper land use. During this time my grandpa Helfenstein began to do custom threshing for the large farming community, because he was one of only a few farmers who owned a threshing machine. Prosperity slowly returned after the decade-long depression, and farmers remaining in the region were again able to produce abundant crops. Unfortunately, on the heels of the depression our country was thrown into World War II following an attack on Pearl Harbor on December 7th, 1941. Throughout the duration of the war our country again experienced food shortages. There was rationing of certain food items such as sugar, coffee, and fresh fruit, as well as many durable goods. I've been told our family dealt with the adversity; they learned to cope with food shortages and became accustomed to ration books, as did most families across the country. I understand it was a time in history when our nation was unified and willing to make sacrifices for the common good. People simply adjusted to doing without certain items for the extent of the war, and our family once again experienced the advantages of living off the land.

By the mid-fifties, farming continued to be lucrative and productive for large farming operations, but it was less profitable for smaller independent farms. Drastic weather events and crop failures were more devastating for smaller enterprises. Farming was and still is considered a risky venture; it's very weather dependent and continues to be a challenging career. Several cousins of my generation returned to their family farms after college. For the few that chose farming as their livelihood, I believe it was truly the love of working the land. Small farms that once enveloped the prairie for over 130 years are now very sparse in this rural community. Many descendants of early pioneers have moved to larger cities in search of better job opportunities. In fact, my generation was the first to explore career alternatives, as well as the opportunity for a higher education.

MOST EVERYONE IN OUR COMMUNITY SPOKE GERMAN when I was a child. As in many households my parents spoke a mixture of English and German in our home. German was usually spoken if a story or joke was being told. I spoke German before English, but unfortunately have lost much of my first language. I'm able to understand the language but have difficulty understanding different dialects. My parents grew up twelve miles from each other and even they pronounced some German words differently. To add to the complexity of our German language, I believe Russian and Yiddish words were often blended into conversations.

When children of my generation started elementary school, we were expected to speak English. Except for my grandparents and several great-aunts and uncles, I don't recall anyone encouraging me to retain my first language. English was the only language to be spoken when my parents attended school; in fact, they were punished if German was spoken during school hours! Most of my parents' generation were only educated through the eighth grade. Their education took place in a rural one-room schoolhouse with one teacher instructing grades one through eight. Starting the cookstove on those cold winter mornings was one of the teacher's many responsibilities. During the winter months teachers might even prepare a large pot of soup on the cookstove to provide lunch for the children. It was customary for teachers to board with one of the families in the community. Single women were hired to teach school, but they were required to give up their teaching careers after marriage—in that era, it wasn't considered proper for a pregnant teacher to instruct children!

Higher education in our farming community wasn't as valued at the turn of the twentieth century as it is today. With few career options for young men, they were expected to follow in their fathers' footsteps and become farmers. A very basic education of reading, writing, and arithmetic was considered to be quite adequate. At a very young age girls were taught to cook, sew, and care for children; of course it was a natural assumption they'd become farmers' wives! Women worked in the fields, milked cows, separated the cream, helped butcher animals, planted and maintained large gardens, cooked, canned, preserved food, raised children, and did all the housework. We shouldn't forget the laundry: clothes were washed on a washboard and hung outside to dry. The age-old saying, "A woman's work is never done," most definitely applied to the earlier generation of women in my family!

My mother spoke of winter blizzards that came up quickly while she and her siblings were at school. She recalled how one family lost all their children while trying to reach their farm during a severe blizzard! Children usually traveled to school with a horse and buggy during the winter. At the onset of an approaching blizzard there'd be early dismissal, assuring a safe return to their farms. After the older boys hitched the horses to the buggy, the teacher covered the children with heavy blankets and sent them on their way. Following that tragic loss in the community, it was determined children should not lead horses during a blizzard. It was always advisable to have the team of horses find their own way back to the farm during a whiteout, since they had a much better sense of direction.

The rural community of Eureka was primarily agricultural; each year crops of wheat, barley, flax, oats, and corn were harvested. Farming was self-sustaining; farmers raised cattle, pigs, sheep, and chickens. Milking was done by hand; automated milking machines wouldn't arrive on most farms until the late fifties. Cream was separated after milking, eggs were crated, and both were sold at the local creamery each week for additional income. Cream and eggs were taken to town on Saturday evenings, and this was also a time for the large farming community to gather for much-needed socialization.

As with my ancestors, my early childhood was steeped in the closeness and warmth of an extended family. There was a strong sense of community: people looked after one another, often relying on family and neighbors for support in times of need or misfortune. This wasn't unusual in the rural Midwest, but after moving to Oregon I discovered that my formative years were fundamentally different than those of my contemporaries. Apparently my childhood had been very unique; it was the first time I realized my best friends were first and second cousins, much the same as my parents and ancestors.

My extended family included twenty-six aunts and uncles and thirty-six first cousins. Countless great-aunts and uncles on both my father's and mother's sides of the family were very much a part of my early childhood. It may be difficult to comprehend but my father had one hundred and thirteen first cousins—I was related to most of the people in this farming community! I'll attempt to give you a perspective of what my life was like in the late forties, fifties, and well into my adulthood. I'm delighted to share my story. Hopefully it will give future generations an insight into their heritage. I believe the age-old proverb, "How do we know where we're going, if we don't know where we came from?"

CHAPTER FOUR

Early Childhood—Eureka

My arrival at the Eureka Community Hospital was on May 10, 1945. Clearly my parents were expecting a boy, and I understand my name was to be Stanley. Stan Opp—I always thought this would have been such a funny name, because it sounded like "stand up"! Finding it necessary to choose a girl's name, my mother named me Dorothy. At the time, maternity patients were hospitalized for about ten days, and there would be a name change before my mother was discharged. It seems my father had great difficulty pronouncing his *th*'s, and he kept referring to me as "Dorty"! This sounded too much like *dirty* to my mother, so she changed my name to Judy Carole, a better choice—no doubt I would have been known as "Dot" or "Dotty Opp"! With my permanent new name in tow I joined my sister Rosemarie, who was two-and-a-half years old.

We lived with my grandparents on the Opp family homestead about twelve miles northeast of Eureka. It was the farm my father and his six brothers and sisters were raised on. When I was a year old our family moved to

Eureka, where my parents would own and operate a pool hall. Our home was an apartment above the business. Opp's Recreation Place was in the middle of downtown on Main Street, and a small movie theater and Wenzel's clothing store were located on each side of our pool hall. Several grocery stores, the Eureka State Bank, a Rexall Drugs, and the Luncheonette were on the same side of the street as our business. A hardware store, a bakery, the Northwest Blade (our local paper), and the Nu Way dry cleaners were across the street. During the forties and well into the mid-fifties Eureka was an active, bustling community; locals and farmers did all their shopping on Main Street. Throughout the day and late into the night people frequented our pool hall—it seemed to be the hub of activity! Approximately twelve hundred people lived in town, and hundreds of rural families identified Eureka as their hometown.

Ours was a very religious community. The many churches included Lutheran, Baptist, Methodist, Congregational, Evangelical, Catholic, Seventh-Day Adventist, and our family church, Reformed. Doctrines of each church were carefully taught; even within the protestant faith there were differences, and the congregation was expected to adhere to their fundamental principles. At times the minister and elders of our church became involved with parishioners' personal lives. A member of the congregation might even be expected to declare their sins in front of the congregation or be excommunicated from our church for committing a particular offense.

Two or three grain elevators remained from the industrious wheat production of the late 1800s; they were the tallest structures in Eureka. A hospital, a small Lutheran college, and a grade and high school added to the landscape. On the west side of town, locals enjoyed fishing for pike and catfish in Lake Eureka. A small dock and swimming area was an ideal place for kids to cool off during those hot, humid summers. I waded in the lake only once or twice because I discovered it was also a home for enormous bull snakes! A baseball diamond north of the lake had a small grandstand where many relatives gathered to watch the hometown Cardinal team. On the east end of town a nine-hole sand golf course was situated next to the country club. Most everyone belonged to the country club, because it wasn't prestigious to be a member; annual dues were only twenty-five dollars! Membership entitled usage of the club for weddings, family reunions, and dances, and it was the only facility in town spacious enough to accommodate large groups of people.

The most impressive site to me as a young child was the city park. Located in the center of town, it was only a few blocks from our pool hall. The city park and country club were among several WPA projects built during the depression. Both sites were constructed with large rocks and mortar; still in use today, they've withstood the test of time. There were two entrances to the park, with steep stairways that descended onto a beautiful sunken grassy area—at least at a young age, those steps seemed incredibly steep! Our city park didn't have swings, slides, or play structures. The site was mostly used for picnics and large family gatherings. Huge oak trees surrounded a few picnic tables and the park seemed to be covered with a thick carpet of colorful oak leaves each fall. Piling leaves as high as we could, my friends and I found great delight in jumping onto them from the top of picnic tables!

The Midwest has definite seasons, and fall was my favorite. As the tall oak trees began to shed their leaves, leaf burning would begin in people's backyards. On those cool, crisp autumn days the aroma of oak leaves seemed to envelop the entire town! Early inhabitants of Eureka had planted the many oak trees to help beautify the city, as well as to provide shade during those hot, humid summer days. I remember crab apple trees, gooseberries, and choke cherries being abundant in people's yards. Always looking for a quick snack, I'd often help myself to a crab apple, sometimes coming face to face with a big fat worm! It wasn't uncommon to find bugs or worms in fruit or on vegetables because pesticides were never used. Another favorite outdoor snack was a stick of tart rhubarb: found in most gardens, it was used for making jam, pies, and custards.

Streets in downtown Eureka had wide boulevards. There were no traffic lights, just a few stop signs strategically located at several intersections. A number of houses had screened porches to keep flies and mosquitoes at bay during those warm summer evenings. Many homes were situated on oversized lots providing space for large gardens and outbuildings. Every fall, basements were stocked with a surplus of canned and root vegetables. Gardens might include a melon patch containing musk melons, sweet watermelons, and pickling melons. A few residents in Eureka even had a milk cow and chickens in their backyards! It was common to retire from farming and move to town at the age of forty or fifty; not wanting to entirely give up the farming way of life, people found it desirable to have the fresh milk, cream, butter, and eggs that farmers had become accustomed to.

The butchering of cows, pigs, and chickens occurred each fall. This process usually took place on family farms. A great amount of pork sausage, blood sausage, head cheese, ring baloney, liverwurst, and summer sausage was made to supply families throughout the year. On those large lots in Eureka, some people had their own smokehouses to cure meat. Our source of drinking water in the earlier years came from wells. Hand pumps were still found in a few kitchens or on the back porches of homes. Retrieving well or cistern water was done by using a pulley system, in which a pail attached to a long rope was dropped deep into the well to retrieve water. This brief description of Eureka might give you a visual image of where I spent my early childhood.

Judy, age two

What Will People Think?

My earliest recollections were at about two or three years of age. Captivated with the floor plan of our apartment above the pool hall, I had an awareness that our home was a different type of housing. The living space had a sizable landing from the back steps, and another stairway led to the downstairs pool hall. Our apartment had two bedrooms, a bathroom, and a small kitchen. The front room (living room) was at the end of a long hallway overlooking a busy Main Street. There was a fascination with furniture placement, as well as colors and textures of fabric, but I was mostly intrigued with the aromas, noise, and great outbursts of laughter coming from our pool hall downstairs! I wasn't restricted from this space unless it was later in the evening, because after all my sister and I were supposed to be in bed. Most evenings I found it difficult to fall asleep—it sounded like people were having a lot of fun!

My parents were very socially active in the community, so I suppose it was fitting for them to own a recreational pool hall. Most nights after closing, they entertained people in our apartment, or we'd visit friends and family in town or on farms. You will notice in my writings that I make frequent references to "visiting"; it was a favorite form of entertainment for people in our community. As young children we were taken everywhere with our parents; I don't ever recall having a babysitter. I have a distinct memory of trying to sleep on a bed piled high with coats while my parents were partying at someone's home. I wouldn't be the only child attempting to sleep on the bed—children were expected to adapt to their surroundings. In the early morning hours we'd be woken up to leave for home, and there was always such difficulty putting on my coat because I'd been sound asleep. There's a clear memory of my sweater sleeve being caught inside my coat sleeve, sometimes up to my armpits—I found it really bothersome! During the winter, Dad usually warmed up our car prior to leaving, and the blast of cold night air would momentarily wake me until I nestled down in the warmth of the back seat for the drive back home.

Sticky hands! I suppose that's another annoyance and vivid memory at about age three. After being given something like a Hershey's chocolate bar, my hands were soon covered with sticky melted chocolate. I've been told I stood in one spot with both hands raised to my shoulders with fingers separated, anxiously waiting for someone to wash my hands! My mother said she never worried about me touching anything, including the clothes I was wearing. Perhaps it was an intentional move to keep me from getting into mischief!

When visiting someone's home on warm summer nights, children usually fell asleep in the back seat of the family car whenever they got tired. There were never concerns of children being left in cars during the day or night while their parents were visiting, shopping, or possibly socializing in our pool hall. In fact, cars and houses always remained unlocked in our small community. Everyone was very trusting, and it was one of the extraordinary aspects of growing up in a small town during that era.

Our pool hall was the gathering place for most of our relatives. It was a favorite place for them to hang out, shoot a game of pool or snooker, play pinball, enjoy a beer, or possibly try their luck at gambling. At the time, punchboards were a legal form of gambling in Eureka, and I understand this activity happened to be quite lucrative for our business. Children were allowed to be in our pool hall with their parents—again, no need for babysitters, since the large booths were another place for kids to sleep until their parents were ready to go home. While hanging out in the pool hall, there were numerous snacks that were very tempting for us children. My cousins and I enjoyed munching on a box of Cracker Jack, usually washing it down with a bottle of Nehi Grape or Orange Crush soda pop! I loved the sweet popcorn, but the real intent was to quickly consume the contents, because there'd be a wonderful prize at the bottom of a Cracker Jack box! My greatest finds were rings, bracelets, or necklaces. I'd wear my Cracker Jack jewelry until the metal turned my fingers, wrists, and neck an interesting shade of green!

Another activity at Opp's Place that paired with drinking beer and playing pool was smoking cigarettes. Chain-smoking was considered an inexpensive, normal activity for most men. I'd watch the thick clouds of blue smoke envelope our pool hall most days and nights! Late at night, cigarette smoke drifted upwards into our living space where I was supposed to be asleep, but I don't remember cigarette smoke being offensive to me. It's possible additives to cigarettes in later years may have created an intolerance to the unpleasant odor. In our community there was definitely a double standard with the use of cigarettes: smoking was considered to be unacceptable for women! I'd hear references made to women who were seen smoking, and how absolutely shameful it looked! Rumors and gossip were very prevalent in this small town, and there was much discussion and speculation about who was doing what—people generally made it their business to know about everyone else's business!

Mom worked in the pool hall with Dad. Throughout the evening she'd make frequent trips upstairs to check on my sister and I, making sure we were asleep. Instead of sleeping I really wanted to be downstairs—it seemed like there was always a big party taking place! With all the beer drinking, pool and snooker playing, pinball machines, punchboards, and smoking, I knew people might also be chewing sunflower seeds. I loved chewing seeds, because this fun activity included spitting shells on the floor of our pool hall! Long before customers arrived, my parents spread a sawdust compound on the wooden floor to help "sop up" all the sunflower shells. Men, women, and children enjoyed this salty habit of chewing and spitting seeds. I acquired the sunflower-seed habit at about three or four years of age.

Being a proficient seed chewer meant you'd be able to secure seeds on one side of your mouth while spitting out shells from the corner of your mouth! I'd closely watch people who had mastered this skill, but I never achieved that expertise. Instead my tongue was sore after several hours of attempting to crack open seeds. At the end of a busy evening I understand the entire floor of our pool hall was covered with shells from all that chewing and spitting—it sounds really disgusting as I share our favorite pastime! After closing hours my parents used a push broom to sweep up the pile of sawdust and shells, which was then tossed into the basement furnace. I suspect those salty sunflower seeds might have actually increased the beer consumption, which was a bit more profitable for Opp's Place.

One of my earliest discoveries in the pool hall was an enclosed glass cabinet at one end of the bar. I was drawn to the colorful selection of candy bars and gum. Lots of time was spent with my nose pressed against the display case gazing at all those mouth-watering treats! I was most interested in the five-stick gum packages by Wrigley's; flavors were clove, black jack, juicy fruit, spearmint, and doublemint. Beemans was another favorite. Gum was just as popular as chewing sunflower seeds, and I was finally allowed to have a stick of gum—once it was determined I wouldn't be swallowing it! If chewing gum before bedtime, I'd place the large wad of gum on the dresser and resume chewing the next morning. Another item in the cabinet was the breath freshener Sen-Sen. These miniature black square mints had a very intense anise flavor. There must have been an attraction to this product because of the packaging: Sen-Sen came in a tiny red-and-gold foil envelope with a black bow. Clearly way too much sugar was consumed. All those tempting sweets were at my eye level: the large candy bars, Cracker Jack, Sen-Sen, gum, and bottles of pop cost only a nickel!

The glass cabinet also contained cigarettes, cigars, and chewing tobacco. The assorted brands of cigars were displayed in wooden boxes with colorful Native American headdresses embellished on sliding covers. I took a particular interest in cigars because each cigar brand had a distinctive decorative metal band attached to it. As cigars were purchased, customers tossed the bands on the floor. I'd quickly pick them up and attach them to my fingers! Colorful Cracker Jack rings and cigar bands adorned my fingers—it was the beginning of my ring fixation! As cigar boxes were emptied I'd retrieve them to hold all my treasures. Several gallon jars on one corner of the bar were also of interest to me. One contained sunflower seeds, which were scooped out with a ladle and sold to customers for, you guessed it, a nickel a scoop! The second jar was far more intriguing: filled with pickled hard-boiled eggs, I'd watch in absolute amazement as customers plopped a whole egg in their mouths, chasing it with a beer!

Early Childhood—Eureka

ANTICIPATING A BUSY NIGHT IN THE POOL HALL, MOM began each Saturday morning by preparing a huge pot of barbecued hamburger. Twenty pounds of ground beef with a mixture of onions, celery, tomato sauce, Heinz 57 sauce, and spices simmered in a commercial-size roaster for most of the day. During the evening, BBQ was served to customers on a hamburger bun with potato chips for twenty-five cents. I understand the tasty BBQ sandwiches were always sold out long before closing! Opp's Place didn't serve hard alcohol or wine. Ours was strictly a beer hall, and the beer being served was Grain Belt, Pabst Blue Ribbon, and Hamm's: "from the land of sky blue water comes the beer refreshing…Hamm's!" I loved listening to the radio in the pool hall and quickly memorized all the catchy radio jingles advertising beer and various cigarette brands. Two sizes of beer on draft were available in our pool hall. The large glass cost a dime and the small glass was only a nickel! Another popular drink in our pool hall was red beer, made with equal parts beer and tomato juice. Years later, I learned few people outside of the Midwest were familiar with red beer. It's still a favorite, but I only drink it when I'm in Eureka—it just doesn't seem to taste as good anywhere else!

Saturday was my favorite day of the week. It was a fun-filled day with sunflower seeds, BBQ aroma, and hundreds of relatives visiting our pool hall all day and late into the night. It was the day most farmers came to town to sell their cream and eggs at Barney's creamery. After doing weekly grocery shopping, people usually spent the rest of the evening in our pool hall. I was allowed to play downstairs during the day and early evening, and it was great fun to run around in the pool hall with all my cousins. Sometimes I'd attempt to rack up balls on the snooker and pool tables, and our customers were entertained watching me reach for pool balls in the center of the table!

During the winter our big furnace was cranked up in the basement, and it managed to keep our pool hall comfortably warm even during subzero temperatures. The large square decorative cast-iron floor register was in the center of the pool hall. Running around in the pool hall came to an abrupt end at age three when I fell on the hot register. It was my first serious injury and I clearly remember how distressing it was to see the charred skin hanging on my hands and legs! Mom treated the burns with salve and wrapped my legs with gauze. My father bought me a little red wagon, and I was pulled around in it until I was able to walk without discomfort.

Early play activity in our apartment was mostly with my sister. There's memory of turning over red upholstered chrome kitchen chairs and covering them with blankets. It was fun crawling through the maze of chairs. Our kitchen window faced the side of the old movie theater. My very vivid fear was that during a cowboy feature film, all the bad guys would somehow be able jump off the big screen… I was convinced they'd use the nearby fire escape to climb right into our open kitchen window!

Dad had built us a double swing behind our two-story building. It was at the base of the stairs which led to our apartment. From this vantage point I'd watch service trucks make daily deliveries to our pool hall as well as the other businesses in the alley.

A very memorable Easter morning occurred while living in our apartment; actually, it was disappointing as well as memorable. Apparently my sister was somewhat doubtful of the bunny delivering our Easter baskets. On this very busy Saturday night, while Mom made many trips upstairs to take care of business, I was asleep but my sister was wide awake, determined to wait for the bunny to make his appearance! This would be the year without an Easter basket for both of us! Sometime during the night there'd been a light snowfall, and evidently a cat had left a trail on the back steps, coming up to the door and returning down the stairs. Mom convincingly told my sister the bunny had left the trail, obviously aware she'd been awake all night, and had left our home without a basket delivery!

Judy and Rosemarie, 1949

What Will People Think?

AT AGE THREE OR FOUR I TOOK BALLET FOR A BRIEF period of time. Dance instructors traveled from the city of Aberdeen to give ballet and tap lessons to children in Eureka. Recitals and competitions were held on the second floor of the old city hall, and there's a clear memory of being onstage but nothing at all about performing, competition, music, or if I even enjoyed ballet. There was much more excitement about the aubergine taffeta tutu my mother had made for me—I absolutely adored the shimmering fabric! Several years later there were more performances. My sister had begun to play the accordion, and it was decided I was to sing along with her! Mom would enter us in various local competitions; she enjoyed this activity much more than I did. One of our standard songs was "Beautiful, Beautiful Brown Eyes." Rosemarie hadn't been playing the accordion very long, and I just remember having to hold a note for the longest time until she was able to find the right key! The accordion playing and singing continued until I was about eight years old and my sister and I announced there'd be no more competitions.

My first playmate was a little boy who lived across the alley in a large brown stucco house. I remember him to be my first nonrelative friend. Nils climbed our back stairs every morning and rang our doorbell at 7 a.m.; he'd arrive with scissors and stacks of magazines. Mom wasn't pleased; it was too early to be woken up in our house because my parents kept late hours in the pool hall. Nils's household was awake much earlier since his father was one of the doctors in town. But Nils was never sent home, instead Mom directed him to our front room where he looked at magazines until I was awake. After I'd had breakfast we'd spend hours cutting car ads out of all the magazines! Whenever visiting Nils's house, I always found it so amusing to see their pet cats and dogs roaming around inside their home, and at times cats were on the kitchen counters! No one else in our community ever allowed their pets inside their homes, it just wasn't done. Nils's family was originally from New York City—so I figured it must have been totally acceptable there!

I met Janet (another nonrelative) when I was about four years old. She and her family were new to Eureka. Her parents had purchased the local dime store, which was only a block from our pool hall. Janet and her family had the same type of housing as ours: they also lived in an apartment above their business. We became good friends but I don't recall spending much time at her house. Janet's parents seemed very strict—they didn't appear to smile very often, and there was an awareness that my new friend wasn't living in a happy home.

Nils, Janet, and I were inseparable for several years. One of our favorite activities was checking out the huge display of merchandise in the new dime store. During this era, independently-owned dime stores were located in small towns. Stores carried miscellaneous household items such as kitchenware, ceramic knickknacks, perfumes, hair products, clothing, magazines, toiletries, and lots of candy! The stores were called dime stores because originally most everything in the store cost about a dime! Most merchandise was made in the United States or Japan and seemed to be stocked with surprisingly good products. Larger cities had national chain dime stores, namely Woolworth's and Newberry's. Both stores were in Aberdeen, which was our closest large city and about seventy miles away. The stores had sizable lunch counters where soda jerks prepared and served sandwiches, milkshakes, banana splits, sodas, and ice cream sundaes. The national dime stores have vanished from the landscape, and they've been replaced by Walgreens, Rite-Aid, and CVS stores, minus the lunch counters.

Not too surprisingly, my favorite place in the dime store was in front of the candy counter, where I'd be focused on the large selection of sugary treats. The long aisle of penny candy was intentionally located at eye level for children, and was also very accessible to our reach! Nils, Janet, and I were continually reminded by Janet's father to be quite certain of our selection, because once we touched the candy it was ours! We'd scan over a hundred different items, including candy cigarettes, root beer barrels, butterscotch rounds, wax lips, and wax Coke bottles filled with a sugary liquid. There were various sizes of jawbreakers, suckers, bubble gum, and assorted types of chocolate and licorice. With far too many choices and very little money there were difficult decisions to make, but usually the selection included my favorite stick of chocolate licorice. After searching my pockets for several pennies, I'd be able to buy about eight pieces of penny candy!

More expensive chocolates and caramels were located in an enclosed glass cabinet in another section of the dime store. A scale was used by Janet's parents to weigh those items, and we were permitted to watch the weighing process but continually reminded to not touch the candy case. Our fingerprints and noseprints on the glass were evidence we didn't always follow instructions! Next to the premium candy and scale, a large white enamel cabinet contained assorted warmed nuts and cashews. Although it was way beyond my reach, I'd be mesmerized watching the lighted revolving tray of roasted nuts, while taking in the mouth-watering aroma. After wandering up and down the aisles "inspecting" all the new inventory, Janet's father would suggest that Nils, Janet, and I should move on to another activity. I don't remember if we ever broke anything, but we were usually eating candy and probably touching some of the merchandise! Predictably the three of us were escorted out of the store. We never really minded, because there might be a game of hopscotch or jump rope waiting for us, or possibly a visit to the park which was only a block away. Actually—just about everything in Eureka was only about a block away!

Family photo, 1950

CHAPTER FIVE

Life on the Farm

After owning Opp's Recreation Place for five years my parents had established a profitable business. That would change abruptly when the city passed an ordinance in 1950 to eliminate gambling and the use of punchboards. After putting so much of themselves into their commercial enterprise, it must have been a disturbing turn of events for my parents. With the new law in place my parents were finding it increasingly difficult to earn a living wage by selling only nickel and dime beer!

The prior summer of 1949 our family had taken a vacation to California, and we'd also traveled to Portland, Oregon to visit my father's sister and family. Uncle Richard and Aunt Esther had opened a restaurant in southeast Portland three years earlier. During this visit our relatives encouraged my parents to move to Portland, apparently offering them an investment opportunity in their restaurant. My parents declined the business offer, because at that time their pool hall was a profitable business, but most importantly Eureka was their home. One year later my parents were struggling to support their family. With limited

Life on the Farm

options and employment opportunities they decided to test their skills at farming. I understand my mother didn't share my father's enthusiasm about the prospect of farm life. In making that fateful decision they didn't realize their financial struggles had only just begun.

My parents purchased a farm about fourteen miles northeast of Eureka. Used farm machinery, milk cows, several work horses, sheep, and chickens were acquired after our move. My father would be seeding barley, corn, flax, oats, alfalfa, and wheat crops. Having both grown up on farms my parents knew of the challenges and physical work facing them, but they'd always been accustomed to hard work. My parents, or at least my father, must have thought of this move as a new beginning and a promising business opportunity. The year was 1951. I was six years old and remember thinking the move was going to be a great adventure!

At first glance our large, two-story white farmhouse seemed enormous to me, and my sister and I excitedly began to explore every room of our new home. The entry, also known as the forehisely (German), was used as a mud room before entering the main house. Most farmhouses had this type of room: this was a place to remove and store soiled clothing, shoes, and work boots. The kitchen, sizable dining room, and front room (living room) were located on the first floor. A small bedroom adjacent to the front room was separated by a heavy tapestry curtain my mother had made. I was captivated with the floor-length curtain of forested trees! A large screened porch was accessible from the front room. From the kitchen, a steep stairway and landing led to the second floor where three bedrooms and a bathroom were located.

The dirt basement had an abundance of storage with a canning cellar across from the furnace. Our furnace burned coal, which would keep us warm and comfortable in the coming winter months. Dried cow manure would be used as fire starters in our furnace—obviously cow patties (as we referred to them) were plentiful! Drying in the pasture during the hot summer, cow patties were turned over with a pitchfork. When completely dry the dinner-plate-sized patties were collected from the pasture and stacked in our basement. Surprisingly, manure was odorless when completely dry, and it was in fact an excellent source of heat.

Our ancestors didn't have the use of coal for warmth; with limited firewood, dried cow and sheep manure were used as their primary heat source. I've been told sheep manure was smoothed out and scored in the sheep shed, and when completely dry it was stacked for future use. Obviously it was an unpleasant and laborious task but there were few options. Out of necessity they utilized the few available resources to provide warmth for their families during those long, cold winters. Indeed, this was the ultimate in recycling—but that word wasn't in their vocabulary.

It was fun exploring the numerous outbuildings on our farm. Our barn had a huge hay loft, and from there a block and tackle allowed me to grab the rope, then drop onto a large pile of hay outside the barn! A huge tractor tire on the south side of the barn quickly became a substitute trampoline—it was a favorite outdoor activity! A small sheep shed was located on one corner of the barn, and sheep accessed it from the north side of the building. Inside the barn I discovered a very small room with a strange-looking machine. This was where cream was separated from the milk. Not far from the barn, the windmill and cattle tank were at the base of the hill next to the pasture. The remaining two buildings were a granary and a freestanding garage which were closer to our house.

There was one other tiny building in the middle of our farmyard. We were told it was the outhouse. The outdoor privy was a three seater—obviously only one person occupied the outhouse at a time! There just happened to be three different-sized holes, which I quickly referred to as papa size, mama size, and baby size. After our move I began to have numerous anxieties about that tiny house. The most disturbing thing other than the slivers and smell was the fear of accidentally falling into the hole. I was told that was exactly the reason there were three different-sized holes! A wooden latch had been attached to the outside of the door, preventing the strong prairie wind from banging the door open and closed. It seemed like a pretty good idea until I realized a person could be intentionally locked inside. If it happened to be me, I'd scream until someone released the latch! Being stuck inside this dark, windowless outhouse was alarming—I'd be quick about doing my business! Occupying this small space with an infinite number of flies was another concern. Adding to my discomfort, we didn't use toilet paper; instead a stack of old Sears Roebuck, Spiegel, and Montgomery Ward catalogs were strategically placed in one corner of the wooden floor!

Catalogs were delivered to our farm three or four times a year. In that era catalogs measured nine by twelve inches and were about five inches thick. Naturally the softer index pages were the first to be used, but inevitably all that remained were the glossy, colorful pages in front of the catalog! I was confused—why were we using an outhouse if we had a bathroom inside our house? Our oversized bathroom had a lovely claw-foot tub, toilet, and large pedestal sink. It was also conveniently located across the hall from the bedroom I shared with my sister. My parents explained that the plumbing had never been hooked up in the house. I was told it would be too costly to turn it into a working bathroom. I then realized our indoor bathroom must just be for "show"!

As I watched my mother unpack kitchen items I noticed she repacked the small electrical appliances. She did this because we also didn't have electricity on our farm! We wouldn't be able to use the upright mixer, coffeepot, toaster, or waffle iron; those appliances were stored in the basement. Our farm did have limited REA, a rural electric power supplemented by a generator in the basement. There were bright lights throughout our house but late in the evening lights became noticeably dimmer. As soon as Dad fired up the generator in the basement we'd once again have lights to finish whatever board game we were playing. Our stove and oven worked by using bottled gas (propane), which explained the large white tank I'd noticed below the kitchen window.

Without plumbing I wondered where we'd get our water for drinking, cooking, bathing, and washing our clothes. Apparently water would be drawn from the well, which was down the hill next to the windmill—the operative word was "down!" Water was carried up the hill in a ten-gallon pail and heated on the stove as needed. I was beginning to realize farm life for our family was going to be noticeably different than what we'd been accustomed to. Inconveniences were certain, but it was going to be a lot of work for my parents.

In one corner of the basement I noticed a large tubular device resembling a hot-water tank, and after opening the door of this strange-looking metal apparatus I noticed three or four shelves inside. A pulley was attached to the top of the fixture. Lowered deep into the ground, it held our perishables. Food was kept cool but not as cold as a refrigerator. After our move I started drinking chocolate milk; the "cooler" didn't keep milk as cold as I liked. When retrieving perishables, someone had to go down to the basement to crank up the fixture, much like a dumbwaiter. It might have been more conveniently located in our kitchen. This strange cooling apparatus was our only refrigeration until winter arrived!

A white oversized cast-iron sink was in one corner of our kitchen. My very creative mother had made a fabric curtain which she'd somehow attached to the edge of the sink. The colorful curtain did a fairly good job of concealing the slop pail. Most farmhouses had a slop pail that contained…well, it contained slop! I guess it was our garbage disposal. Food and many liquids found their way into this pail. When the slop pail was full, or most likely too smelly, contents were tossed outside, where our farm animals eagerly waited to eat this mixture! I found the slop pail to be terribly offensive, but realizing my newly acquired dog Netty might be consuming this slop made it much worse. On the yuck level, the slop pail was a very close runner-up to the outhouse!

Although there were three bedrooms upstairs, my sister and I continued to share a room. The smallest bedroom was used for storage and as our playroom. The closet contained old clothing, lace curtains, hats, platform high-heels, purses, and other garments used to play dress-up. Once in costume we'd make up plays, using a bathroom window to deliver our dialogue. The oversized latched bathroom window opened up onto the steep stairwell, and we envisioned the stairs as our theater. Since the bathroom wasn't of any particular use, it now became our stage! At times we'd perform Romeo and Juliet, entertaining our cousins who'd taken seats on the steps. The only dialogue we knew of this Shakespearean play was the phrase, "Romeo, Romeo, wherefore art thou Romeo?" A long, narrow adjoining closet connected our bedroom to my parents' bedroom. It was an ideal hiding place when playing hide-and-seek after our performances.

The screened porch on the first floor was another playroom, where our dolls lived in their baby buggies. A hide-a-bed on one end of the porch was used for additional sleeping when relatives visited. An antique Victrola about the size of a jukebox had been left on the sun porch by previous owners; it's possible it was too heavy to move! No one needed an old Victrola for listening to music, because people were now playing their vinyl records on turntables. It would be another fifteen years before anyone realized the value of antiques such as our Victrola. At the time, most old stuff was thought of as junk.

Relatives once gathered glass oil lanterns, copper washboilers, oak wall phones, and other old "useless" items. Everything was taken out to the pasture where it was thrown into a big hole and buried! I was told those outdated things were destroyed because they took up way too much room and just reminded everyone of hard work. Fortunately our Victrola had escaped the fate of the junk pile, at least while we lived on the farm. A large stack of seventy-eight rpm records had been left in the mahogany cabinet of the large music maker, and I remember that the records shattered like porcelain if we accidentally dropped them! Hours were spent on our sun porch dancing to the collection of old scratchy records, and every few minutes we'd have to wind up the Victrola. I don't remember the type of music we listened to but if we wound up the Victrola too tightly, music played faster and voices were at a much higher pitch.

Our farmyard had several large oak tree groves. Planted years earlier, they provided protection from the frequent prairie winds. Trees served as a shelter belt, which was an effective measure to protect surrounding farmland from erosion. On hot summer days my sister and I found it inviting to play in this cool shaded area of oak trees. Naming our forest camps A, B, and C, we'd busy ourselves dragging branches and tree limbs around to create and design rooms. A number of trees had fallen from previous storms. One tree resembled a stairway, allowing us to walk to the top of another tree! Our dolls were often brought to our camps; it's where we'd spend many long summer afternoons.

A large junk pile was behind our granary. Most farms had a scrap pile containing broken-down farm equipment and discarded household items. I discovered it was an excellent place to treasure hunt. The sizable junk pile had been there when we moved onto our farm. It had once been someone else's stuff, which made it all the more appealing to me! I'd use extreme caution when roaming through the junk pile, because I knew it was one of the likely places to come across a skunk or snake—I had a terrible fear of snakes. After moving onto our farm I'd been told we didn't have poisonous snakes in our area. However, I knew the Missouri River area had rattlesnakes, and it was only about fifty miles west of us, not really far at all; how could they be that certain? Supposedly the only snakes in our vicinity were garter snakes, large gopher snakes, and bull snakes, but it made no difference to me: I'd always be very careful when I went outdoors! I once came very close to stepping on a big fat bull snake while running barefoot in our farmyard—it's the last time I was shoeless outside! Skunks were often seen on our farm. We'd been warned it was wise to keep our distance, but our dogs weren't as lucky. They once got a bit too close to a skunk, and the stench was awful!

While carefully navigating my way through the junk pile, my favorite place to play was in a black, rusted-out Model A Ford. After carefully scanning the interior of the car for snakes and skunks, I'd climb onto the worn leather bench seat, close the door, and pretend to drive! The hand-operated windshield wipers and horn were in working condition, and luckily the four windows still rolled up and down. There were several buttons to push on the dashboard and I could easily turn the steering wheel. Although my feet never reached the brake, accelerator, or clutch, many imaginary road trips were taken in that car!

Close to one grove of oak trees, we discovered rock walls about five feet high. A doorway and several windowpanes were still visible in this small dwelling; it had been the remains of an early settler's home. About twenty-five feet from the rock building we noticed an earthen mound with a very small door, and opening the door we discovered steps descending underground. Our parents told us settlers had used this cool dark space as a root cellar to store vegetables. I wasn't aware of it then, but this small hole in the ground would be used for shelter whenever a tornado approached our farm! Gazing into that dark abyss, I remember thinking there was no way I'd ever go down into that hole. I just knew it must be the home of spiders, lizards, and snakes! Indeed, this cellar was used numerous times—we were unaware our farm would be assaulted by tornadoes every year!

As much as I enjoyed the freedom and open space of our farm, there were certain elements that caused me concern. Obviously snakes topped the list, but milk cows and our two large workhorses came in a close second, because the sheer size of those large animals was very frightening to me. My parents routinely milked about twelve cows. Milking took place early in the morning and again towards evening. Milk machines were used by only a few farmers in our area; like my parents, most farmers were still milking cows by hand. Our milk cows were Holsteins (black and whites), which were known to be the best milk producers. Having both grown up on farms, my parents were very skilled at milking and experienced being around farm animals. A few cows were skittish, and Dad was the only person who'd be able to milk them. I'd watch him approach them very slowly and quietly. He'd cautiously place the milk stool close to the cow's udder. Dad gently patted their big bellies while talking to them softly, saying things like "Whoa bossy," and "Come on—come on." Only then would he carefully begin the milking process. I guess Dad was sort of a "cow whisperer!"

Some of our milk cows had names. The cow I've referred to as being difficult to milk had been named "Lightning" by my father; he'd given her that name because of her mean disposition. Agitated cows such as Lightning usually had kickers placed on their back legs before they were milked. Supposedly the metal clamps kept them from kicking the milker, and of course kickers needed to be placed on cows very carefully for obvious reasons. On one occasion a relative from a neighboring farm was milking our cows while we were gone for several days. Lightning happened to be in her usual temperamental mood, and as Clarence attempted to milk her he was kicked across the barn, knocking him unconscious for several minutes!

We'd be reminded to never run through the barn because it might spook the cows, apparently having an affect on their milk production. That was never a problem for me—I'd watch the evening milking process from a safe distance. My favorite part of this activity was waiting for Dad to aim a stream of milk directly into a hungry cat's mouth while milking; he was on-target most of the time! Numerous cats were always scurrying around in the barn. They'd be waiting for fresh milk, but their main task was to help with the mouse population.

Unlike Nils's house, our dogs and cats were never permitted to grace the doorstep of our farmhouse. Pets were considered farm animals, which meant they were to be outside with the other farm animals. During severe blizzards we might not see our dogs and cats for two or three weeks. Supposedly they sought shelter and warmth in the barn by lying next to, or on top of, the cows. Most of the time it was an effective way to stay warm, but unfortunately that's how we lost several kittens when a cow rolled on top of them! Nourishment for our many cats was mice and milk. Our dogs were given milk after the milking process and they also ate table scraps and waited for the infamous "slop pail" to be tossed outside! We never purchased dog and cat food. If available it would have been considered an unnecessary expense. Our dogs Netty and Spotty also hunted field rabbits, or at least that's what our parents told us so we wouldn't worry about them being hungry.

Despite the harsh elements, most of our pets survived those long, cold winters and we'd eventually be reunited. Spotty, a black-and-white cocker spaniel, was my sister's dog; he'd been given to her when we lived in Eureka. My dog Netty was part collie. He'd been acquired after our move to help round up cattle in the pasture at milking time. Dad was determined to train both dogs, but we soon realized neither would ever be particularly skillful as working dogs. Both dogs hopped into the back seat of our car when we drove out to the pasture to get the milk cows, and after we opened the back door they eagerly jumped out. There might even have been a bit of running and barking, but they made a very pitiful attempt to chase the cows towards the barn! Minutes later and definitely dog-tired, Netty and Spotty approached our car—we always gave them a welcomed ride back to our farmyard!

Our pets needed to fend for themselves; I don't recall our dogs getting a much-needed bath. I once asked my mother about their grooming, and she said they must have jumped into the cattle tank when they could no longer tolerate themselves! Spotty and Netty also never had distemper shots or visits to the veterinarian. Veterinarians were only called in absolutely dire situations; incurring an expensive vet bill was avoided if possible. When cows had difficulties birthing, Dad attempted to help with deliveries. There were successes but occasionally we'd lose an animal.

Netty once had a litter of puppies. We discovered one pup had distemper, and regrettably my father had to put it down. Clearly, it was a disturbing event for me, but I also remember how visibly shaken my father was at having to shoot the puppy. Sadly, there were no other options.

A portion of my parents' busy workday was spent milking cows and separating the cream. A considerable amount of milk was collected. Cows normally produce five to seven gallons of milk each day. Milk collected was transferred to the small separator room where my mother was in charge of the entire process. I'd manage to find a corner in the tiny room to watch the mechanics of discs, filters, and screens separate the cream. Cleanliness and sanitation were essential, but it was more challenging in the spring and summer because flies were everywhere. To improve the situation, I'd volunteer to spray the barn with a pump canister filled with DDT to help eliminate the fly population! I thought it was a fun activity, but how frightening—DDT was more dangerous to our health than the annoyance of flies!

A favorite family story about the infamous separator room was a comment made by a young relative. She said, "Yes, we have a separator room too, that's where we separate the flies from the cream." How true: the flies were relentless! Mom used soap and boiling water to clean and rinse the separator equipment. This process took place twice a day. Initially, water was carried from the well to the house where it was boiled, then brought down to the separator room to clean all the equipment. I now realize the end result of this tiresome task amounted to only two-thirds of a cup of cream from each gallon of milk. Cream collected was poured into a five-gallon can and sold at our local creamery each week.

Another method to eliminate flies was with the use of fly strips. Sticky scented rolls hung from the ceiling and walls of the separator room as well as our barn. It was a futile effort, because cows were constantly swishing their tails in an attempt to keep flies off of them. I felt sorry for the cows. I remember asking my mother why cows' tails weren't longer so they could swish the flies off of their eyes, noses, and mouths? Mom said the cows' tails were plenty long—they often slapped their tails across her face while she was milking them!

Life on the Farm

BASIC FARM MACHINERY WAS USED TO HARVEST OUR wheat, barley, flax, corn, oats, and alfalfa crops. We had several tractors, a plow, a seeder, a header, a binder, a disc, and several implements to cut and rake hay. There was very little automation on our farm; most everything was done by hand. After Dad cut and raked hay, he stacked it with a pitchfork. Without a hay bailer, haystacks were scattered throughout our pasture. Mechanized farm machinery now cuts, bails, and stacks hay, in fact most farm machinery is computerized to do much of the work. Farmers in the twenty-first century are also experiencing the comfort of air-conditioned farm machinery. Farming in 1950 was labor intensive and far more difficult for my parents, but they often spoke of how their parents broke the land with a hand plow pulled by horses.

Our farm animals grazed on hay and pastureland during favorable weather, but caring for them during the winter months was far more challenging. Cows, horses, and sheep needed hay and water provided for them when the pasture was covered with snow. My father stored hay in the barn loft with a block and tackle, and from there it was dropped into cows' stalls and the sheep shed with a pitchfork. In addition to milking and separating cream, Mom often helped Dad with seasonal fieldwork. My parents shared the workload and responsibilities. Together they kept our farm running as efficiently as possible.

Mom's large garden was next to the windmill and water pump. It contained pickling cucumbers, potatoes, cabbage, green beans, wax beans, peas, beets, carrots, lettuce, radishes, and onions. We had all those amazing greens in our garden, but surprisingly we never ate crunchy lettuce salads; it was never part of our meal. Lettuce and/or cucumbers were often used as a cold soup that included sour cream, green onions, and vinegar. At the time people referred to lettuce as rabbit food because rabbits loved nibbling on it! I think lettuce was planted for the rabbits to keep them away from other vegetables in the garden.

After harvesting her garden in late summer, Mom would begin the canning and pickling process. This was done with the continual task of retrieving water from the well. Countless quarts of dill pickles and wax beans were put up. Carrots were usually pickled with wax beans, and they were a particular favorite of mine. I remember the wonderful aroma of fresh garden dill in our kitchen on pickling day; it stirs fond memories! From homegrown cabbage Mom made sauerkraut, which fermented in a small crock in the basement. Our cornfields provided us with all the corn we could eat. We had lots of corn on the cob. Corn was also canned, and of course popcorn was a favorite snack; it was considered a staple.

A large melon patch in a fenced area of our pasture is where musk melons, pickling melons, and sweet watermelon seeds were planted each spring. Many summer evenings we'd drive out to the melon patch to check on the ripeness of sweet watermelons. Dad used his jackknife to cut a square plug out of the melon, and after taking a bite he'd determine if it was sweet enough for picking. If not the desired sweetness he'd carefully replace the plug, and it continued to ripen on the vine! Without proper refrigeration, watermelons were served at room temperature, and salt was often sprinkled on melons to enhance the sweetness.

From our melon patch Mom also pickled whole small melons. After removing the rind they were dropped into a large ceramic crock of pickling brine. Both crocks of sauerkraut and pickling melons were kept in our basement where temperatures were much cooler. I also remember it was considered healthy to have scum or mold spores on the surface of the open pickling crocks! After the pickling and canning process was completed, butchering took place each fall. A surplus of food was needed to sustain us through the long winter. Most beef, pork, and chicken was either canned or smoked. We also made our own pork sausage and summer sausage: put into casings, it hung in the smokehouse to cure.

Laundry day was demanding for my mother. Every week, water was retrieved from the well, heated on our kitchen stove, then poured into a wringer-type washing machine. After garments were cleaned, each article of clothing was fed through rollers to remove excess water, and clothes were then hung on the outside wash line with wooden clothespins. Garments dried quickly on hot summer days because of the strong prairie winds. I have memory of falling asleep on line-dried bedding. Sheets and pillowcases captured the scent of the fresh-cut grasses or wildflowers in bloom—spring and summer air was sweet and fragrant!

After laboring all day doing very physical field work, my father was able to rest after the evening milking. On the other hand, it seemed my mother rarely had time to herself; I often wondered if her work would ever be done! With her many tasks and responsibilities, Mom still managed to prepare all our delicious meals from scratch. All the cream, homemade butter, and fresh eggs were readily available for cooking and baking. Sweets were a big part of our lives; cakes, pies, cinnamon rolls, or brownies were baked two or three times a week, and desserts were served after each meal. Kuchen, our traditional German dessert, was normally prepared for large family gatherings. The sweet yeast dough had a custard-fruit filling, and the pie-shaped recipe yielded about twelve kuchens! I understand this customary kuchen dessert has recently been named the official dessert of South Dakota.

Most mornings would begin with one of my favorite breakfasts: an "egg in hole" was prepared in a cast-iron skillet with homemade bread, churned butter, and fresh eggs. Dinner was served at noon. It was our largest meal of the day, and we always referred to our evening meal as "supper." We'd frequently have lunch, but it was served late at night—I'll get back to you later about that.

I never tired of my favorite dinner of creamed chicken (free range, of course) and dumplings. Our chickens were fed close to the chicken coop, so they'd be scratching around for food all day, which made them very accessible for butchering! An unsuspecting bird would be butchered only a few hours before our meal. I'd be close by and was curiously drawn to this entire process. While scanning her large flock of chickens, Mom would decide which one was to be eliminated. I'd observe her carefully making the selection and I don't believe it was random! Chickens with a gimp or other physical abnormalities usually had their lives cut short. I know this to be true because I'd try to hide Petey, my crippled pet chicken, whenever Mom was butchering. Apparently I wasn't careful enough because Petey did end up on our dinner table! I'd named Petey as a baby chick; he was easily spotted in the brooder house with the rest of the chicks because of his gimp. Therein lies the problem: one should never name an animal that will eventually be butchered!

I suppose all the chickens' lives were going to be cut short, but some seemed to have shorter lives than others. With a sharp butcher knife in one hand, Mom picked up an unaware chicken with the other, and in a split second she'd twist its neck with one rapid movement and quickly chop off the head. It appeared to be swift and lethal! It always amazed me how the body continued to flop around the yard! Boiling water was then poured over the chicken, making it easier for feathers to be pulled. After the bird was gutted, pin feathers needed to be removed. This tedious chore was made easier if the skin was singed with a match. If my sister and I were close by we'd pull out pin feathers; this activity produced a very distinct and unforgettable odor.

My dog Netty eagerly watched the chicken butchering. It was his job to clean up the mess, and he accomplished this task by devouring the whole head, which included feathers, beak, and comb! One day, my mother and aunt butchered sixteen chickens in preparation for canning, and to our amazement Netty consumed every one of the chicken heads! Hunger for our dogs was likely an everyday occurrence. I'm sure my dog waited for the annual butchering day; he loved feasting on chicken heads. It shouldn't have been a surprise that both Netty and Spotty developed an appetite for live chickens. Our dogs were allowed to eat the heads while mom was butchering, but she'd be furious if they helped themselves to a live chicken from the henhouse, often threatening to shoot both dogs for snatching one of her chickens in the middle of the night! Obviously, Netty had developed quite a taste for chicken blood. How was he to know that he could only eat them some of the time?

As it turns out, both dogs eventually met their demise for eating one too many chickens after we moved to Portland. Apparently the farm they ended up on didn't take too kindly to chicken snatching either! Basically our dogs were just trying to survive by scrounging for food wherever they could find it. I know Netty was hungry much of the time; sometimes I fed him onions and radishes from the garden, yet another good reason for being an outside dog!

Farmers often hired butchers to slaughter animals. Thankfully I was probably in school when that activity took place on our farm, because it was ghastly enough watching the chickens being butchered! I'm not sure if we were purposely sheltered from observing the butchering of large animals. It was also puzzling that I never watched a cow birthing or the birthing process during lambing season while living on the farm. The same is true for our dogs and many cats. The only explanation is that it might have prompted far too many inquiries regarding the reproductive process—it's possible those were questions my parents weren't prepared to answer.

Because of our ages, my sister and I had very few farm chores. Our main job was to set the table and wash and dry dishes after each meal. A favorite chore was churning butter every couple of weeks. Fresh cream was poured into a square glass butter churn, and a metal cover with wooden paddles and a handle covered the jar. After my sister and I took turns rotating the handle of the butter churn for twenty minutes or so, the cream thickened and became butter. Butter in its natural state is white; sometimes we'd add yellow food coloring to make it more appealing to the eye. If Mom's bread baking happened to coincide with our butter churning, we'd be snacking on fresh warm bread topped with homemade butter; it was the best!

Gathering eggs from the henhouse was one of my chores. It wasn't a regular activity but I'd often do the collecting during the summer. I remember the distinctive smell of the chicken coop on a hot summer day—another particularly pungent odor that's difficult to describe, and also hard to forget! My immediate concern, other than the smell, was how to retrieve eggs once inside the henhouse. I naturally assumed the chickens would and should just hop off of their nests to give up their bounty! While cautiously approaching a nest, hens always started to peck at my hand. Of course egg gathering was to be done with one quick motion of shooing the hen off her nest, then quickly grabbing the eggs. With a great deal of angst I'd somehow manage to collect the eggs, but as I left the building our mean old rooster would sometimes fly at me from a rafter of the chicken coop! While running and screaming with the rooster chasing after me, I might drop a few eggs from the wire basket. Broken eggs were never a problem, because we always had more eggs than we could use.

One of my favorite quiet pastimes was watching the light, fluffy popcorn shapes of cloud formations. They appeared to look different in the Midwest, and it was fun to lie on the ground and envision animal shapes in them! I'm so grateful to have experienced those times of complete solitude in my life. Everything moved at a much slower pace. Summer days were long and filled with excitement, and my vivid imagination carried me away to faraway places. I don't remember being bored too often, but have since read that boredom can also be a window to creativity.

In the early fifties many small farms dotted the countryside of McPherson County, South Dakota. Neighboring farms were in close proximity, sometimes within a mile or two of each other. All our neighbors were relatives, and after our move I was excited to discover over sixty second cousins living on farms very near to us. Most every evening after finishing our chores we'd "go visiting" or someone would visit us. Every farm was unique, and as nighttime approached all of us kids loved to play hide and seek in the dark farmyards. We loved to hide in barn hay lofts and numerous outbuildings with the intention of scaring each other!

Our farming community looked forward to Saturday night. Milking and farm chores were done early, allowing extra time to get cleaned up to go to town. "Cleaning up" in our household meant it was time for our weekly bath. Daily sponge or spit baths were taken with a soapy basin of hot water, but our Saturday bath took place in a large galvanized washtub right in the middle of the kitchen! After a large amount of well water was heated to fill the tub, my sister and I were usually the first to take our baths. Mom was next and Dad was normally the last to bathe. The bathing order was determined by whoever happened to be the dirtiest! Usually it was my father, because after working in the fields all day he'd be covered with dirt and grime. Additional hot water was added between bathers. Recycling water was a necessity, and it's something we were quickly becoming accustomed to. Carrying water up to the house was not an easy task, and we were taught to not waste this precious resource.

With chores completed and being much cleaner than we'd been all week, it was time to get dressed up to go to town. Women always wore dresses, because pants were considered too casual; they were only worn to do house and farm work. Girls could wear pedal pushers or pants when going to town but my sister and I usually wore dresses on Saturday nights. Pedal pushers? This was an article of clothing for girls and women introduced in the early fifties, also known as clamdiggers and now referred to as capris. Pedal pushers were originally designed by White Stag (a Portland-based company) for bike riding.

Our first stop in Eureka on those Saturday evenings was at Barney's Creamery, where we'd sell crates of eggs and cream collected during the week. I'm not sure how many dozen eggs were in each crate, but Mom recently reminded me we were paid only eight cents for a dozen eggs! Cars were lined up at Barney's with farmers waiting to have their cream tested. Everyone hoped for a high test count, which resulted in more money. After our cream and egg sale my parents were paid about ten dollars in cash! It seems unimaginable, but the egg and cream money was used to purchase groceries, gas for our car, and essential items for the coming week.

Saturday nights often included a stop at Schaeffer's blacksmith shop where we'd drop off a machinery part to be repaired. Much of our farm machinery was dated, and it seemed equipment was always breaking down. Everyone called our smithy "Old Man Schaeffer," but I doubt he was even fifty years old. Following my father into the shop, I'd be spellbound watching the smithy forge steel over the open fire. The smithy would hammer and work late into the night to finish repairs for farmers. As work was completed, names were attached to each part and placed on the ground in front of the blacksmith shop. Old Man Schaeffer trusted that people would settle up their payments whenever they came back into town. We'd pick up our repair before we left town on Saturday night. If we happened to forget, we'd stop by the next day after church, and the part would still be there.

Most farm families wanted to get to town early on those busy Saturday nights, since they were interested in securing a good parking spot on Main Street. The "good" parking was in front of the Luncheonette or the pool hall we once owned. Parking in those prime spots on warm summer nights was ideal for women and children who wanted to sit in their cars. With car doors open to the sidewalk, women could visit with friends and relatives, their young children could fall asleep in the back seat, and everyone would be quite comfortable. Saturday nights brought most of the farming community to town, and sidewalks would be packed with hundreds of relatives. I also remember that Dad seemed to have good parking karma!

It's difficult to comprehend that ten dollars covered our expenses for the coming week. Our farm provided us with much of our food, but staples needed to be purchased. Each week we managed to buy several large boxes of groceries. Not too surprisingly, my very industrious mother rendered the lard after butchering to make our bar soap and laundry detergent—there wasn't a need to purchase many cleaning products. Special treats sometimes found their way into our grocery box: chocolate-covered marshmallow cookies with a cherry center come to mind! Potato chips were another favorite treat, and so was Wonder Bread! It's hard to imagine that I preferred that bread because Mom made us delicious homemade bread every week.

After grocery shopping, my mother, sister, and I usually went next door to Wenzel's, which was a favorite meeting place for women. The small department store sold work-related clothing, shoes, fabric, notions, and a limited selection of household items. Mom was always interested in looking at new fabrics and pattern books. Years earlier she'd taught herself to sew, making many of our clothes as well as her own dresses. Every Christmas, Easter, and Fourth of July, matching outfits were made for my sister and I. If there was extra money, a pattern and several yards of fabric and thread might be purchased for her next sewing project. Fabrics such as dotted Swiss, cotton prints, or corduroy might be selected with matching trims of rickrack, ribbon, or colorful buttons to adorn our newly created outfits. My mother was an excellent seamstress, but the nagging question remains: when did she find time to do all this work? It's astonishing that she was able to be so resourceful and creative on such a limited budget. There didn't appear to be any leisure time for my mother and yet she always seemed to have an abundance of energy. Mom usually had multiple projects going on at one time, always completing them with perfection!

Ten dollars! There was always money left over for Dad to enjoy a few beers and cigarettes at the pool hall with his cousins. As an occasional treat my sister and I might each be given a quarter for the movies, and many of our farm cousins might also join us. A new theater had been built across the street from the dime store, and it was a welcomed addition to our community. Admission to the new Lyric Theater was merely ten cents for children. Once inside our first stop was the snack bar for popcorn and soda pop, each costing a nickel! Our new theater had a small glass-enclosed balcony. Mothers could now take their babies out of the main theater if they were fussing. We called it the "crying room!"

As the large red curtain opened at the Lyric, a theater full of children were entertained with three or four cartoons. My favorites were Mr. Magoo and Tom and Jerry. Lengthy newsreels were next, with news about the ongoing Korean War. Numerous previews followed, and lastly we'd enjoy a double-feature movie. Throughout the evening, unruly children were frequently reprimanded by Mr. Wenzel, the proprietor. It was common for movie reels to break, resulting in house lights being temporarily turned on, which was an opportunity for the same unruly kids to toss popcorn at one another! Booing and hissing noises might continue for five or ten minutes while Mr. Wenzel busied himself splicing the movie reel in the projection room. I really loved going to the movies: over five hours were spent in the Lyric on those Saturday nights with my eyes riveted to that large screen.

    I'm convinced the Lyric was the only babysitter our parents had. Extended theater time provided them with the only kid-free time of the week. At about 11:30 p.m. all us kids raced out of the theater to check in with our parents at the pool hall. We always knew where our parents were—again, it was only about a block away! Remembering I still had a nickel in my pocket, I'd run next door to the Luncheonette for a yummy soft ice cream cone. Sometime between the ice cream and going back to our farm, there might even be time to chew and spit sunflower seeds with my cousins.

    Long after midnight our family would leave all the excitement in Eureka and return to our farm. If we were really tired my sister and I might fall asleep in the back seat, but I don't remember that happening too often. This was usually the time to start a family sing-along. Popular songs such as "Moonlight Bay," "Sincerely," or "Yellow Rose of Texas" come to mind. My mother harmonized with us but Dad couldn't carry a tune, because he was monotone, so instead of singing he'd begin to hum. If we happened to

Life on the Farm

take the back road to our farm, Spotty might be waiting for us next to our rural mailbox, about a mile from our farm. Spotty must have known it was Saturday night. He'd be eager to greet us, and we always gave him a ride back to the farm.

As if there hadn't been enough excitement for one night, much more was waiting for me on those warm summer nights. As we arrived home the moonlit sky was filled with bright twinkling stars, and a thick Milky Way illuminated our farmyard! It felt like I should be able to reach out and touch those stars—they seemed that close to me! Neighboring farms could easily be seen on those bright starlit nights. I remember our farmyard and the landscape to be a vivid color of midnight blue, and there appeared to be an endless horizon. Glancing towards the marshy lake beyond the windmill, I'd notice what looked like a small city of twinkling lights. Our lake happened to be aglow with thousands of fireflies! A mason jar was kept in the forehisely for those special occasions. After quickly scooping up a few fireflies close to the house, they'd be my night-light as I fell fast asleep.

After a very late night, Sunday mornings always arrived too quickly. We'd attend church in Eureka after completing our morning chores. My earliest recollections of our church day began with a German service, after which there was an English service, followed by Sunday school. A few years later the German service was discontinued, but it was still a long time for young children to sit quietly, at least I had great difficulty doing so. Most of my early church memories are about our minister; he always seemed angry or annoyed with the congregation during his sermons. At times he'd raise his voice and slam his fist on the pulpit, working himself into a feverish pitch. His face would get beet red while he proclaimed we were all doomed and going to hell; apparently he was exasperated about all the sinning that was going on. I've since wondered if he'd driven downtown on Saturday night and noticed people were having lots of fun in the pool hall!

Predictably, sometime during the lengthy sermon I'd become bored and restless from sitting too long. Mom always anticipated my actions, and out of her purse came a hankie which I'd begin to fold and fashion into two babies rocking. I'd also play, "This is the church, this is the steeple, open the door and see all people." I'd busy myself interlocking my fingers, opening my hands to reveal the steeple and all the people! Indeed, there were a lot of people in church on Sunday mornings; most everyone in our community attended church regularly.

I'd been told that years earlier only men sat on the right side of the church sanctuary, while women and children were seated on the left. I wonder what was up with that? I'm only guessing, but maybe it had something to do with only men being on the "right" side of God! I've been told several rebellious members of the congregation determined this was sheer nonsense, so they decided to shake things up a bit by having their families sit together! It apparently created quite an uproar in our church community. It took some time but ultimately the entire congregation became accustomed to the new seating arrangement.

Reflecting on my early church experiences, I found it frightening and disturbing that we were being reprimanded by the minister. While listening to the lecturing, I'd try to recall what I'd done wrong the prior week, wondering if I'd really been that bad. I was only six years old and was worried about hell; the minister had described it often enough and it didn't seem like a good place! I'm convinced fear was the motive used to effectively control parishioners, and I believe it continues to be a powerful tool used by some organized religions. Sadly, most of the preaching I remember as a child was about the fear of God instead of the love of God. While attending this church, the most positive experience for me was the music: there were the familiar sweet, melodic, and inspirational hymns with assuring lyrics of a peaceful and loving God. The music I enjoyed during church didn't at all correlate with the minister's troubling sermons. After what seemed like an eternity, I'd finally be released from church, and after a short break children were sent off to Sunday school. The minister's wife was at times our teacher, and sadly, she often had the same disposition as her husband. During Sunday school we read psalms, sang, and began our studies of the catechism. Catechism study was preparation for our eventual confirmation, which in our church occurred at age thirteen.

Sunday was to be a day of rest, and except for milking cows and feeding livestock, there wasn't to be other farmwork done on the sabbath. All businesses in Eureka were closed, and if we forgot to buy something Saturday night it would just have to wait until our next visit to town. Certain leisure activities might be limited in very religious households on Sunday—as well as every day of the week. I knew people who weren't allowed to dance or go to movies at the Lyric, and playing cards might be allowed if the Jack, King, Queen and Joker weren't used—those cards were thought to be the works of the devil! Apparently the use of scissors was also restricted in some households on the sabbath, and I recently learned my grandma Opp wouldn't use scissors on Sunday. I'm not sure if it was based on her religious beliefs or merely superstition, because I don't think anything would have prevented her from doing needlework or sewing. Actually, I recall Grandma was a bit superstitious. If eating utensils were accidentally dropped she'd quickly glance at the floor. If a knife was dropped she'd claim there'd be a gentleman caller, if it was a fork, a woman would be visiting, and a spoon would supposedly bring a child to the door!

After church our family returned to our farm to enjoy a leisurely Sunday afternoon. I'd be anxious to read the comics in the Aberdeen Sunday paper, which we referred to as the "funny papers." We'd soon initiate a plan about who we intended to visit late in the afternoon. People rarely called anyone to extend an invitation to their home, so visiting was a spur-of-the-moment thing. It was a natural assumption that guests would be staying for a meal—in fact, it was their intention to drop in for dinner or supper! It may seem ill-mannered, but no one seemed offended by this practice. Women never appeared flustered about unexpected dinner or supper guests or found it necessary to fix something extra special. A large stockpot of soup might have been prepared the day before. Maybe an additional jar of canned chicken, pork, or beef would be opened. There was always homemade bread and a few more potatoes were often added to stretch the meal. Of course there were always dill pickles—lots of pickles! Saturday was baking day, after all you never knew who might be dropping in on Sunday. Delicious pies, cakes, kuchen, cookies, and bars seemed to magically appear from kitchen cupboards to feed the uninvited guests!

Impromptu visiting could be tricky. At times we were in our car ready to visit someone when our plans abruptly changed, because glancing toward Highway 45 we noticed a car heading straight for our farm—someone was paying *us* a visit! Our family raced back into the house, quickly putting away our coats and hats. Sometimes it was disappointing for my sister and I if we anticipated visiting favorite cousins. My parents were determined we not tell our guests we were actually planning to go somewhere ourselves—what would people think? Unfortunately, Mom now had to put her apron on and begin to prepare a meal. Women always helped with cooking and cleanup whenever visiting someone's home. Homemade aprons were provided and a large stack of flour-sack dish towels were close by to dry the many dishes. Working together in the kitchen was an ideal time for women to socialize and it might also be a time to catch up on the latest gossip.

After church there might be a family gathering at the Helfenstein home in Eureka; this usually occurred on a holiday or celebration. My grandparents' home was large enough to accommodate the entire family for dinner, and over twenty people would be enjoying Grandma's chicken noodle soup. Grandma made her own egg noodles and the delicious soup was always served with ketchup and cinnamon. The meal included homemade bread, some type of "wurst" (sausage), pickles, and either kuchen, pie, or cake for dessert; it was the best! Obviously, not everyone was able to be seated at the same time. Men gathered around the dining table first, and children followed. Women were the last to eat. Fortunately at the Helfenstein house there was always an abundance of food.

CHAPTER SIX

Starting School

As the end of summer was approaching I was excited to begin school. Without a kindergarten program I'd be starting school as a first grader. A rural, one-room schoolhouse was located several miles from our farm. About fifteen of my second cousins attended the school, and I was anxious to join them. Instead, my parents announced my sister and I would be attending school in Eureka, claiming we'd receive a much better education. Of course I wanted to stay home and go to school with the farm kids, but there would be no discussion about the matter. We'd be living with my father's parents in Eureka, and coming home on weekends, vacations, and summer months. I was only six, so the thought of living away from home was very unsettling to me. There were reminders that Nils and Janet would be starting first grade with me, but it made no difference—I wanted to stay home! Our closest neighbor and second cousin would be joining us. Mary Jane and her brother Tom would live with their aunt, and we'd be the only children in our rural district to attend grade school in town. Being drawn together by this circumstance formed a strong friendship;

Starting School

it would become a lifelong bond. Living away from home seemed to be more difficult for Mary Jane and I. Less than one year apart in age, we both dealt with separation anxiety from our parents. Curiously, my sister didn't appear to be upset about going to school in Eureka.

I must have been in my grandparents' home many times, but realizing I'd now be living there made me see everything differently. My father's parents appeared to be old and very frail, and I quickly realized there'd be challenges communicating with them; they only spoke German and claimed to not understand a great deal of English. Although my sister and I understood everything they said, we'd lost much of our ability to speak German fluently. It's since occurred to me they may have understood more than we thought, hoping it would encourage us to speak more German.

My grandparents' house was directly across the street from the grade and high school. Their small home had only one bedroom, so my sister and I slept on a hide-a-bed in the front room. An oil furnace in one corner of their tiny kitchen provided warmth for our new surroundings. Always interested in bathroom accommodations, I discovered it was accessed by going through my grandparents' bedroom. Delighted to see a bathtub, I noticed it was filled with quilts and pillows. Grandma explained it was much too wasteful to fill the tub with water, so instead we'd be taking sponge baths while we lived there. Since the tub wasn't used in a conventional way, it instead provided a sleeping area for babies and very small children who visited their home.

When Grandma was cooking or washing dishes, water was retrieved from a water pump in the tiny kitchen. I was most surprised to see the brightly patterned linoleum kitchen floor completely covered with a layer of newspapers. This was done to apparently keep the floor clean! Once a week soiled newspapers were thrown out and replaced. It was puzzling, because I'd never seen another kitchen with newspapers all over the floor; I'm assuming this was done because Grandma wasn't able to scrub the floor. I just remember being very careful while walking through the kitchen; it's amazing my frail grandparents never injured themselves while walking on all those slippery newspapers!

On my first day of school, along with Nils and Janet, I was pleasantly surprised to discover six second cousins in my first-grade class. Looking for warm, fuzzy feelings from my teacher, there didn't appear to be any—she seemed very strict! Taking in my new environment, I immediately noticed a much older girl sitting in the back of our classroom. I certainly wasn't the only child somewhat bewildered by her presence; it appeared the girl was a classmate but nothing was mentioned about why she was there, and somehow we understood not to ask any questions about her. Obviously we should have been told to not stare at her, which of course is what I remember doing! The girl sat in a much larger desk that had been brought over from the high school. Marilyn was sixteen years old and mentally challenged; she had apparently been in the first-grade class for years. There weren't special education classes during this era, at least they weren't provided in the Eureka school system. Without another placement she'd spend yet another year in a classroom with five- and six-year-old children. Marilyn often lowered her head onto her wooden desktop to sleep, but much of the time she blankly stared at all of us children. As the school year progressed, I suppose we became accustomed to her solitary presence in the back of our classroom. Sadly, Marilyn was disregarded for the entire school year. No one seemed to interact with her, not even our teacher. I've thought of her often, wondering how many more years she spent in that classroom.

The school year had just begun, but living away from home was proving to be very difficult for me. I missed my parents terribly, and anxiously waited for each Friday so I could go back home. I made many tearful phone calls to the farm, pleading with my parents to come get me! My constant state of unhappiness must have been very troublesome for my parents and grandparents. As we were brought back to town Sunday evenings I'd be in tears; Grandma always did her best to console me.

I thought my grandparents were really old, but I now realize they were only in their sixties. I suppose they seemed old because of their numerous health problems. Grandpa was afflicted with a severe lung condition; as a young man a hay wagon had fallen on his chest. Following the accident his breathing became extremely labored at times, and the injury would impact his health for the remainder of his life. Grandma also had a number of medical issues, the most obvious of which was her difficulty with swallowing food. Everything she ate needed to be puréed or dipped in broth or coffee. Her throat condition brought on relentless coughing spells whenever she ate solid foods. It was frightening when she began to cough, and I would worry about her choking! Because of her difficulties with eating I doubt Grandma weighed more than ninety pounds. Both of my grandparents seemed to be in very fragile health.

What Will People Think?

Grandma and Grandpa Opp

AS WITH MANY MIDDLE-AGED WOMEN OF THAT GENERAtion, Grandma thought of herself as old. Her thinning grey hair was pulled back into a bun, and she wore long, dark print dresses, sensible shoes, and heavy cotton hose rolled down to her ankles. I remember her as being very sweet and soft-spoken, but she seemed to worry obsessively about her health. I now realize Grandma's behavior was eccentric and reclusive; she only attended small family gatherings, purposely avoiding large groups of people. Grandma was very religious but rarely attended church, claiming there were too many people in one area.

Grandpa was more social. He'd be anxious to visit people in the evening, and reluctantly Grandma agreed to go with him, but when it was time to leave she'd claim to have a headache. Her headache mysteriously disappeared when it was too late to go anywhere, and she'd soon be well enough to use her treadle sewing machine or begin crocheting. Grandma was perfectly content to stay home creating crochet doilies and sewing colorful aprons, and all the beautiful intricate needlework would be given to her children and grandchildren. If Grandma went outdoors, it was to tend to her garden. She delighted in caring for her vegetables and flowers, but even on warm days a coat and scarf were worn. Grandma also seemed to be concerned about sunlight because the house appeared dark much of the time. Windows and doors of their home were rarely opened. It seemed Grandma was always worried about a slight draft; she was very fearful of catching a cold. I remember being confused by her unusual behavior.

My grandparents didn't own a car. I assume groceries and supplies were brought into their home by aunts, uncles, and my parents. Meals in their home were noticeably different than what I was accustomed to; obviously food wasn't a dominant interest for Grandma because of her throat condition. My sister and I were food grazers, so having us eating frequently must have made it challenging for Grandma to satisfy our growing appetites. Sometimes I'd ask her to make popcorn, since it was my favorite snack, but it was usually burned! Most every Friday morning Grandma made dry-curd cottage cheese, and from this tasty dry cheese she made cheese buttons. Much like a large ravioli, the dough pocket was filled with a cheese/egg mixture with green onions, and it was then fried in butter and bread crumbs.

Along with this German-Russian dish we also enjoyed a cheese button soup with chicken broth. I waited for cheese buttons on Friday, because this was Grandma's signature dish. Friday was quickly becoming my favorite day of the week; along with Grandma's cheese buttons, it was the day my parents would take my sister and I back home!

Most breakfasts were cream of wheat and oatmeal, but sometimes Grandma made us chocolate pudding. It took on a grayish color because she was quite frugal with her use of cocoa, but still it was a special sweet treat, and after all who wouldn't enjoy pudding for breakfast? I would learn Grandma made my father the same gray pudding every morning when he was a child! We must have shared our food woes with our mother, because we were accustomed to her wonderful cooking and there were always seconds if we wanted. Mom soon began to supplement our diet, and there was more food appearing in our grandparents' refrigerator. One of our favorites was iced cocoa: this delicious drink was made with whole milk, and sometimes we added malt powder because we loved malted milkshakes! Unlike Grandma, Mom used lots of cocoa in our nutritious milk drink. We'd consume a gallon of this rich chocolate milk every week.

Sitting at the little green kitchen table while enjoying the warmth of the oil furnace is where I experienced my first coffee drink. Grandma drank a lot of coffee and I suppose she thought I might also enjoy it. After she put a small amount of coffee in my cup, heavy cream was added, followed by several teaspoons of sugar—definitely ahead of my time, I was drinking something that resembled a latte! I enjoyed a cup of this hot, sweet drink before I went off to school each morning until Mom discovered what Grandma was serving me. She was not pleased, and my caffeine habit ended abruptly!

While living with my grandparents, I was introduced to chamomile tea. The flowers simply flourished in Grandma's large garden. After we picked the small white flowers, they were dried on newspapers. Grandma used a lot of newspapers—and when completely dry, chamomile was kept in a covered mason jar. Grandma thought chamomile tea was a cure-all for just about anything that ailed me. Tea compresses were applied to my eyes whenever I had pink eye, and hot tea was also used as an aid for indigestion. When I had a tummy ache (particularly on Sunday evenings), chamomile flowers were brewed and a spoonful of honey was added for sweetening. I found it very soothing, and this was a hot drink my mother approved of.

Visiting Eureka forty years later, I discovered chamomile growing where my grandparents' house had once stood. Chamomile flowers were everywhere—they were seeds from the large garden Grandma had taken such good care of. When I planted the seeds in Portland, I had little success; apparently chamomile didn't like our warmer Northwest climate. I felt strongly about preserving my grandmother's tea, because it was the same strain of sweet chamomile our ancestors brought with them from Germany and/or Russia. I've been told women had carefully sewn chamomile and vermouth seeds into the hems of their coats and dresses before their departures!

Chamomile and vermouth had been essential to our ancestors' comfort and well-being, so I assume they were determined to find a clever way to conceal the seeds. Their concerns were valid, because I'm certain the seeds would have been confiscated upon their arrival to America. As our ancestors began to homestead on the Dakota prairie, chamomile and vermouth seeds were planted in their gardens. Both hardy plants seemed to thrive in the region because of similar climate and soil conditions to their homeland. Together with other natural remedies, they were used as medicinal treatments to help relieve ailments and chronic illnesses. Early settlers may have been aware of inadequate medical care in the region they'd be calling their home; it would be several more decades before doctors began to practice medicine in McPherson County.

The farming community I grew up in has dramatically changed. Most small farms I remember as a child have disappeared. While visiting a vacated farm years ago, all that remained was the foundation where a house had once stood. To my surprise hearty chamomile flowers continued to thrive next to the foundation!

Searching for information about our family tea, I visited the Stash Tea Company in Northwest Portland in the mid-eighties. The company had been cofounded in 1972 by tea master Steve Smith. Steve greeted me as I entered the building. He was intrigued when he saw me carrying a mayonnaise jar containing dried chamomile flowers! After he analyzed seeds in his laboratory, a cup of tea was brewed. Taking a sip of tea he stated it was the purest chamomile he'd ever tasted! The company's sources for chamomile were from various regions throughout the world, and I was told our tea far surpassed what was available to them at Stash.

After learning how I'd obtained the tea, Steve expressed interest in sharing the story about our family's tea in their upcoming Christmas catalog. He was particularly fascinated with how the seeds had arrived in this country, and suggested they needed at least thirty pounds of chamomile to begin this venture! It was exciting to imagine the unlimited possibilities of promoting our family tea but it was also concerning. Harvesting chamomile was very labor intensive, because our tea needed to be handpicked. The probability of providing Stash Tea with thirty pounds of chamomile flowers and promoting this business venture seemed highly unlikely.

I WAS EXCITED TO SHARE MY TEA DISCOVERY WITH SEVeral people in Eureka, but there was curiosity why anyone would go to the trouble and expense of harvesting tea when it was available at the health-food store in Aberdeen. I explained that our family tea was an entirely different strain of chamomile. Many people consider chamomile to be too invasive, and with the use of weed killers they've been fairly successful in getting rid of what they refer to as the "chamomile weed"! I'm pleased a number of relatives in rural Eureka continue to share my enthusiasm about our ancestral tea; they value the gift and understand the need to preserve this part of our heritage. Steve Smith eventually launched the Tazo Tea Company. It's been over thirty years since he analyzed our family tea, but I recall his last comment regarding our ancestral tea. He said, "Whatever you decide to do with your family's chamomile, don't ever throw away the seeds in the bottom of that mayonnaise jar, they're alive and well!"

Sitting next to Grandpa's rocking chair every Wednesday evening I'd watch him stoke his pipe while we anxiously waited for our favorite radio program, *Amos and Andy*, to begin. He claimed to not understand English, but obviously enjoyed the dialogue, laughing whenever he heard

Rochester's gravelly voice! Coincidentally, it was usually the time Grandma began to use her sewing machine. Grandpa would be irritated, because the treadle sewing machine in this small room was making too much noise for us to hear the radio, and there'd usually be some scolding in German. Grandpa often walked downtown to buy thread at Wenzel's for Grandma's needlework projects. He'd often return with a different color thread or the wrong thread count, and there might be more scolding: "Newh, newh, newh!" It seemed he was expecting her response when he came home—with a twinkle in his eye and a mischievous grin, he'd again be on his way downtown to exchange the thread. I've suspected Grandpa may have intentionally bought the wrong thread so he could spend more time socializing with his friends. If that was his intent, he experienced terrible breathing problems after returning from walking that short distance.

As the school year continued I'm sure my parents were hoping I'd adjust to being away from home, but the new living arrangement with my grandparents wasn't getting easier for me. I'd be so happy to see my parents each Friday, but when brought back to town on Sunday evenings my tummy ache and tears returned. As winter arrived, snowstorms often prevented my parents from coming to town, so another week or two would go by without seeing them. I was learning to be concerned about weather at a young age! I always hoped for a big blizzard when home on the weekend so our family would be snowbound together. There were a few times we were snowbound for about three weeks!

If there was a heavy snowfall my parents usually found a way to get us back to town. We'd be taken to the Wittmayer farm with horse and sleigh, because it was only a mile away and very close to Highway 45. Snowplows normally cleared that road, as well as Highway 10, allowing Mary Jane's parents to drive us kids to town. My constant state of homesickness had to be troubling for my grandparents, because it required more of their time and energy. I can only speculate why they were asked to take on this responsibility, but my sister and I continued to live with my grandparents for the entire school year of 1951.

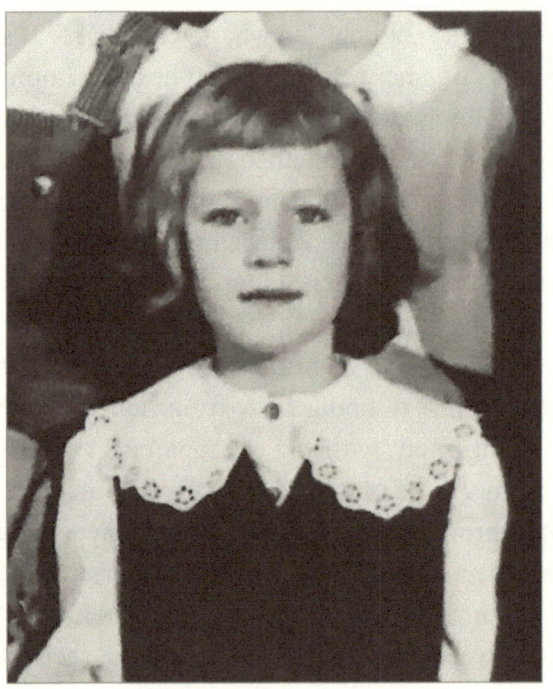

First Grade

THERE WERE A NUMBER OF THINGS I LIKED ABOUT MY school in Eureka. I was intrigued with the structure itself:

it was the largest building I'd ever been in. The building was three stories: first, second, and third grades were on the main level, and the second floor held fourth, fifth, and sixth graders. A very small lunchroom was in the copula on the third level. Most students went home for lunch, but on extremely cold days children brought their lunches to school. It wasn't a problem for my sister and I; we'd run across the street to eat at Grandpa and Grandma's house. The large bell on the school building was our reminder to get back to school after lunch. In fact, the school bell was often our wake-up alarm if we overslept in the morning, because the bell was very loud and could be heard throughout town. The first bell allowed us about twenty minutes to dress and quickly eat breakfast before the tardy bell rang.

The grade school had a large basement where the music room, projection room, bathrooms, and furnace room were located. A long, dark tunnel connected our school to the high school gymnasium, but thankfully there wasn't a need for us younger children to go to the high school too often. An enclosed fire escape slide exited from the sixth-grade classroom on the second story, and a metal cover affixed to the bottom of the slide kept children from climbing inside. There were frequent fire drills. Concerned the cover hadn't been removed during a drill, I envisioned children being stuck inside the tunnel on top of each other!

Bathroom concerns followed me into the first grade. Our teacher had instructed us to raise a hand when needing to use the bathroom. We were instructed to hold up one finger or two depending on what kind of bathroom business we needed to take care of—it was terribly embarrassing! I've since discovered she wasn't the only teacher of that era needing to know what bodily function was about to take place. It suddenly occurred to me—how is she going to know?

Searching for opportunities to leave the classroom I'd eagerly volunteer for eraser duty, which was a favorite activity. Finding my way to the basement with a bucket of dirty erasers, I'd locate the huge eraser-cleaning machine. The device had a large brush which rotated as the handle was turned, and while holding an eraser against the brush with one hand I'd turn the handle with my other hand. There'd be a huge cloud of chalk dust. A bin below the machine was designed to collect dust, but instead much of it ended up on the floor and all over me. I'd come back to the classroom with a bucket of clean erasers but covered with white chalk dust!

Halloween was new to me, and I discovered it was one of the positive things about living in town. After school I'd be at one of my cousin's homes rummaging through boxes of discarded clothing to assemble a costume. Our plan was to trick-or-treat all over town, but my grandparents weren't excited about me being out after dark—because of the language barrier, they never knew when I'd be home! Our Halloween treats were usually homemade cookies, popcorn balls, apples, or penny candy; no one was ever concerned about children eating anything homemade. Each year a woman gave trick-or-treaters a nickel, and children were lined up at her front door! In 1950 a nickel bought us a lot of candy, an ice cream cone, or even half of a theater ticket.

CHAPTER SEVEN

Winter on the Plains

With the arrival of winter I discovered the convenience of a chemical toilet in our farmhouse basement. It was located close to the warmth of the furnace, and as an added bonus there weren't any pesky flies to bother me! Actually, it would have been impossible to use the outhouse for much of the winter; extreme cold was a factor, but for most of the winter this small building wasn't visible—it was completely covered with snow! I enjoyed the luxury of our indoor toilet during the winter. With the arrival of spring our outhouse would again be open for business!

The first winter on our farm brought record amounts of snowfall. Sometimes my father had to tunnel his way out of the house; a shovel was kept in the forehisely for that purpose. If a heavy snowfall appeared on weekends, I'd hurry outdoors to make a snow angel, build igloos, and dig tunnels. After extended blizzards it wasn't unusual to see huge snowdrifts reach the roofs of our barn, granary, garage, and chicken coop. As snow hardened from extreme cold, I'd soon be able to walk onto the roofs of several outbuildings! It was very challenging to stay warm while playing outdoors; my bulky snowsuit, cap, mittens, and overshoes were worn for only brief periods of play. An itchy wool scarf was wrapped around my neck, covering everything except my eyes. The bright sun and crystal blue sky seemed inviting but it was deceiving: once outside, the frigid air created a burning sensation in my lungs! Within minutes the scarf was frozen to my face from condensation and I'd be numb from the cold. Frostbite was always a concern, and I'd soon be indoors sitting next to the heat register to warm up. On those bright cold winter days there'd be several attempts to play outdoors when temperatures were far below zero—all that beautiful snow was waiting for me!

If our family was snowbound there were never concerns of depleting our food supply. Anticipating a long winter, all the butchering and canning had been done in the fall, and an abundance of food had been stockpiled. A large barrel located next to our house contained frozen packages of beef and pork, and it served as our outdoor freezer during the winter! Contents in the barrel were protected from animals by placing a large rock on the lid. When we no longer had freezing temperatures, Mom canned the packages of meat that remained in the barrel. Boredom was rarely an issue if snowbound; a puzzle on the card table in one corner of the front room might occupy our family for a week or so. An intense game of Monopoly might even take several days to complete, and other favorite board games such as Sorry, Clue, and Chinese Checkers also helped pass the time. Most nights while playing board games or cards we enjoyed our favorite snack of popcorn: served in a large tub, it was topped with homemade butter and salt. Popcorn was considered a healthy, inexpensive snack.

What Will People Think?

The coal-burning furnace in the basement kept our farmhouse comfortably warm during the coldest of temperatures. There was limited heat from registers on the second story of our farmhouse, so other than sleeping, not much time was spent upstairs during the winter. We slept on feather beds and kept toasty warm with homemade goose down quilts. On extremely cold nights a large rock was heated on top of the furnace; wrapped in a heavy cloth, it was used as a welcomed bed warmer. I'd jump out of bed on those chilly, wintry mornings, locate my wool slipper socks, and quickly race down the long flight of stairs. Wearing my heavy flannel pajamas, I'd park myself on a rug in front of the wall heat register in the dining room—I discovered it was the warmest place in our house!

Judy next to heat register

Winter on the Plains

My mother shared stories of their cold bedrooms when she was growing up on the Helfenstein homestead. Heat registers weren't opened on the second story of their farmhouse during the winter, so she'd wake up with frost on her blanket from the condensation of her breath! Girls slept in one bed and boys in another, and body heat kept them warm during those very cold nights. Chamber pots were used during the winter for bathroom needs, and apparently the pot was frozen in the morning! I also remember the use of a chamber pot in our bedroom; it was very much a welcomed convenience in the winter months.

During an extended blizzard, the radio in the front room was our only communication with the outside world. Powered by limited REA, it was at times difficult to get a clear station, so we'd be anxiously waiting for the latest weather forecast. Strong winds often brought down power lines, interrupting both radio and telephone service. Weather was always a concern for farmers, but it was vital information during the winter months while caring for livestock. The stock tank was often frozen, so Dad would use an ax to chop holes through the ice, allowing livestock to access water. Animals instinctively knew when bad weather was approaching, so the barn door was kept open allowing them to seek shelter. If farm animals weren't able to reach shelter during a severe blizzard their nostrils might freeze, causing them to perish in a snowstorm!

It was extremely difficult to do daily chores if experiencing a fierce blizzard. Our barn was only about a hundred feet from the house but there were many times it wasn't visible! Although weather conditions were dire, farm animals required feed and cows needed to be milked. To safely reach the barn, Dad tied a rope onto the front door of our house. Carefully holding the rope, he'd attempt to walk towards the barn in the blinding snow. It took quite a while to walk that short distance, and he needed to be careful because a strong gust of wind might easily separate him from the rope—it was his lifeline! After the exhaustive effort of walking through three or four feet of snow, Dad tied the rope onto the barn door. Mom anxiously waited for Dad to tug on the rope, which was a signal indicating he'd safely reached the barn. During those severe blizzards he'd do all the chores, while Mom stayed in the house with my sister and I for safety reasons. Parents worried their young children might venture outdoors and become disoriented in a blinding snowstorm! The fear of house fires or other emergencies were additional concerns if children were left alone in the house.

Completing the milking and separating was a lengthy process for Dad. Mom would estimate how long it might take him to do the work, and I'd sense her concern as she began to worry about Dad's well-being. It was important to be vigilant and aware of potential life-threatening weather conditions. Losing sense of direction during a whiteout was frightening, and each year we'd hear of someone perishing in a blizzard while doing outdoor chores. After storms subsided the unfortunate victim was often found only several feet from shelter! I have vivid recollections of my mother, sister, and I looking out of the west kitchen window hoping to catch a glimpse of my father. We saw nothing but blinding snow—I remember anxiously waiting for his safe return!

The early fifties brought dangerous blizzards to the plains of the Dakotas, and temperatures frequently reached thirty or forty degrees below zero for extended periods of time. References were never made to windchill temperatures, as that was an unfamiliar term; this was the Fahrenheit temperature! With such treacherous conditions it was extremely difficult to do even minimal farm work.

Laundering bedding and clothing was more challenging for my mother during the winter months, and outer garments weren't changed every day to minimize work. Our clothes were once frozen on the wash line, so Mom brought everything indoors, and clothing was leaned against the dining-room walls! Garments were usually hung in the basement during the winter, where everything dried quickly because the wash line was close to the furnace. Trudging through deep snow to retrieve well water for laundry and other needs was painstaking work. Sometimes we'd retrieve buckets of new snow by simply opening the front door—it melted quickly indoors!

Typically, a clear blue sky appeared following an extended blizzard. Bright sun reflecting on massive amounts of snow was at times blinding! It was always tempting to play outside, but after checking the temperature gauge we'd discover it was much too cold. After days of heavy snowfall and strong winds I'd notice interesting sculptures of huge snowdrifts throughout our farmyard. During this brief period between storms our family would initiate a plan to visit neighbors close to our farm. All farm roads and our closest highway were at times completely blocked and as a result, the only means of transportation was with horse and sleigh! Travel was limited to neighbors who lived within a mile or two of our farm; we didn't want to be far from home because weather could change quickly. Traveling by sleigh allowed our family an evening of much-needed socialization; having been housebound for two or three weeks, we'd be anxious to see people outside our immediate family.

To begin our adventure Dad hitched the workhorses to a sleigh. Our sleigh wasn't something you'd envision from a Norman Rockwell painting—instead it was a flat sled used for hauling manure and picking rocks in the spring! Yes, rocks were picked—each year they came to the surface of the soil during spring plowing. The German word for our sled was "ruutch." Any remains of manure had been cleaned, and furthermore it was much too cold to detect an odor! Adding to our comfort, Dad secured an old bench car seat onto the sled, where my mother, sister, and I would sit. We'd be bundled up in our snowsuits and covered with old wool blankets. A tarp protected us from snow being kicked up from the horses' hooves—or anything else they might send our way! Being completely covered kept us comfortably warm while traveling that short distance.

I'd be excited to hear the bells tied onto the horses' manes, because it meant we were finally on our way, and as Dad shouted commands to the horses we'd begin to glide across the deep mounds of snow! Without a seat for himself, he stood in front of our bench seat with a firm grip on the horses' reins. It always amazed me how Dad managed to balance himself over the rough terrain. There weren't hills around us, but the huge snowdrifts created during the blizzard made it feel as if we were no longer on flat Dakota prairie! I'd be anxious to catch a quick glimpse of my surroundings and sometimes peeked out from beneath the heavy blankets. The brilliance of the Milky Way in the night sky seemed to cast a magnificent blue sparkling effect on the snow; it was stunningly beautiful! The brightness of the moon and twinkling stars helped lead our way in the night.

On those cold, crisp, still nights, sounds could be heard a mile away. I'd be waiting to hear the familiar crunching sound of snow beneath the sleigh as the horses encountered huge snowdrifts. The horses would be snorting heavily, and those sounds were amplified as the they struggled to pull our sleigh over the deep snow. While attempting to navigate a large snowdrift, their hooves often kicked a clump of snow on top of our sleigh. If I caught another quick glance, snow might hit my face—it never bothered me, I was much too excited! I remember those sleigh rides as being absolutely breathtaking and magical! Not too surprisingly, my favorite horse-drawn rides were visits to the Wittmayer farm, where after approaching their farmyard we'd be dropped off at the house. Dad continued to their barn where horses were unhitched from the sleigh, and given hay and water so they'd be well rested for our return trip home.

Having been snowbound for a number of weeks, it was so exciting to see people outside our family. Our parents would spend the evening playing cards; their games of choice were pinochle or the familiar card game of "high low jack." My sister, Mary Jane, and I loved playing board games while snacking on popcorn. I also have fond memories of Hulda (Mary Jane's mother) having a huge display of yummy food on the kitchen table! My parents would occasionally look out the window to check on weather conditions because an approaching storm might shorten our visit. Long past midnight after a fun-filled evening, we'd begin the familiar sleigh ride back to our farm, where the brilliance of the moon and stars would again be our guiding light!

I was becoming accustomed to severe winter weather while living in this rural community, but found it frightening to hear of people being stranded in their cars during blizzards. During the winter of 1951 the Wittmayer farm was a safe haven for two people whose car became stuck in the snow. Mary Jane's father was able to reach them on Highway 45 with his tractor. After being brought to the Wittmayer home, they were given food and shelter while the blizzard raged on for three weeks! These travelers were extremely fortunate because several people in McPherson County would perish as a result of this storm. Ours was a community where people would always be helping one another in times of need or misfortune, reminiscent of our ancestors first setting foot on the plains of South Dakota.

Weather permitting, a welcomed telephone call kept us in communication with friends and relatives during those long winter months. Our large oak wall phone was in our dining room. While standing on a chair I'd be able reach the speaker and handheld receiver. Our fence party line included ten or twelve families (all relatives) in our neighboring farm community. Everyone always "listened in" on each other's phone conversations; it was a favorite pastime and an opportunity to catch up on the latest gossip! No one was offended by this practice. Multiple people entered into the conversation, and it was a normal activity. Whenever someone picked up the receiver to listen in, they'd scratch the receiver with their fingernail to let everyone know someone else had just joined the party!

The telephone switchboard was located in the Wittmayer home. Many years earlier Mary Jane's mother had accepted the responsibilities as the switchboard operator. Hulda's duties were to connect calls twenty-four hours a day, seven days a week to people who weren't on our fence party line. She was paid eight dollars a month! Whenever visiting their home I was very interested in checking out the mechanics of this fascinating device, but was told it wasn't a toy, and reminded to keep my curious fingers off all those plugs and wires!

The phone-ring pattern for our farmhouse was two longs and three shorts. There weren't numbers or prefixes to remember; neighbors on our fence line each had a different combination of longs and shorts. People in Eureka had only three or four digits for their phone numbers. The operator in town connected all local calls, and of course she knew everyone. When placing a call to our farm I'd be careful about who or what I talked about, always aware that a number of people might be listening to my conversation. I'm certain the rural community knew of my homesickness because of the frequent phone calls to my mother!

I ONCE CALLED MY MOTHER FROM MY GRANDPARENTS' house to let her know I'd forgotten to pack my day-of-the-week underwear for the coming week. I suppose there should be an explanation about day-of-the-week underwear: during the fifties, it was a popular choice of panties for little girls. Each day of the week was colorfully embroidered on the underwear except for Sunday. Never having thought much about it as a child, I later learned it was considered sacrilegious to have the word *Sunday* embroidered on underwear! So yes, there were only six pair of panties in a package. I suppose the obvious question remains: what did I wear on Sunday? During this difficult phone call I tried to explain what I'd forgotten to pack without mentioning the word *panties*. Understandably, my mother was frustrated and annoyed with my guessing game during her busy workday, so I embarrassingly blurted out the missing article of clothing. Wouldn't you know it—the very next Saturday night in town a number of women came up to me and said, "Judy, make sure you don't forget your panties when you go back to school!" I was mortified; what would people think! There could be no secrets when everyone listened in on your phone conversations. As I've mentioned, in this community people always made it a point to know your business!

Several months before the Christmas season catalogs were delivered to our rural mailbox. Excited about their arrival, we'd begin to earmark pages in those giant "wish books." Sears Roebuck, Montgomery Ward, and Spiegel catalogs were our connection to the outside world. What an excellent pun—those catalogs did end up in the outhouse! Paging catalogs was a favorite pastime. Admiring the latest fashions brought my sister and I hours of amusement. The all-too-familiar dialogue would begin: "If you had to choose a favorite dress on this page, which one would it be?" "What would be your second choice?" This activity continued, one page after another, with us always evaluating likes and dislikes regarding style or color of clothing. I'd be bored after ten or twelve pages and eager to do something else, but my sister would have been content playing catalog for days. At a very young age it was apparent my sister had a keen eye for design and color. She became a graphic artist and also designed clothing early in her career. I believe this type of play helped expand creative thinking, as well as develop our vivid imaginations.

I was so happy to be home for our three-week Christmas vacation. Anticipating many visitors during the holiday, we'd begin to bake kuchen and a variety of cookies; and of course there was lots of fudge and divinity candy! Mom made most of our Christmas decorations, and she'd also put finishing touches on our Christmas dresses. A small fir tree was purchased from the grocery store, and we'd string popcorn and cranberries to decorate our tree. I don't recollect having traditional ornaments; instead, a single string of multicolored bulbs with reflector backings illuminated our tree. The final decorative touch was a box of glittery silver tinsel draped over the branches. The tinsel was carefully removed after the holiday and saved for the next year. I thought our tree was magnificent!

Church activities dominated the holiday season. Weeks before Christmas each child in our congregation was given a verse to memorize, which we'd be expected to recite at the Christmas Eve service. Every year my cousins and I were concerned about how long our verse or piece (as we called it) would be. Standing alone before the congregation was worrisome; what if I forgot my piece—what would people think? That phrase was repeated often during my childhood. Being concerned about what people thought seemed to be of great significance. Always aware of the importance of doing well, as we nervously finished our piece we were given a brown paper sack from beneath the large Christmas tree adorning the alter. The sack was filled with oranges, apples, nuts, peppermint candy canes, and hard rock ribbon candy. It was a special treat each year!

Buying gifts wasn't a major part of our family's holiday tradition. Economics were a factor, but the emphasis was on celebrating Jesus's birth. Christmas season was also a time for many family gatherings, and not too surprisingly there was an abundance of food; it seemed to be the primary focus of most gatherings! In our family, like many others, we splurged on specialty food items instead of buying lots of gifts. It may seem simplistic but it obviously made for a less stressful holiday. As we left for church on Christmas Eve, Mom always found a reason to go back into the house. She'd retrieve a hat, gloves, or scarf while we patiently waited in the car. Mom was consistent with her story each year, and/or apparently very forgetful! Our unwrapped Santa gift was placed beneath the tree, and it was our only Christmas present.

Without exception my roller skates were my favorite Santa gift, but I remember the most disappointing Santa gift happened to be the Holy Bible! Although my name was engraved in gold on the cover, it made no difference—I was still unhappy about my gift! My thoughts were kept to myself. They weren't even shared with my sister, but I wondered if she was also disappointed, because she got the same Santa gift! Consumed with guilt for a VERY long time, there were the usual concerns about what people would think if they found out I was unhappy about getting a Bible for Christmas?

My father always did his Christmas shopping for Mom on our way to church every Christmas Eve. There'd be a "quick" stop at the Rexall drug store, and while Dad made his purchase the three of us waited inside the car. If parked in front of the store we'd watch him through the store window! Dad's selection was usually the first item he saw—Mom would get so irritated with him! One year he purchased a lovely blue powder-puff music box. Opening the back door of the car, he tossed the package onto the back seat; the lid popped off and the music began to play! It was definitely an icebreaker for Mom, and we all laughed about the spoiled surprise.

The following year, his last-minute shopping didn't have the same happy ending. The gift my father purchased at Rexall was a *Betty Crocker* cookbook. Mom was terribly offended, and accused Dad of not liking her cooking; she mistakenly assumed the cookbook was purchased to improve her cooking skills! Quickly coming to our father's defense, my sister and I explained that Mom didn't have a cookbook, and it also had beautiful pictures of interesting recipes. It made little difference, because the *Betty Crocker* cookbook was taken back to the store and Dad never heard the end of it!

Uncle Ted and Aunt Ida's ranch was the usual gathering place for the Opp family Christmas dinner because their house was spacious enough to accommodate the family. I have fond memories of their big beautiful farmhouse. It was unusual to have an open oak staircase and built-in oak bookcases with leaded glass doors in our rural community. A sunroom on the main floor and a balcony on the second story also made their house seem very unique. As a child I thought their house was huge, but years later I was astounded to discover how small the rooms were! In later years the, the Lazy O Ranch became known for raising prized registered Herefords. My aunt and uncle still live on the ranch. Having reached 103 and 105 years of age, they recently celebrated their eighty-third wedding anniversary!

Christmas Day at the ranch found our mothers in the kitchen busily preparing food for our large family. After supper, us kids anxiously waited for the Christmas box to appear; every year a huge box of gifts was sent to the ranch from our relatives in Oregon. The box contained about thirty-five gifts, one for each member of the family. After supper and a great deal of pestering by us children, the box finally appeared in the front room! It was really exciting to see the colorful packages with Christmas paper and matching ribbons because this was my only wrapped gift. We'd begin to shake our packages, trying to guess what was inside! Aunt Esther was very creative. She'd sew aprons for the women, and men in the family might unwrap a colorful tie she'd made. All us children might discover a new board game or puzzles. I remember how those simple gifts brought us so much joy!

My aunt and uncle and their daughters had moved to Portland years earlier as our country was coming out of the deep depression. For a number of years Uncle Richard held numerous jobs and owned several small businesses, and he struggled to provide for his family. As our country entered the Second World War, my aunt found employment in the shipyards. She once told me they lived very frugally on my uncle's salary while hers was saved to start their future business. The postwar years brought a healthier economy to the area, along with the eventual success of their steak house which was established in 1946. It now allowed them to give back to their extended family in the Midwest. I've never forgotten their kindness and generosity; it meant a great deal to me as a young child. After our family moved to Oregon, I was involved with the ritual of Christmas shopping and wrapping gifts for our relatives in South Dakota; I remember feeling such pride to be a part of this annual family tradition!

Following the Christmas season our community eagerly waited to celebrate New Year's Eve. As with each holiday it was spent with family, and food was again an important part of every gathering. Arriving home far past midnight and having been asleep for only an hour or two, we'd be woken up by very loud noises around three or four o'clock in the morning! Waking people up in the early hours of New Year's Day was a customary practice by our adult relatives; it was a German tradition. Young men roamed the countryside traveling from farm to farm "shooting in the new year." They'd be blasting car horns and shooting rifles in the air! One New Year's Eve several people were actually on the steep roof of our farmhouse attempting to wake us! Our uninvited relatives were making all that noise to announce their presence, and their intent with all this disturbance was to be invited inside for drinks! I loved being woken up in the middle of the night by this rowdy group! Of course they'd be welcomed indoors and given a shot of schnapps in hopes that they'd soon be on their way! After reciting a traditional New Year's verse in German, this band of revelers would be off to the next farm for a repeat performance.

Another food memory was waiting for "lunch" to be served. The infamous lunch wasn't only served during holidays, it was a normal occurrence after an evening of visiting and typically occurred around 11:00 p.m. Kitchen or dining room tables were covered with what appeared to be an endless display of food. This late-night lunch often consisted of a variety of sausages, bread, cheese, whipped Jell-O, potato chips, pickles, pickled watermelon, cakes, pies, brownies, cookies, candy, beverages, and of course, most always our traditional kuchen. Children had every intention of staying awake for lunch, but sometimes we were just too tired, and one by one, kids dropped off to sleep on a bed piled high with coats. It was difficult for me to stay up that late, but if I fell asleep I'd miss lunch! It didn't take long to discover who served the best lunches, so I'd do my best to stay awake for this fabulous late-night treat.

When lunch was served at our home during the winter, it usually included homemade ice cream with hot fudge. Our ice-cream maker was a hand-crank device and we were never without the ingredients. Cream was as fresh as the day the cows were milked, there was an endless supply of eggs, and of course ice was all around us! Sugar, vanilla, and rock salt (for the ice) were the remaining ingredients needed to complete the recipe. As Dad churned the ice-cream maker, my sister and I were always close by—the beaters needed to be licked! Ice cream was kept in our "outside" freezer until ready to be served.

While home on weekends during the winter months there were occasional gatherings for a steak fry in our basement. Grilled round steak was a rare treat. Placed on a wire grill and barbecued in the open furnace, it was served with sliced sweet onions and ketchup on homemade bread. Another food memory was roasted corn on the cob. After being grilled in the furnace for several minutes, a few kernels might actually pop on the corn cob. It was dipped into melted butter, then salt and peppered.

As you've noticed, the subject of food does seem to dominate my writings. "Real" food was, and still is, a significant part of the culture I grew up in. I suppose it's because farmers were acutely aware of their food source, from the caring of their livestock to the butchering process and preservation of food. Finally, there was the preparation and social interaction of sharing all that delicious food with friends and family. In retrospect, my innumerable food memories are some of the most treasured times of my childhood. It's apparent there was an association with sharing all this good food with the people I loved!

Winter on the Plains

AFTER EXPERIENCING A LONG, COLD WINTER, EVERYONE eagerly waited for a few early signs of spring. Mother nature wasn't always ready to give up on winter that easily, and we often experienced late snowstorms in April or May. Unexpected spring blizzards came up quickly, but usually lasted only a few days. If farmers were in town at the onset of the storm they were often stranded in Eureka. It was wise to stay with relatives until the storm had subsided, rather than risk traveling back to their farms in hazardous conditions. If phone lines were down due to weather problems there might be concerns about whether loved ones had reached a safe shelter. Unfortunate travelers stuck on a snowy country road might be stranded overnight in their cars, and in that event it was always advisable to have an emergency supply of food and blankets in their vehicles.

CHAPTER EIGHT

Spring and Summer of 1951

With the arrival of spring, mounds of snow melted and early field work would begin for farmers. My sister and I might still be able to enjoy ice-skating on a small pond close to one of the tree groves. Our skates weren't conventional ice skates. Dad had made them by attaching two metal runners onto a piece of wood, and a wide leather strap secured the unique skates onto our overshoes. Our skates were very basic in design: we were only able to skate in a straight line, but with the help of a long metal rod we could easily glide across the ice! As temperatures got warmer, melting occurred below the surface of the ice. We referred to this as "rubber" ice. Water below the thin layer of ice moved in a wave-like motion, creating lots of fun while skating! It might sound dangerous to be skating on melting ice but we never broke through; our skating pond was only about two feet deep, so it was never really a safety concern for us.

Spring and Summer of 1951

My sister and I on homemade skates

WHILE HOME ON WEEKENDS IN EARLY SPRING I'D NOTICE a number of additions to the livestock. There'd be baby lambs in our farmyard and new calves in the pasture. Newborn lambs were sometimes rejected by their mother, and this meant we'd need to care for them. I'd be excited to discover several lambs in our forehisely, where they'd be kept toasty warm while curled up on old blankets in an oversized box. Since they required nourishment on a regular schedule, I'd volunteer to help with bottle-feeding and cuddling! Within several weeks they'd be strong enough to join the rest of the flock. Newborn calves needing additional care were kept in a small fenced area of our farmyard. I'd attempt to bottle-feed them through the fence, but it was always challenging. Being very aggressive, they'd often snatch the milk bottle right out of my hand!

Spring season and milder weather turned out to be somewhat helpful with my homesickness. I had new roller skates and miles of sidewalks in Eureka; skating quickly became my favorite pastime. Every day after school my friends and I strapped on our skates, and we skated until suppertime. My grandparents weren't pleased about my skating. They worried about my safety, and there were concerns I'd injure myself while on their watch; as a grandmother I now know this to be true! Communicating with them continued to be a challenge, because they never knew where I was going or when I'd be home. As I left the house, Grandma and Grandpa shook their heads as they watched me jump off curbs and lunge over cracks in the sidewalks with great speed! There might have been an occasional fall, but other than a few cuts and bruises, there was never a serious injury from my fearless roller-skating!

My Kingston Deluxe adjustable metal skates were made by the Chicago Skate Company, and they were my only pair of skates. As my shoe size changed, the wrench which was part of my skate key easily adapted the skates to my new shoe size. The skates had excellent ball-bearing wheels, so I was able to move quite freely with them. A leather ankle strap and side clamps did a fairly good job of securing my shoes onto my skates, but every few blocks I would have to stop and tighten my skates. Always concerned about losing my skate key, I attached it to a shoelace that became a necklace which was never removed! Most evenings my friends and I skated after supper until it was too dark to see where we were going. We briefly enjoyed skating at a roller rink in a Quonset hut on the west side of town and were so disappointed when it closed. I suppose it would have been fun to have a bicycle but none of my friends had bikes when I lived in Eureka; skates were more affordable. After our move to Portland, my cousins gave my sister and I their old Schwinn bicycles, and I would learn how to ride a bike when I was about twelve years old!

Chicago Roller Skates

My favorite place to skate was the sidewalk in front of the funeral home—it had the smoothest concrete in town. After dark, a distant streetlight illuminated what appeared to be glitter on the sidewalk. My friends and I suspected glitter had been added to the concrete to give the place the appearance of heaven! The front door of the funeral home was always unlocked. Straub's Mortuary was open 24-7 for visitation, and on many occasions we'd climb up the four or five steps and boldly skate around inside. We were intrigued with the mysterious smells and tranquility in this building. Truthfully, I suppose we were most curious about the "new" dead people! We'd skate from one casket to another until we heard the mortician make his way up the basement stairs. He was really old, and by the time he reached the first floor we'd be out the front door, down the steps and skating as fast as we could! We were never caught, but there was the element of excitement and fear in knowing he might just find out who we were. It was by far one of the most daring things I ever did!

Most of my skating escapades were with my second cousin Barbara. We were friends and classmates. One particular day while doing a skate through at the mortuary, we discovered Barbara's first cousin Vickie in a little casket! Vickie was younger than us. We were horrified—there weren't supposed to be little kids in caskets! Even so, there she was all laid out in her best dress with her long blonde locks of hair beautifully combed. Absolutely terrified, we quickly skated back to Barbara's house, where her mother told us that Vickie had died of sudden kidney failure. I suppose it was the first time we realized death wasn't just limited to old people; it was the last time Barbara and I skated inside the funeral home!

Several years ago my mother discovered my infamous skates in one of her outbuildings. Having not seen them for over sixty years I assumed they'd been given away or thrown out. Thrilled to be reunited with my skates, I was surprised to discover how heavy they were. I wonder how I was able to move so freely with them? After I cleaned my skates with great care, they now have a prominent spot in our den. My skates still bring a smile to my face, and incidentally I still have my skate key!

Spring and Summer of 1951

LIVING IN AN AGING COMMUNITY, WE ATTENDED WAKES and funerals as children. Never sheltered from illnesses or proceedings leading up to someone's death, we'd often visit relatives in the hospital or nursing home with our parents. When a death occurred we'd sometimes be included in visits to the mortuary and funerals. I remember church bells tolling in Eureka whenever someone died. My grandparents listened to the bells to determine which church they came from, speculating who'd been ill or recently hospitalized. In our community it was customary to have an open casket for the deceased because everyone always wanted to see how good they looked. I'd hear the same comment, "don't they look good," at every visitation or funeral! The strange custom of taking pictures of the deceased usually occurred during visitation to the funeral parlor; I guess people felt they needed to capture one last photo with their Brownie cameras!

My earliest recollection of attending a funeral and wake was at about three years of age. I have a vivid memory of a wake at the Helfenstein homestead and of seeing the deceased laid out in the parlor. The image has stayed with me. It was unsettling, because I'd never seen a dead person in a house! In that era the deceased was cleansed and prepared for burial by a family member. I have memory of people visiting the home to bring food and pay their last respects to the family. In those days it was expected that a member of the immediate family would keep constant vigil with the deceased until burial. During the late forties, burials took place in the country church cemeteries, and the practice of being laid out in homes was discontinued after the mortuary opened in Eureka.

There were wakes and funerals of elderly relatives, but at the age of seven I was greatly affected by the death of my sixteen-year-old cousin, Maxine. There'd been an auto accident, and my cousin was the only fatality. I found it distressing to see my parents and extended family so emotionally distraught, and it was yet another realization that young people can also die. We did visitation to say our goodbyes to Maxine. Because of the nature of the accident it should have been a closed casket, but it was not to be. The very graphic image of my cousin has stayed with me all these years. Again a camera appeared—just in case we'd forget!

As spring was approaching, farmers seemed to be reenergized as plowing and seeding began. Pastureland seemed to come alive with wildflowers and there was an abundance of grass to feed the livestock. With each year, farming on the plains of Dakota was considered a risky venture; there were no certainties of a successful harvest or a profitable year. Still, there was renewed hope and optimism that this might be the year of a bumper crop. The arrival of spring was always a new beginning.

Our sheep wandered throughout our farmyard nibbling on grass. We kept a watchful eye for one in particular, who we'd named Tony. He had a reputation for being very aggressive! For some reason my mother happened to be Tony's target. He'd torment her whenever she went outside to do chores, particularly when she hung laundry on the wash line. It seemed as if Tony was waiting for Mom, and after spotting her he'd begin to chase her around the farmyard! One day he chased her onto a rock pile, preventing her from getting back into the house. Coming to her rescue, Dad diverted Tony's attention, allowing her to escape. After that incident, Mom carried a baseball bat whenever she went outside to do her chores. Tony was introduced to the bat the next time he chased her: she managed to hit him squarely on the head. Clearly stunned by the encounter, he never bothered to chase her again!

Sheepshearing took place every spring. While home on the weekend I liked to watch them get their annual haircuts. Uncle Gust and Cousin Myron might do the shearing. One person held the animal while the other did the shearing. It was desirable to have wool come off in one or two pieces, but that was more difficult with the use of hand clippers. With sheep wiggling and squirming while trying to free themselves, shears sometimes nicked them and they'd begin to bleed. A total transformation took place: after shearing they were half their former sizes! With their heavy coats removed, and having received a few unfortunate cuts, they'd begin to shiver. I remember being upset to see that they were injured and cold. Sheep wool was bundled, tied, and taken to Barney's creamery with price determined by poundage. Raw wool was then sent to Chicago where it was washed, combed, and eventually made into blankets and other articles of clothing. At the time the entire shearing process really appealed to me, and I was determined to learn how to shear sheep one day—without nicking them! I've since discovered it wouldn't have been a profitable livelihood, because sheepshearers were paid only ten cents to shear one sheep!

As my first year of school came to an end, my report card stated, "Invariably needs to work harder" and "Inclined to give up too easily!" I had difficulties with arithmetic, and the reason for the comments was that I simply didn't know how to do my arithmetic homework or blackboard assignments. No one made me accountable or seemed too concerned, not even my teacher. Rather than attempting to do my arithmetic homework, I found it was much more fun to roller skate! Asking my grandparents for help wasn't an option because of the language barrier. Did I ask for help from my parents on the weekend? Probably not. I was so happy to be home, why spoil my weekend working on my least favorite subject? Thankfully, my first year of school was ending, and I wouldn't have to think about arithmetic all summer. I felt absolute joy and delight. Summer vacation was about to begin and I'd finally be going back home!

Vacation would have to wait, because there'd be two weeks of Bible school before going home for the summer. Apparently this occurred at the end of every school year. Bible school was held in the old Reformed church, next door to the high school. My sister and I would be staying with our grandparents for an additional two weeks. Bible school was required study for our eventual confirmation, and the conclusion of this process was memorizing the catechism. My concerns before beginning Bible school involved memorizing my Christmas piece, but now it was the entire catechism? I was only six, and confirmation seemed like an eternity away, so I'd worry about that later. Bible school was a full day of study, much like regular school, but at least I wouldn't have to deal with arithmetic!

With summer upon us our outhouse was once again open for business. New spring catalogs were stacked on the floor, and almost on cue, the enormous flies returned! As the weather got warmer mosquitos also showed up; it's as if there was competition between them to make us miserable! Large, pesky flies were annoying and unsanitary, but the mosquitos were relentless. They seemed to be in a feeding frenzy and a biting mood on those humid summer evenings. After being outside for only a short time my arms and legs were covered with welts, and intense itching soon followed! Without insect repellent, a temporary measure to alleviate itching was to place an X over the welt with my fingernail, but it provided only interim relief. I'd scratch the welts until they bled and scabbed over. Mosquitos would be an annoyance throughout the long summer. Our lake was an excellent breeding ground for mosquitos, but on the upside, it was also the same lake that provided those amazing fireflies on warm summer nights!

Despite mosquito bites, I was so happy to be home for the summer. Most every evening we had company or went "visiting" after doing our chores. Us kids loved playing outside at night, even though we knew the mosquitos were waiting for us! We'd busy ourselves with outdoor games such as "ghost make a sound." Uncle Ted and Aunt Ida's ranch was an excellent place to play this game after dark. The *it* person would begin to count: one o'clock, two o'clock, and so on, up to twelve o'clock, while everyone else hid. They'd then say, "Ghost make a sound!" We'd make crazy sounds from our hiding spots in various outbuildings throughout the farmyard as the *it* person began to search for us. The object of the game was to reach home base before being tagged. As the youngest in the Opp family I'd usually hide with an older cousin, since it was too scary to be alone! I also remember being careful running around the farmyard; with only one yard light, there'd be concerns about stepping on a fresh "cow patty!"

Another favorite game was "Andy, Andy over." It was played during the day in a farmyard. We'd attempt to throw a ball over the roof of a house, and if the person on the other side caught the ball they'd run around the house to tag us. If the ball didn't clear the rooftop, we'd yell, "pig tails." Most farmhouses were two levels, and I recall how challenging it was for us younger children to throw a ball over a steep roof!

When playing "Captain may I," it was best to have a large group of kids participating. The captain had a row of people lined up about twenty feet away, giving commands such as, "Take one giant step forward," "Take two small scissor steps," or "Take one baby step backward!" If the person began the command without asking, "Captain may I?" they'd have to return to the end of the line. When brave enough to play the game "statue," the outcome usually resulted in some sort of injury! The object of the game was to remain in a statue position after someone twirled you around to make you dizzy. I once landed against a wall radiator at my grandparent Helfenstein's home, and the result was a head injury. My grandmother was alarmed when she saw all the blood, but there wasn't a visit to the doctor; she calmly treated my injury and wrapped sterile strips around my head. It was my last game of statue!

Home treatments for injuries were common. I remember stepping on rusty nails while living on the farm. The nail usually went through the sole of my shoe and punctured my foot. Epsom salt was used to clean the wound, but there was never a visit to the doctor for a tetanus shot. My mother related her worst injury as a young child: while attempting to hurtle a rusty barbed-wire fence, her nose was split open! There wasn't a visit to the doctor; her mother cleaned the wound, reshaped her nose, and proceeded to treat her with homemade remedies. I understand strips of sterilized old sheets were wrapped around her head to help keep her nose in place. Amazingly her injury healed without sutures or complications, and the end result was a tiny scar that was barely visible.

During lengthy cold winters children searched for inventive indoor activities to entertain themselves. We found creative ways to play with empty wooden spools of thread. Many women made their own clothing and did some type of needlework. At the time, sewing and crochet thread was on wooden spools instead of Styrofoam or plastic. Most homes had a surplus of empty spools, and they came in various sizes and were often used as building blocks. Kids sometimes rolled them across a linoleum floor with the intention of making as much noise as possible!

Linoleum? I have a vivid memory of colorful linoleum. In our community, like many others, I suspect it was a standard floor covering in most homes during the forties and fifties. Fascinated with intricate patterns and colorful designs, I remember unique linoleum flooring with Asian motifs. Large oval-hooked rugs were usually placed over linoleum in front rooms, and they were made by crocheting strips of recycled fabric. Smaller hook rugs, also referred to as "rag" rugs, were used in other rooms. They were very slippery on linoleum floors, and it was fun using them to slide clear across a room! Sometimes I'd use small rag rugs, pillows, or possibly a down quilt to slide down our steep wooden staircase—when my parents weren't in the house!

One of my favorite toys was a dollhouse Mom had made for us when we lived in Eureka; it was one of our prized possessions. She'd built this one-of-a-kind dollhouse out of two wooden orange crates. The two-story house had a shingled roof, cellophane window panes, curtains, linoleum flooring, and painted rooms. Our mother was so creative, she'd somehow constructed a matching upholstered sofa and chair from a wooden cigar box. Floor lamps were made of wooden spools of thread and Tinkertoys and they were then painted with nail polish. It was a time when individual pieces of dollhouse furniture could be purchased from dime stores or catalogs, so we managed to acquire a sizable collection of store-bought furniture to interchange with furnishings from our very unique dollhouse.

Paper dolls were another fun, quiet activity for little girls when I was a child. Hours were spent dressing our paper dolls with numerous outfits, matching handbags, shoes, and other accessories. Movie stars of that era were often portrayed by paper dolls and illustrated in coloring books. Not surprisingly, toys were very gender-specific when I was a child; it wasn't encouraged or the norm for girls to play with trucks, cars, or toy guns. We frequently visited my second cousin Bob and his family, since they lived only a half mile from our farm. Bob always shared his toy metal dump trucks, tractors, and cars with me; it was really fun to play with those toys on the huge dirt pile in their front yard! I'm not sure Bob shared the same enthusiasm about playing with girl toys while visiting our farm—probably not, what would people think?

At the age of seven or eight I managed to acquire a double holstered "Roy Rogers" gun set with pearl handles. The gun set had accidentally been left behind by a young boy after he and his parents visited us from a distant town. I suppose it was a case of finders keepers; I'm thinking the gun set wasn't worthy of return postage! It must have been a distressing loss for the little boy, but the Roy Rogers guns soon became one of my favorite toys. The guns came with a roll of caps which were fed into the chamber, and as I pulled the trigger there'd be a small puff of smoke and the smell of sulphur! Lots of time was spent perfecting my quick draw, twirling my guns, and dropping them into my holster!

Children did numerous farm chores at a very early age. It was expected that young boys learn how to milk cows and help their fathers with field work, but most amazingly they'd also be driving tractors and pickup trucks! It wasn't uncommon for seven-year-old boys to drive farm vehicles. As long as they could see out of the windshield, reach the pedals, and drive in a reasonably straight line, they could get behind the wheel! Wooden blocks were sometimes attached to the clutch, brake, and accelerator with pillows placed on seats to help children reach the pedals. Of course driving was only done around the farm to help with field work. I recall how excited boys were to be doing real farmwork with their fathers.

Girls learned to do all household tasks at a young age, and as they got older they'd also be milking cows, separating cream, and helping with field work. Other than setting the table, doing dishes, churning butter, and attempting to collect eggs, I had few chores. In the five years on our farm I tried to milk a cow only a few times, but with limited success. My father wasn't very eager to have my sister and I milk cows; he was always concerned about our safety around our farm animals, and so was I!

Following a busy harvest season there'd usually be a number of family weddings, and naturally us children attended the church ceremony, reception, and dance. If it was a traditional German wedding celebration the party might even continue for several days! The reception and dance were typically held at the country club or the Quonset hut on the outskirts of town. The bride's family and close relatives provided all the food; most likely a pig or cow would have been butchered for the occasion. Large roasters filled with pork sausage and hulupsy (stuffed cabbage rolls) would manage to feed hundreds of guests. Additionally, the wedding supper might include numerous hot dishes (a Midwest term), hot German potato salad, homemade buns, and an assortment of colorful Jell-O salads to complete the menu.

Jell-O! This product seemed to be on many dinner tables during the fifties, even though it contained little nutritional value. Colorful Jell-O salads always appeared at weddings with one or more of the following ingredients: shredded carrots, celery, coconut, cottage cheese, fruit cocktails, bananas, apples, olives, raisins, walnuts, and even mayonnaise! Who knows, maybe it was a clever way to get children to eat their veggies and fruit. License was taken to add just about anything to a basic package of Jell-O, and it always intrigued me how those added foods seemed to be suspended in that congealed mass! Women seemed to take great pride in creating those colorful, layered, molded Jell-O salads. Personally, I found it challenging to eat around the veggies, especially shredded carrots; I'd usually spit out things that had no business being in Jell-O! Thankfully, we didn't have those strange Jell-O salads on our dinner or supper table. Instead, my mother made whipped Jell-O with lots of whipping cream. Sorry to get sidetracked, I just needed to share my thoughts regarding Jell-O—let's get back to the weddings!

As adult guests arrived to the wedding reception they'd be served a shot glass of traditional hocht seid schnapps (wedding liquor). Homemade schnapps was made with 190-proof Everclear alcohol, burnt sugar, and anise extract. This potent liquor was appropriately named "Red Eye!" One glass was used to serve all guests, but no one seemed too concerned;

apparently the high alcohol content killed the germs! Most of our relatives were beer drinkers, and there'd usually be several kegs at the reception. Children were served soda pop in glass bottles. I remember we could have as much as we wanted—but that wasn't always a good idea! A traditional wedding cake was served at the reception but it wouldn't be the only dessert, kuchen was also served. Next to the assorted fruit kuchens there'd be large platters of homemade dill pickles. Those two items were always served together, because it was a sweet and sour combination we'd become accustomed to.

Wedding gifts were opened during the reception, but they weren't unwrapped by the bridal couple; it was considered an honor for friends of the couple to unwrap and display gifts. I'd be sure to secure a good spot to watch all the presents being opened! I don't remember traditional thank-you notes being sent, and I suspect the lengthy reception was an opportunity for the couple to thank their guests for the gifts. Wedding gifts were typically homemade items such as quilts, down pillows, hand-embroidered dish towels, pillow cases, tablecloths, or intricate crochet doilies. In later years gifts often included store-bought items, but they were usually practical in nature. The tradition of auctioning the bride's shoes might even occur during the wedding reception, but of course shoes were given back to the bride after the bidding! Guests might pay twenty-five cents for a piece of wedding cake and perhaps the same amount to dance with the bride and groom, and all funds collected were given to the newly married couple.

Sometime during the extended wedding festivities, families went back to their farms to do milking chores. After they returned several hours later, the wedding dance and partying continued until the early-morning hours! While our parents danced and partied, us kids roamed around the dance hall eating too much food and drinking way too much soda pop. When it got dark we'd go outside to play ghost-make-a-sound or hide-and-seek with our cousins. I understand that if beer kegs weren't empty by the early morning hours, the wedding reception would continue the following day with more celebrating and dancing!

Children weren't restricted from overindulging with food or soft drinks at weddings. If we made ourselves sick from eating too much of a good thing, it would be a valuable lesson learned for the next big celebration! Our parents also never told us it was time to call it a night, that was entirely up to us. Being too tired to take another step or possibly ill from overeating, we'd begin to search for our cars, and if we were lucky, a blanket and pillow might be waiting for us in the back seat. Children were always expected to adapt to their surroundings! All of us kids felt very secure, and there were no concerns about our safety in Eureka.

In anticipation of their eventual wedding days, many of my older cousins had acquired a cedar chest at a young age. Girls were taught to sew, quilt, and embroider; it was an expectation that their hope chests be filled with quilts, embroidered towels, and assorted needlework for their eventual marriages. After all, it was a natural assumption that everyone was going to get married! I recall a few of my great-aunts referring to young women as "old maids" if they hadn't married by the age of twenty! The hope chest tradition seemed to have lost its popularity with my generation. Generations earlier it was common for women to have a dowry when they married; parcels of land, horses, cows, pigs, sheep, chickens, ducks, and furniture might be included.

At the turn of the century apparently some marriages might even be facilitated. I've been told that if a young man was thinking of marriage, his father would escort him with horse and buggy to a neighboring family with daughters of marrying age. Horses' manes were sometimes decorated with brightly colored ribbons to impress the young women! After introductions were made the couple would decide if there was to be a match. It was customary for the oldest daughter in the family be the first to marry.

I'd often hear phrases and bad words in German as a young child; they seemed to be used quite freely! I was familiar with the swear words but fortunately wise enough to never use them, because girls were to be on their best behavior—what would people think? Most boys weren't that concerned about good behavior or what people thought, and bad language was used even if it resulted in some form of punishment! "Dunner veder" was considered to be a bad word, and if a child said that word it might result in a quick slap across the face, or a bar of soap in one's mouth! The English translation is thunder weather! If a certain emphasis was added, such as "aast dunner veder," it would be considered a much greater offense!

Another inappropriate word was "dunners dawg." The translation was Thursday—simply a day of the week! It was absurd, and I have no idea why they were considered bad words, but none of us kids had the courage to ask about the logic, because we'd been taught to never question authority. I remember hearing hilarious songs, stories, and jokes; they always sounded funnier in German. If the same story was repeated in English, it seemed much of the humor was lost in translation!

As a young child of that era, children were to be seen and not heard, to know their place, and to never question an adult. Attempts to explain one's actions or opinion were considered talking back. We'd often hear the phrase, "Why don't you act your age?" As a six-year-old, whenever I was told to act my age, I really wanted to say, "I am!" It was puzzling: how is a six-year-old supposed to act? Evidently children weren't supposed to cry if they were upset or spanked. We'd sometimes be told, "If you don't stop crying, we'll really give you something to cry about!"

I have recollections of being very frustrated whenever greeted by a particular relative. She'd always ask me the same question: "So...what do you know?" If I answered, "Not much," or "I don't know," she'd reply, "Well you better start learning something!" After repeated encounters I decided to try a different tactic. The next time she asked me the same question I stated, "I know a lot." Angry with my response, she replied, "Don't have such a smart mouth!" Clearly, nothing I said would be the right answer to suit her, so I finally just avoided being around her!

I remember an increased level of discipline after our move to the farm. It was a time when most parents regarded some degree of physical punishment as being appropriate in disciplining children: apparently "Spare the rod, spoil the child," was stated in the Bible. I don't have memory of physical punishment while living in Eureka, but after our move there seemed to be a gradual but noticeable change in my mother's disposition. As with most siblings, my sister and I had disagreements and argued; she was far more creative and convincing and seemed to have a much better story for Mom. During those altercations I felt powerless and absolute frustration in being set up. I'd attempt to explain my side but Mom was very quick to anger and not inclined to listen to explanations of who did what to whom. Her usual response was, "I'll spank you both to make sure I got the right one!" I never understood what motivated my sister's actions, since she knew she'd also be punished. We were never disciplined by our father, so obviously the burden always fell on our mother.

I recall people telling Mom about how well-behaved her little girls were; her quick response was, "I try to spank them at least once a week to make sure I've covered everything they've done wrong!" She used a switch, a strap, or an electric cord, and I clearly remember how angry my mother was. One very hot summer afternoon after a spanking, I decided to run away from home. I recall packing my little red Cinderella suitcase and the long walk to the gate of our farmyard. I was hoping my mother would come after me, apologize, and ask me to come back home. Disillusioned, I sat on my suitcase in the hot sun for what seemed like an eternity! When it became apparent Mom wasn't coming after me I began to slowly walk back to the house. When I entered the house she simply asked, "What are you doing back home, I thought you were running away?" I told my mother I was much too little to open the gate!

Searching for answers regarding my mother's behavior, I'm convinced the daily struggles of living on our unproductive farm and continual financial stress had taken a toll on her emotions. I now have a better understanding of how difficult life must have been for her, but as the adult it was also her responsibility to control her anger. My sister and I just happened to be drawn into her internal conflict. I know my mother regretted her actions and I believe she did the best with what was happening in her life at the time. After much uncertainty, I felt it was important to include events in my memoirs that had a significant impact on my life.

Hesitant to reveal discipline encountered during that period of my childhood, I was concerned my mother's infinite good qualities might be overshadowed. I've instead chosen to remember all of her wonderful attributes and have long ago forgiven her for that troubling period in her life. Those unsettling events are notable but they're only a small part of my early life, because most of my childhood was filled with much happiness. I believe everything that transpired in my childhood, whether it was good, bad, or indifferent, made me the person I am today. This brief period in my young life would prove to be instrumental in my own parenting skills, and for that I'm grateful.

On a far more positive note, I recall baseball being a dominant national pastime in the early fifties. It was evident in Eureka as well as the surrounding farming community. Each year many of our relatives were on the Eureka Cardinals home team, and in fact Uncle Harvey was their catcher for a number of years. Many summer Sunday afternoons found our family and relatives sitting in the small grandstand cheering for the Cardinals. My father and some of his cousins had at one time played on rural farm teams. I don't have memory of watching my father play the game but he often spoke of the intense competition between the city and farm teams in earlier years. Dad claimed several cousins had the skill to play major league ball, stating they just didn't have the good fortune to be seen by the right people!

I enjoyed the game of baseball but much of my focus was also on the snack bar, where a nickel might come my way to buy candy or popcorn! Sitting in the grandstand was another place where the chewing and spitting of sunflower seeds took place; it was a natural combination. People in our community often caravanned to surrounding towns attending regional baseball tournaments, and most every year the Cardinals were in the state playoffs.

Each fall, anticipation of the World Series brought excitement and a much-needed diversion to our community. Several of Dad's cousins who were avid baseball enthusiasts and their families might be invited to our farm to listen to their favorite team on the radio during the series, since there weren't televisions! While home on weekends I'd be excited to join in on the fun. I remember the New York Yankees and Brooklyn Dodgers dominating the series during that era. Listening to the World Series on the Philco radio in our front room was preferable but sometimes we didn't have the best reception. To remedy the problem our parents climbed into our four-door Plymouth to tune into the game on the radio!

While our parents listened to the game, us kids played outside. With the volume blaring we'd be able to hear the game, and when our favorite team scored a home run there might be several blasts on the car horn to add to the excitement! Beer, pop, pretzels, popcorn, and of course sunflower seeds helped create a festive baseball atmosphere; I guess it was our version of a tailgate party! No matter where we listened to the game, it was our way of being connected with the rest of the country during the World Series each year.

Harvest season was the busiest time of the year for farmers, and once again a pitchfork, shovel, or other hand implement was involved in the manual labor. Many farmers had combines to harvest crops but there was little automation on our farm. Prior to the use of combines, binders and headerboxes were used for harvesting, and as we approached our first harvest season I learned we'd be shocking our crops. I suspect there was an urgent weather concern requiring our whole family to be involved. To begin the process of shocking, a binder machine cut and tied wheat stalks into bundles. After four or five bundles were tied, a lever was tripped, dropping stalks onto the ground. Our job was to walk behind the binder to pick up shocks of grain. We'd place wheat shocks upright in a tepee fashion, allowing shafts of wheat to dry more quickly. Harvest season occurred during the hottest part of the summer, so to help shield us from the direct sun Mom made my sister and I yellow calico bonnets. We wore long-sleeved shirts, pants, and gloves to protect us from the newly cut stubble fields, but despite precautions our arms and legs were scratched from sharp stubble that managed to pierce our clothing.

    Being involved in our first harvest for three or four days was really exciting for me. I was only seven years old and it was the only time I did any physical farmwork. I'm sure my sister and I didn't work more than five or six hours a day. It was very tiring but I felt so proud to be helping my parents. Shocking for that short period of time definitely left a lasting impression! The first year on our farm was the only time we shocked our crops, because a small combine was purchased the following year to harvest our crops: automation had finally arrived!

OUR FAMILY FREQUENTLY TRAVELED TO NORTH DAKOTA on Sunday afternoons to visit my cousin Velma and her family; they lived about fifteen miles from our farm. We were always eager to reach their farm before they returned from church with the intention of surprising them. Dad always parked our car behind their barn so they wouldn't see us as they approached their farmyard, and after they were inside their house we'd sneak up to the front door and yell, "Surprise!" They were very familiar with this routine—we happened to surprise them regularly!

My cousin had a collection of salt and pepper shakers, and in her young life she'd accumulated about a hundred sets. I'd never heard of anyone having a collection of anything. Shakers were wrapped in tissue paper and stored in shoeboxes to protect them from breakage. Predictably, sometime during each visit we'd go upstairs to unwrap the shakers, admiring them as if we'd never seen them before! The all-too-familiar dialogue would begin: "If you had to choose one as your favorite, which one would it be?" After admiring the entire collection we'd carefully repack the shakers for our next visit. It was one of my favorite activities when visiting their farm.

My Aunt Edna and Uncle Walter lived on the Helfenstein homestead about six miles from our farm, and I'd spend several summer days with my cousin and her family. I have memory of Marsha and I making countless mud pies that were left to dry in the hot sun! Another fun activity was playing in the summer kitchen about thirty feet from the house. This kitchen was used for laundry, canning, sausage making, and as a place to feed threshers. Using the summer kitchen kept the main house cleaner and cooler on those hot, humid summer days.

During those visits it was great fun to hear about the latest activity involving Marsha's younger brother. Jeff was about three years old, very mischievous, and always looking for his next adventure. He once dumped dozens of eggs into a five-gallon cream can, along with his father's watch. It was discovered at the creamery the next Saturday night! On another day Jeffrey fed four or five freshly baked loaves of bread to his dog! His culinary skills started early as he mixed flour, sugar, ketchup, and other ingredients on the linoleum kitchen floor while his parents were milking cows! I suppose attention deficit disorder might possibly explain his actions, but no one talked about any type of disorders back then, or seemed too terribly concerned. Everyone just said, "He is very busy!" This energetic little boy managed to keep the drama going on in their household, and it was always fun to share another Jeff story when I returned home.

Annual dental appointments were scheduled in Ashley every summer with the town's dentist. The office was occupied by only one person—the dentist! Without a receptionist or an assistant, my appointments were lengthy in his very hot dental office, where there was no air-conditioning! Several summer afternoons were spent in that dental chair; sometimes it felt like I'd never be released from his office. Frequent telephone calls interrupted my appointments. The doctor used phone time to mix amalgam for my next filling, which was a slow process because he still used a mortar and pestle! The anesthetic normally wore off long before my appointment was over. Noticing my apparent discomfort, the doctor continually asked, "Does this hurt, does that hurt?" Well of course it hurt—so another stainless-steel syringe packed with Novocain would show up. This was long before the use of high-speed drills, and I have explicit recollections of the slow, groaning, smoking drill and the unpleasant smell of burning enamel—another memorable, distinctive odor that's difficult to describe! The best part of my dental day, other than leaving the dentist's office, was a chocolate milkshake at the drive-in following my appointment!

Summer Sunday afternoons often included a fishing trip to Long Lake where the bullheads were plentiful. Located about twenty miles from our farm, we'd meet three or four families (all relatives) at the lake. Bullheads, commonly known as catfish, were abundant; they were the only type of fish I remember eating in South Dakota. With ten or twelve children fishing, our fathers kept busy baiting the girls' bamboo lines with worms! We once caught 135 bullheads, which was our largest catch at Long Lake; there wasn't a required license or a fish limit.

After our fishing adventure everyone went home to do evening milking chores, but they'd soon return to our farm for the much-anticipated fish fry. The fathers cleaned fish while our mothers busily salted and peppered the bullheads. Dipped into an egg batter, they'd be dredged with a mixture of flour and cornmeal. The aroma of fish frying in large cast-iron skillets brought all of us children around the dinner table! Our fish-fry dinner might include potato salad or macaroni salad, pickles, pickled watermelon, and homemade bread, and of course there was always dessert—another special food memory! With over twenty people enjoying the bullheads I don't remember leftovers. If there were any, I'm sure our dogs Netty and Spotty were first in line!

The fish man occasionally visited our farm in the spring and summer, and it was always exciting to see his truck pulling into our farmyard. I assume he must have traveled from neighboring Minnesota. His refrigerated truck appeared to be filled with fresh pike, sturgeon, and smoked fish. I'm not sure if we ever knew his name; we just called him "the fish man!" My parents always bought a piece of smoked fish. We'd enjoy our late-afternoon snack with cheese and saltines, which were always referred to as "soda crackers."

Another visitor that sometimes appeared in our farmyard was the Watkins man. I remember his visits as welcomed interruptions to Mom's busy day. We'd watch him unpack all the mops, brooms, cleaning products, ointments, and lineaments. There was always the newest snake oil, which he claimed would cure just about any affliction! Part of his sales pitch always included a demonstration of a new product, and we'd anticipate his clever presentation. As a young girl my mother remembered the Watkins man visiting the Helfenstein homestead, and after my grandmother selected numerous items she'd proceed to pay him with two "live" chickens! After tying the legs of the chickens onto the outside of his car he'd drive off to the next farm! This was during the depression era when people didn't have cash, but the bartering system seemed to work well and was commonly used.

Before the beginning of each school year our family traveled to Aberdeen to do our school shopping. Two important purchases were a warm winter coat and school shoes. It wasn't necessary to do a lot of shopping, since Mom made most of our clothes. We also had wonderful hand-me-downs from our cousins, Patti and Doreen. Every year a box of clothing arrived from Portland. Our cousins had very interesting clothes, unlike anything we'd see in Aberdeen department stores or while paging catalogs. With a population of about twenty thousand people, Aberdeen was the largest city close to us, and was about sixty miles away.

We'd usually get an early start after doing our morning chores, and another family often joined us for the daylong trip. All shopping was done in the downtown department stores, because there weren't suburban malls. I loved shopping for shoes, and there were several family shoe stores on Main Street. My favorite store had a machine that showed an X-ray of our feet! The device was featured as a novelty for shoppers, and perhaps a place to keep children occupied and entertained. It was so fascinating to look at the bones in my feet, of course, and we were allowed to stand in the machine as long and as often as we wanted! I remember how disappointed us kids were when that fun "X-ray machine" disappeared!

Aberdeen was a vibrant, bustling city. It was exciting to see the bright neon signs, busy street traffic, colorful window displays, and the many choices of clothing. I was especially interested in the pneumatic tubes traveling across the ceiling in large department stores. As a purchase was made, sales clerks placed cash inside an enclosed vacuum tube from the sales counter, and it was then sent upstairs for the cashier to make change. Minutes later the tube was sent back down to the sales clerk with the change and receipt. I never minded the wait, because it was really entertaining to watch numerous tubes crisscrossing the ceiling from the many sales counters. I'd anxiously wait for the familiar sound of compressed air in the pneumatic vacuum system!

All retail purchases were made with cash; credit cards didn't make an appearance until the late sixties. Apparently the first credit card was the Diners Club card, introduced in the fifties. I understand it was quite a status symbol. Gasoline credit cards arrived in the early sixties, and American Express and an avalanche of credit cards soon followed. Several department stores in Aberdeen offered layaway plans, allowing customers to make a down payment on a purchase, but there was no immediate gratification—stores held the item until final payment was made. It was very common for stores in Eureka to run a tab for their customers, and bills were paid monthly. Legal contracts were used, but sometimes business transactions might even be completed with a handshake! In this small community you knew everyone, and people were trusted that they'd keep their word. Those were more innocent and uncomplicated times, but all that has changed, even in Eureka!

Eating in a restaurant was a rare treat for our family, but sometime during the shopping excursion in Aberdeen we'd have dinner at the Virginia Cafe. Not too surprisingly our standard fare was a hamburger, fries, and a milkshake. If it was determined that my sister and I had been well-behaved on this daylong outing, paper dolls or a new piece of furniture might be added to our dollhouse. After a full day of shopping we sometimes visited with my great-aunt and uncle who lived in Aberdeen. There might be one last stop at the Dairy Queen for a soft ice cream cone before we left for home.

CHAPTER NINE

Helfenstein Household

As summer came to an end, I dreaded the thought of being away from home for another school year. But to my surprise, there'd be different living arrangements for the upcoming school year: we'd now be living with Grandma and Grandpa Helfenstein. Perhaps my father's parents were having additional health problems and unable to care for us. It's also possible my parents were hoping the change might put an end to my homesickness, tears, and general unhappiness. It was a good decision: I immediately felt much more at home with my mother's parents. I absolutely adored my grandparents; they were affectionately referred to as "Ma and Pa!"

Ma and Pa were younger than my Dad's parents, and they'd retired from the family homestead in their late forties. Both were very energetic and enjoyed an active social life. I was especially pleased that everyone in the household spoke fluent English, but like with my parents, German was at times blended into their conversations. Ma and Pa still had three sons living at home when my sister and I joined their household: Ervin was sixteen,

Harvey fourteen, and Curtis was only twelve years old. They were often referred to as the second family because of the significant age difference between them and their older siblings. Being closer to my age, I suppose my uncles seemed more like big brothers, and I instantly loved being a part of their family! When I wasn't in school I'd follow Ma around the house, watching with great curiosity as she went about her daily work. I must have annoyed her at times with my many questions and inquisitive nature but I certainly never sensed it. Ma was very soft-spoken, patient, and loving. There was never a cross word spoken to me. I felt an immediate bond and strong connection to her; she was like my second mother.

The Helfenstein house was located on G Avenue, right down the hill from the fire station and city park. The large, two-story house was situated on a corner lot with a sizable garden in the west side yard, and it would provide us with an abundance of canned vegetables for the coming winter. Large oak trees adorned the front and side yards along with a small patch of grass, and pink hollyhocks bloomed below the dining-room window. I associated the flower as being Ma's favorite, but it's possible this hearty perennial was one of the few flowering plants that survived the long, cold Dakota winters. As the oak trees lost their leaves in the fall, Lake Eureka was visible from the upstairs bedroom I shared with my sister.

Helfenstein Household

Helfenstein House

A small, covered porch just off the front room was a favorite spot when weather permitted. It may seem a bit odd, but I distinctly remember the squeaking porch screen door—somehow that familiar, comforting sound made me feel very safe and secure! While sitting on the porch bench, I'd often watch cloud formations in the late afternoon. On sunny days, a colorful transom window of blue, yellow, and purple stained glass cast a warm glow of light into the front room. A pump organ occupied one corner of the dining room. It may have once belonged to my great-grandparents. I understand Great-Grandpa Wolf had been the musician in the family. There were frequent attempts to play the keyboard, even though the foot pump was difficult for me to reach. A matching decorative organ stool changed heights when spun around. I loved twirling on it until I got dizzy! Sweets were close by—the dining room table always held a well-stocked candy dish filled with either pink and white peppermint candies or lemon drops. An oversized white swinging door separated the dining room from the kitchen, and this is where Ma came up with one amazing meal after another!

I've often wondered what my uncles thought of my sister and I joining their household; after all, they'd been displaced from one of the two upstairs bedrooms. Ervin and Harvey now shared a bedroom while Curtis slept on a cot in the adjoining closet/sewing room, and although this very small room had a window, it must have been very confining for him. My sister and I were given the largest bedroom with a white iron double bed, and surprisingly our room also had a half bath—I was delighted! Patriotic images surrounded two large photographs of former US Presidents. I remember being captivated by the intricate, ornate gold frames of convex glass that held the antique photos hanging on our bedroom wall. A sizable landing held a sofa, desk, and several bookcases, and this area was used as a playroom when my friends came over after school.

I rarely interacted with Ervin; as a sixteen-year-old he was busy with his friends, sports, and high school activities. Although there was an eight-year difference in age, Harvey and I seemed to have a closer bond; we also shared a love of chocolate licorice! I was interested in my uncles' dinner and supper conversations, and it was really fun to hear about their latest escapades! Curtis didn't seem too enthralled with having two little girls living in his house. We were only five years apart in age, and he was no longer the youngest in the household. I'm sure he felt we were invading his space; after all, he had been sleeping in a closet since our arrival!

Ma could always be found in the kitchen wearing one of her colorful homemade aprons; in fact, I rarely saw her without an apron. Women wore aprons to protect their wash dresses while doing household chores. I have no idea why those colorful cotton-print dresses were called wash dresses, but they were worn every day except for Sunday. Several pockets adorned Ma's apron, and they usually held a stray button or several linen hankies. Hankies? They're archaic items that were used for personal hygiene purposes or blowing one's nose! Years ago, very few people left home without putting this item in their pocket or purse! Women carried hankies and men had handkerchiefs, and every week there'd be dozens of men's handkerchiefs and women's hankies in the laundry.

A large portion of Ma's busy day was spent in the kitchen cooking for her family. Her teenage sons had huge appetites, and like my mother Ma was an amazing cook; of course everything was homemade. Also like my mother, there was little relaxation time for Ma. Her busy day included cooking, baking, cleaning, sewing, laundry, and gardening. Modern conveniences we've become so accustomed to in the twenty-first century simply didn't exist; washers, dryers, dishwashers, blenders, food processors, and numerous other appliances hadn't been invented. Caring for Ma's large household and preparing three meals each day was more than a full-time job for her; she'd barely finish breakfast dishes when it was time to prepare the dinner meal. Large dinners continued to be served at noon, because that's what they'd become accustomed to while living on the farm.

Wednesday was bread-baking day. A large amount of bread dough had been prepared the night before, and we made sure there was enough for schuff noodla (dumplings). Additional dough made sweet treats such as baked custard bread, cinnamon rolls, or schlitz kuechla, more commonly known as fry bread. I always looked forward to our Wednesday dinner of creamed chicken and dumplings. As I rounded the corner of the fire station on my school lunch hour, the aroma from Ma's kitchen seemed to envelope me! All seven of us gathered around the kitchen table at 12:00 noon, and if anyone happened to forget it was time to eat, a loud siren was heard throughout town; the siren would be heard again at 6:00 p.m. for supper! We always referred to the siren as the noon and supper "whistle," and rarely would anyone in town deviate from this eating schedule.

    Waiting for us on the stovetop were two large cast-iron Dutch ovens of chicken and dumplings. One held the light and fluffy dumplings with gravy, while the other was filled with golden crispy dumplings. Both Dutch ovens also contained potatoes. I'd eat until I was stuffed, but there was always room for possibly one more dumpling with peanut butter syrup! After overeating, the five of us walked very slowly up the hill to school. I wanted nothing more than to take a long nap. I have countless food memories, but this weekly dinner at Ma and Pa's was the very fondest of my childhood!

    When Ma wasn't cooking there was lots of laundry requiring her attention. She used the same type of washing machine as my mother, but her laundry day involved more work, since there were more people in the household! After school I'd sometimes watch Ma tackle the huge stack of weekly ironing. All washable clothing needed to be ironed because cotton blends of fabric weren't yet available. Additionally, most dress shirts and dresses were hand starched before being ironed, and those items were rolled up in a large plastic bag. I don't think Ma owned a steam iron; she continually dampened clothes while ironing with the use of a sprinkler that was attached to a pop bottle filled with water. If there was an hour or so of leisure time before bedtime Ma's large sewing basket appeared, which was filled with socks needing to be darned! Socks were never thrown out if there was a hole in the toe or heel; instead they were darned for additional wear. A light bulb was put inside the sock to make it easier to stitch the hole! When socks were completely threadbare they'd be thrown into a rag bin for more recycling; socks and other recycled clothing were used to help create those colorful hook rugs!

My grandparents often visited friends in the evening or entertained guests in their home. During the winter months Ma invited her friends over for quilting parties, where five or six women sat around the large quilt stretcher in the dining room while busily hand stitching a quilt. Always captivated by the intricate skills of the quilters, I'd at times sit under the stretcher watching the busy movement of needles and thread creating colorful patterns! The women were usually working on a quilt for an upcoming wedding, or for the latest newborn arriving in our large family. This was also a social activity for them, and a bit of gossip might even be exchanged while quilting, but at those times German was usually spoken!

My second-grade teacher boarded across the street from my grandparents' home. It was common for homeowners to take in boarders to help supplement their incomes. Sometimes I'd walk to school with my teacher, and upon entering my classroom those dreaded arithmetic problems might be covering the blackboard! If not on the board in the morning, they seemed to magically appear after recess or lunch. My teacher would say, "Whoever finishes their problem first can quickly sit down." Nothing happened quickly for me; usually I'd be the last person standing at the blackboard. Blackboard exercises continued every day, and it was definitely the very worst part of my school day. It's puzzling—why didn't I ask my sister or uncles for help with arithmetic? My moments of achievement were at every spelling bee, which occurred weekly. My fears were not of being in front of the class, because I also loved reading out loud in the classroom. There was empathy for my classmates who had difficulties with spelling or reading, since I was just as tormented while trying to solve a story problem!

Our school playground had swings, merry-go-rounds, seesaws, monkey bars, and slides. Playing on those death-defying steel structures was fun, but kids sometimes fell from them because they were really high. There'd be fewer injuries during the winter because our heavy clothing and soft snow helped cushion our falls. But those metal structures were really hot during warm weather; monkey bars and particularly slides burned our legs because we always wore dresses to school. I also remember how worried we were about our underwear showing while playing on the playground equipment! The merry-go-round was my favorite, but when my girlfriends and I played on it the boys started spinning it as fast as they could, never allowing us to hop off! Screaming and getting dizzier, we'd eventually fly off and land on the ground, which is just what the boys were waiting for! Teachers had first-aid kits in their classrooms, and after treating our cuts and scrapes they'd tell us not to be so careless!

As spring arrived our marble bags were brought to school. Recess was an excellent time to shoot marbles or trade them with friends, and it was an activity enjoyed by both girls and boys. Our favorite game, called "stretch," required the use of jackknives or switchblades, which wasn't a problem because we always carried them with us! When playing stretch, knives were thrown into the dirt to see how far we could stretch our legs. I'd often miscalculate my aim, resulting in the knife piercing the top of my leather shoe or stabbing my foot or toes. I'd then search for more Band-Aids from my teacher! No one was worried about children coming to school with knives or switchblades—it was totally acceptable! Our blade of choice was usually attached to a rabbit's foot key chain. It's been over sixty years since I've thought of or seen a rabbit's foot but most people carrying keys or jackknives owned one when I was a child. Yes, it was a real rabbit's foot that had somehow been preserved and fashioned into a decorative key chain, and it was considered a must-have!

After joining the Helfenstein household I was pleased to find an abundance of food available for my snacking-and-grazing habit. Each fall my grandparents purchased several boxes of apples and oranges. We could have as much as we wanted but were reminded to never waste food. Fruit was kept in the freezer room. This wasn't a cold-storage room but instead a room where the chest freezer was located. A twin bed was on one side of the room, and it was used if someone was ill, allowing Ma to keep an eye on them from the main floor.

Inspecting the freezer room the first time, I noticed a number of mason jars lined up between the studs of an unfinished wall. I was absolutely intrigued with the strange objects inside the jars. Ma said I could look at the jars but cautioned me not to open them because they were filled with formaldehyde! The jars contained tonsils, adenoids, kidney stones, gallstones, appendixes, etc., each labeled as to its contents, and to whom the organs had once belonged! Dr.

Macintosh, our only physician in Eureka at the time, liked nothing more than to present his patients with a sealed jar of their internal body parts that had been removed after surgery! At the time, I thought it was a souvenir of their hospital stay, but most likely it was affirmation that something had actually been removed during surgery! Knowing the mindset of some people in the community, it's possible they wanted to make sure they actually got what they'd paid for! I was curious about this unusual collection, so I'd invite my friends over to compare hospital jars; they also had collections of internal organs at their houses!

    Pa's smokehouse was located on the north side of the house. He was the butcher and a master at sausage making in our family, so he'd do all the mixing of ingredients at the foot of the basement. Raw ground pork and beef was blended by hand in a large washtub, and Pa periodically tasted the raw meat to see if more seasoning was needed. I watched this process while sitting on the top step of the basement stairs because I knew he liked the company. Pa often suggested I come downstairs to taste the mixture, but it didn't look very appetizing. He'd say, "You don't know what you're missing!" Apparently I didn't know what I was missing. It appears on many upscale restaurant menus, and we now refer to this delicacy as steak tartare!

    Pa made other meat specialties such as head cheese, blood sausage, liverwurst, ring bologna, pork sausage, summer sausage, caladets, schwardamaga, and pickled pigs' feet! I'd only eat pork sausage, summer sausage, and liverwurst; I was never interested in tasting the other delicacies! I rarely left my perch from the top of the stairs when Pa's sausage making took place. The basement walls and floor were dirt; there were spiders and mice, and sometimes I'd see little lizards scampering across the wall! When retrieving a jar of canned fruit or vegetables from the canning cellar, I'd race up the steps two at a time; there'd be no lingering!

From the top basement step I'd also watch Pa repair worn shoes. He'd replace the heels and soles of shoes for the family. Metal cleats were nailed to the heels of our shoes to save them from excessive wear; I suppose they were stylish as well as functional. I always liked the rhythmic clicking sound of cleats while walking on a sidewalk! Cleats were used on the heels of penny loafers, which gained popularity in the early fifties; a shiny new penny was inserted on the top of each shoe. Owning a pair of classic penny loafers with cleats was another status symbol in the early fifties, and they were worn by teenage girls and boys.

Rainwater collected in a barrel on one corner of Ma and Pa's house was used for watering houseplants and occasionally to wash our hair. Hair conditioners weren't available, but supposedly rainwater made our hair more manageable. A cistern on the back porch provided water for our garden. A metal bucket with a rope was lowered deep into the well, and the water-filled bucket was then raised to the surface with a pulley. Collecting water from the cistern looked like a fun activity, so I quickly volunteered to do this chore for Ma. While retrieving water one day I was bewildered by the unusual weight, and pulling the bucket out of the well I was horrified to find a fat bull snake curled up inside! I'm sure the whole neighborhood heard my screams as I dropped the snake-filled bucket into the well! Uncle Curtis knew of my fear of snakes and loved to torment me. He once pulled a bull snake out of Lake Eureka, placing it across the street in front of our house. It was over six feet long—I never went into Lake Eureka after that!

My favorite chore was buying milk from our neighbors. My uncles were big milk drinkers and the Obenauer family was one of the few households that still had a milk cow on their property. Ma put coins for payment into the empty glass bottles I was returning, and after a short visit with Mrs. Obenauer I'd carefully carry the milk jars back home. About three inches of thick cream topped each quart bottle; this was whole milk with a high fat content, and no one was familiar with 1%, 2%, or skim milk. I'd watch Ma skim cream from each bottle into a large pitcher. She used all that rich heavy cream for cooking, and it's one of the reasons her food tasted so good!

My grandparents made frequent visits to the homestead to help my aunt and uncle with seasonal farmwork. Each fall they were involved with the butchering of beef, pigs, and chickens on the farm, and after butchering Ma did her canning in the summer kitchen. Pa was relatively young when he retired from farming, and for a number of years he worked part-time doing concrete work. Along with several men in the community he poured many of the sidewalks I skated on in Eureka. If my friends and I knew where they were pouring concrete, we couldn't wait to carve our initials in the new sidewalks!

Pa was bothered with a stomach disorder, and many times after eating I'd notice him moaning and pacing throughout the house while holding his belly! His distress was apparently caused by an ulcer which was diagnosed much later in life. He must have also had acid reflux, because his discomfort usually occurred following a meal. It's not surprising Pa was uncomfortable because many of the foods he ate were very high in fat. His love of fatty foods only exasperated his indigestion, but he chose to indulge anyway! People weren't aware or seemingly concerned about high fat in one's diet, or the need to reduce intake of salt and sugars. No one ever thought about cholesterol, and in fact the word wasn't in anyone's vocabulary until the seventies. Most foods were naturally prepared with heavy cream, butter, and lard because they were readily available in our community. Piecrusts were always made with lard when I was a child, and there was a noticeable difference in taste—they were amazing! Food tasted much better when using those rich ingredients; it's what we'd become accustomed to.

Mom often spoke of the butchering process, where cleanliness was absolutely essential. She said the liver was immediately inspected for abnormalities after slaughtering, and if there were any signs of lesions or disease the entire carcass was disposed of! Eggs were fresh, and chickens were free range and organic, words that would have also been foreign to us. None of our animals were fed byproducts or given antibiotics or hormones to stimulate rapid growth. Everything we ate was made from scratch because of necessity. This was long before prepackaged, prepared food or frozen dinners were available in grocery stores. Additionally, artificial sweeteners and diet, low fat, reduced sodium, sugar free, or gluten free products weren't on grocery store shelves either.

While sitting at the kitchen table in the Helfenstein house I'd carefully remove all fat and gristle from beef, pork, or chicken during every meal. Fat was intentionally pushed to one side of my plate, with the hope that it would be discarded. Pa tried to persuade me to eat the fat, and he'd explain that's where all the flavor was. When it became apparent that I wasn't going to eat the congealed mass, he'd scoop it off my plate with a piece of bread. I couldn't believe how he managed to eat all that fat! Predictably, within a short time the pacing and moaning would begin, and indigestion would cause Pa great discomfort for much of the evening. A kitchen drawer was well stocked with his latest antacid remedies, in hopes that he'd find some relief from indigestion.

    I have fond recollections of Ma waking us each morning. She would have been in the kitchen for quite some time preparing breakfast for the family. Standing at the base of the stairs she'd repeat a phrase in German: "Dupfa, dupfa, cuumin sie ruunder" (hurry, hurry, come on down). Ma was our alarm clock. I remember it being such a sweet and endearing way to be woken up each morning! As we came downstairs, our hot steaming oatmeal was waiting for us, and every morning Ma would say, "Eat all your oatmeal, it will stick to your ribs!" Accompanying the oatmeal was some kind of sausage, such as liverwurst, ring baloney, or pork sausage. Topping off the meal there'd be hard-boiled eggs, bread, and of course cheese; throughout the years cheese has always been a part of my breakfast. While vacationing in France years later, I observed cheese being served with our breakfast every morning. Apparently we had adopted the custom from our European ancestors! Along with Ma's hearty oatmeal breakfast, there was always a plate of cookies on the table. It may seem a bit unusual, but they were typically homemade cookies of a healthier variety. In fact, cookies were served with each meal, not as a dessert but just as part of the meal!

    Ma made her own noodles, and they were used for the hearty chicken noodle soup she frequently made. Watching her cut the noodles with a sharp knife was always very concerning; with her moving the knife faster than the eye, I was certain she'd lose her fingertips! Noodles were placed

Helfenstein Household

on a large sheet that was draped across her bed, and every few hours Ma fluffed up the noodles so they'd dry evenly. This looked like something I might enjoy, but I was only allowed to watch, and reminded to not touch them!

Those tasty noodles were also used for a recipe served on meatless Fridays; after sautéing onions in butter and bread crumbs, creamed eggs and noodles were added, and lastly steamed prunes were combined with the rich noodle mixture. I occasionally make this dish with leftover spaghetti; it's a comfort food that takes me back in time! Meat was served at every breakfast, dinner, and supper in the Helfenstein house, so this meatless noodle dish was something I looked forward to every week. I found it confusing, because at the time only Catholics avoided eating meat on Friday, but I never asked anyone about it. Perhaps it was a carryover from our ancestors, since I understand they practiced Catholicism several hundred years ago.

Ma didn't refer to recipes, and she also never used measuring cups or spoons. Handfuls of ingredients were her form of measurement: a pinch of this and a dash of that made all her meals and baking perfect! Without a Mixmaster, all the heavy mixing of dough was done by hand—and there was a lot of dough! While observing the mixing of dough and the kneading process I'd anxiously wait for the yeast do its magic. As I watched Ma slice off a piece of dough with a sharp knife, there was always the familiar sound of the sticky mass as it was slapped into the bread pan. The well-seasoned cast-iron commercial loaf pan held four loaves of bread, and the house was soon filled with the aroma of fresh-baked bread!

I'm certain my constant shadowing of Ma's activities required a great deal of tolerance on her part, but I never sensed her impatience with me. It's not surprising I'm able to recall such infinite details and vivid food memories. I lived in the Helfenstein household during my most formative years; it was a very impressionable period in my life. Plainly, I was searching for comfort and security. Ma was able to fill that void, and I'm very grateful she was instrumental in providing the emotional and steadfast presence needed in my early development.

Ma & Pa Helfenstein

Aways being anxious to help Ma in the kitchen, one of my favorite tasks was mixing equal parts of peanut butter and syrup. This sticky concoction was served in a hexagon-cut glass bowl and placed on the kitchen table for every meal. Slathered on breakfast toast and warm homemade bread, it was also used as a dipping sauce for dumplings; I'd replenish the mixture several times a week.

Halva's another item that stirs fond food memories. I was introduced to this sweet delicacy while living with my grandparents, and quickly took a liking to it. Halva is an Arabic word meaning sweet. Made of sesame, it's sweetened with brown sugar and honey. Years later I discovered its origin to be Middle Eastern. Fresh halva was formed in large rounds (similar to cheese rounds) and found in the butcher section of our local grocery store. A covered dish of halva was always kept in the refrigerator, so I'd help myself to a small amount most every day when no one was in the kitchen! I don't know why I was sneaking around, because Ma wouldn't have minded, but I also knew eating too often between meals was discouraged.

While living with my grandparents I learned a word that applied to eating when you weren't really hungry. The German or Russian word "glieshda" meant you were just thinking about food; I guess it pretty much described my grazing habit! The word was used frequently when my uncles, sister, and I were looking in the refrigerator or nosing around the kitchen looking for something to nibble on. Ma would say, "You don't know what you want, du hast (you have) glieshda!"

Bockhenslie was another snack food I was introduced to while living with Ma and Pa. Purchased for the Christmas holiday, it was also referred to as St. John's bread. The strange-looking product resembled a dried flat black banana, and it was very fibrous with large black seeds and had a very distinct, sweet flavor. Bockhenslie seemed to disappear from our local stores in the midfifties, but after recently googling St. John's bread, a picture of bockhenslie (obviously a German/Russian word) appeared. The item was described as a dried carob pod and a product of Turkey.

I recently ordered St. John's bread from a Jewish deli in Flatbush, a neighborhood in the borough of Brooklyn, New York. I was delightfully surprised, since it's exactly what I remember munching on as a child! How interesting that halva and carob pods both have Middle Eastern origins. Who knows, there may be another link to our ancestry!

After receiving my genetic test results in February of 2019, I felt it was important to share the following information. Knowing my heritage to be German/Russian, it wasn't at all surprising to find my ethnic makeup to be 96% European, but it was revealing to find there is indeed a slight Middle Eastern genetic link to my ancestry! These were the results: 59% British Isles, 22% East European, 11% Scandinavian, 4% Southeast European, less than 1% Sephardic (Jewish), less than 2% West Middle East, less than 1% East Middle East.

While living in the Helfenstein household I'd often be drawn to a built-in mirrored medicine cabinet located above the kitchen table, because it seemed like an unusual place for medicines to be located. Being naturally curious, I felt the need to periodically inspect the contents of this latched cabinet, just to see if anything new had been added! While standing on a kitchen chair I'd inspect strange colorful metal tins of smelly black salves, various ointments, tweezers, bandages, Mercurochrome (a mercury-based compound), and iodine, all items to treat our injuries. With some supervision, Ma allowed me to treat those occasional cuts on my feet from playing stretch! Remarkably, many of the salves seemed effective but several stained our clothes and smelled really awful! Fortunately, the FDA would determine some of those unsound cures we relied on would no longer be available!

Helfenstein Household

In the early fifties there were two grocery stores in Eureka: the Red Owl and Super Valu. I'd frequent both stores looking for my favorite, the Big Time candy bar. Filled with chocolate, caramel, and peanuts, the original quarter-pound candy bar cost only a nickel! I know what you're thinking: did everything cost only a nickel? Actually, most of my purchases rarely exceeded that amount! My weekly allowance was a quarter, so I had a nickel a day to spend on candy. Obviously my dentist hadn't shared with me the relationship between sugar and cavities!

Not everyone in town owned a car, so people often walked uptown to do their grocery shopping. Grocery orders were taken over the phone with free home deliveries made the same day in a woody station wagon. I remember groceries being brought into Ma's kitchen and placed on the counter. We've come full circle: groceries are now purchased online with home deliveries. What was old is new again! Groceries weren't placed in bags; after stocking shelves merchants recycled cardboard boxes for their customers' use.

Mail wasn't delivered to homes in Eureka. Homeowners had a numbered ornate brass mailbox inside the post office, and once a day someone in our family walked uptown to get the mail. Sometimes I'd go with Pa or Harvey, but if I went alone there'd be more time to look around. I'd be eager to see the FBI's new most-wanted posters tacked on the large bulletin board. After carefully examining mug shot photos showing front views and profiles of the criminals, I'd read their vital statistics and the crimes they'd committed. I was most interested in the monetary rewards for capturing a criminal! If I closely scrutinized the photo, there might be a possibility of spotting them and collecting the reward. After all, I knew everyone in town, so a stranger would definitely stand out! After lingering on the premises I'd open the mailbox with the combination or ask the postmaster for our mail. Before heading home I'd check my pockets for a penny because the dime store was across the street, and chocolate licorice was always waiting for me!

Roller-skating continued to be a favorite outdoor activity, but I was no longer skating every day until dark, as I had the prior year. I had learned to read, so visiting the city library to check out three or four books each week was a new activity for me. Our small library was in the basement of a building on Main Street, right next door to the bowling alley! So much for finding a quiet place to catch up on reading, but surprisingly I don't remember it being too noisy. Our librarian, Mrs. Schulkowski, was very sweet. She also encouraged me to read and emphasized the importance of taking care of my books and returning them promptly. I was always concerned about late fees because they might be a penny or two out of my pocket—and that meant less chocolate licorice!

Our bowling alley had only three lanes. I'm not sure if children were allowed to bowl, but my friends and I enjoyed going inside to watch the activity. Bowling lanes weren't automatic; instead, pinsetters were hired to set the bowling pins! Young boys precariously perched themselves on a ledge above the pins when the bowling ball was thrown down the lane. The small ledge was meant to provide protection from flying pins, but oftentimes the pins or the bowling ball might hit the pinsetters! As the ball and bowling pins came to a rest, the pinsetter hopped off the ledge to reset pins, and he'd then roll the ball back to the bowler. The young boys needed to be very alert and agile; it was a dangerous way to earn very little income—they were paid only twenty-five cents an hour! I understand my uncles, Ervin and Harvey, both worked as pinsetters—for only a short time! Several years later a bowling alley was constructed next to the new Lyric theater. Automation had arrived, and with automatic lanes there was no longer a need for pinsetters.

I was always aware of upcoming school functions because my uncles were involved in sports and numerous high school activities. One of the biggest fall celebrations was homecoming, and the weeklong festivities usually involved the entire community. I don't remember going to a football game, but events leading up to homecoming were exciting for us kids! A homecoming parade down Main Street with the high school marching band and floats brought everyone downtown. The parade took place in the morning and again in the evening, allowing farmers to come into town to enjoy the activities. Anyone interested in being in the parade was welcomed, and we'd be dressed up in crazy costumes; there'd even be early dismissal from school to attend the homecoming events!

During homecoming week students gathered at the lake for a huge bonfire while cheerleaders led cheers, and the traditional snake dance would follow. It was comprised of mostly high school kids, and they'd snake dance from the lake into downtown, ending up on Main Street. While holding hands, teenagers serpentined through town in a whip-like formation led by members of the football team. It looked like great fun, and my friends and I were anxious to join them! We were finally allowed to be on the very tail end, but realized that wasn't the most desirable place to be because within seconds of serpentining we were intentionally whipped off the tail and thrown onto the ground! I think my uncles were involved with this particular prank; it must have been a calculated way to dispose of the "little people!" There were minor scrapes as we landed on gravel. Iodine from the medicine cabinet helped treat my injuries, and we decided to not participate in snake dances until we were much older!

With another winter season upon us there were again record amounts of snowfall. I discovered it was more fun to play in town, where there were more kids and some really good hills for sledding. With massive amounts of snow we'd have about five months to enjoy outdoor activities. After christening the first snowfall with our snow angels we'd be anxious to make a fox-and-geese run. The best place to do this was in the huge backyard which bordered Ma and Pa's yard. We'd start the run by outlining a large circle in the snow with a sizable home base in the center; the radius of the circle took up most of the neighbor's backyard! The fox-and-geese run was in a pie-like fashion with numerous dead-end trails, and it was similar to playing tag in a circle. The neighbor's yard would quickly be overrun with about twenty kids. Janis loved having everyone show up in her yard to play fox and geese, but I remember her parents weren't happy about us tramping down their beautiful lawn! Fox and geese continued until we were called in for supper, or most likely too cold and wet to endure the elements.

The Helfenstein house was at the bottom of a steep hill—at least at the time I thought it was really steep! After enough packed snow had covered G. Avenue, Curtis brought his Radio Flyer sled out of the basement. In my mind his sled seemed the size of a toboggan! As the oldest kid sledding with us, he was always in charge of the steering. Our sled run started at the fire station with about five children stacked on top of Curtis; being the smallest child in the neighborhood, my spot was on the very top. It was usually a short ride—at the first sharp left turn onto G. Avenue, us little kids would fly off the sled and land on a huge snowbank. I'm sure it was an intentional maneuver by my uncle! Inner tubes would have been perfect for zooming down that hill, but they weren't available because they were still being used in tires.

Following a heavy snowfall, snow walls were often built for protection during a snowball fight. Snow walls showed up next to the city park, where they'd last throughout the winter with hard snowballs stockpiled for the next big fight. Boys seemed to really enjoy this activity, and sometimes they hid behind the wall waiting for the next kid to walk by! While walking home from school or picking up the mail I'd be sure to walk on the other side of the street, since I never knew if someone was waiting for me to be their next target!

Each year, back-to-school night included parents as well as students. It was an opportunity to show parents our classroom and work we'd completed. This might have been the only time for parents to discuss their child's progress, or lack thereof. Perhaps it would have been an opportunity for my parents to address my arithmetic difficulties and unfinished homework. Weeks before, I reminded them of the event, but my parents never attended a back-to-school night. In my childhood memory, every classmate's parents were in attendance, but I'm quite certain that wasn't the case! It was obviously of great importance to me and very disappointing that my parents weren't there. As a young child there was confusion about their lack of interest and involvement in my school-related activities. At those times

I'd be searching for acceptance and validation. I remember closely observing the structure and interaction of other families and wondered why mine appeared to be different.

There were mixed signals: clearly I was loved and provided for, and there was definitely of sense of belonging, but for some reason my parents weren't able to provide the nurturing and guidance needed for my educational growth. As an adult, I now understand my parents did their very best. They were in continual survival mode; farm life was difficult for them. It's also possible they were uncomfortable interacting with my teachers because of their lack of formal education. On the upside, blessed in so many ways with the richness of my unique childhood, I feel it more than compensated for my parents' lack of involvement.

Sometime during the second grade, my friends and I became aware of the unusual behavior of the third-grade teacher. Our classrooms were next to each other and we'd frequently hear her shouting at the kids! Mary Jane, Bob, and several other cousins gave us daily narratives about their teacher's nasty disposition. Miss B. had just begun her first year of teaching for the Eureka School District but what made her unique from the rest of the faculty is that she happened to be eighty-five years old! It was obvious to us children that she had numerous health issues and seemingly the beginnings of senility. We noticed Miss B. had great difficulty with her vision, but somehow she managed with astounding accuracy to pitch erasers from her desk at children who misbehaved! While walking up and down the aisles, Miss B. carried a wooden ruler, and we were told she used it to hit children's fingers! All of us second graders knew she was really old, and I suppose we were secretly hoping she'd be "gone" by the time we entered third grade!

On extremely cold days recess was normally held indoors, but after Miss B. arrived it seemed she wanted children to be outside, regardless of the weather! We couldn't understand why she was in charge but it finally occurred to us that she was the oldest one, and I guess we thought the other teachers were probably afraid of her! We'd soon be in the adjoining room next to our classroom dressing for the brutally cold recess. Outer garments hung in the cloakroom on coat hooks, and individual cubbies held our snow pants, wool caps, scarves, mittens, and overshoes. Once we were completely dressed, our teacher tied wool scarves over our faces to protect us from the bitter cold. It was quite an ordeal for the whole class to get bundled up for our brief recess, but necessary to prevent frostbite!

With heavy amounts of snow, our "overshoes" were worn every day for much of the winter. They were referred to as such because they went over our shoes! Most children wore overshoes that were mid-calf with three or four buckles. Made of rubber, they kept our feet dry but provided little insulation from the cold. Overshoes were usually purchased larger than what was needed, with the expectation that we'd grow into them! For the first year or so many of us kids hobbled around with overshoes that were too large, and as our shoe size changed we struggled to put them on and take them off! My overshoes were fancier than most, because there was a roll of fur across the top to keep snow from getting inside. I have a distinct recollection of my socks slipping under the arch of my foot whenever I wore those overshoes! Leggings would have solved that problem but they weren't part of my wardrobe. After several years of wear the fur on my overshoes became brittle, causing chafing and blisters on the back of my legs. Vaseline was kept close by to ease the discomfort! That was way too much information about socks, chafing, and my uncomfortable overshoes, but it was the only thing I disliked about winter! Freezing temperatures and steel playground equipment in our schoolyard seemed a perfect combination for boys to dare or double dare someone to stick their tongue on the cold metal! Most every winter there was at least one boy who accepted the dare—it was great excitement for all of us bystanders, but intense pain for the boy! When I first saw the movie *A Christmas Story* I was amazed at how accurately it depicted the exact scene on our playground so many years ago. The movie was set in the early fifties, and in fact it resembled our schoolyard and play structures. However, there was one exception: we quickly notified a teacher about the unfortunate boy whose tongue was stuck on the cold steel, but we'd be asking for help from someone other than Miss B.!

I was anxious to shelve my uncomfortable overshoes after another long winter, and the month of May finally brought nicer weather. I'd be excited about the festive May Day holiday, when we'd create colorful May baskets in art class by weaving colorful construction paper. There weren't too many varieties of spring flowers to place in our May baskets, but luckily my favorite lilac flower might be in full bloom. It was a tradition to deliver baskets of flowers to our best friends at the end of the school day. Racing from house to house with flower baskets, I'd ring the doorbell, place the basket on the porch, and quickly run away! It was exciting to discover May baskets on the Helfenstein porch after returning home.

CHAPTER TEN

Summer—1952

As my second school year ended there'd again be two weeks of Bible school before going back to the farm. It was the summer of 1952 and family members were busily preparing for the Opp-Neuharth family reunion. As with most large gatherings the celebration was held at the country club. My grandfather's siblings were all in attendance, as well as about three hundred of their direct descendants! At that time most of our relatives still lived fairly close to the Eureka area. I remember the reunion as a huge success, and typical of all celebrations there was a lot of food prepared by each family—it was, of course, a potluck! An outdoor group photo was taken on this very hot summer day in July, and the 8x10 black-and-white photo is in my photo collection. I'm able to identify most of my relatives in the photograph—with the help of a magnifying glass. I'm the little girl on the far right front row shielding her eyes from the bright sunshine. I was absolutely mortified when I first saw the photo—my underpants were showing!

The reunion took place over sixty-five years ago, and trying to determine the number of descendants in our family seems an impossible task. Our relatives are now scattered throughout the United States and in many parts of Europe. Throughout the years I've kept in touch with my thirty-six first cousins (paternal and maternal) and a number of close second cousins, but there are many second cousins I've never met. Attempting to count my second cousins several years ago, I concluded the number was a staggering 387! Remarkably, my mother's side of the family isn't included in that total because we lack Helfenstein-Wolf family history.

The second summer on our farm we spent a great deal of time with my second cousin Mary Jane. The Wittmayer farm was a distinct contrast from the living conditions on our farm: their home had electricity and indoor plumbing. In recent years Mary Jane has said she delighted in the unique differences in our home lives and fondly remembers my mother's wonderful cooking! I felt the same, but recall experiencing foods at their house that weren't normally served in our home—strangely, canned tuna fish comes to mind. My mother recently stated the price of tuna at the time was only ten cents a can, but it was still considered a nonessential food item in our household. I enjoyed those delicious sandwiches at Mary Jane's house, deciding my kitchen pantry would one day be stocked with this yummy seafood in a can! Another treat on those hot summer days was found in the Wittmayer basement, where there appeared to be an endless supply of fudgesicles, popsicles, creamsicles, and orange push-ups in their freezer!

A manicured lawn, flower beds, and a garden surrounded the Wittmayer farmhouse, and on hot summer days we enjoyed cooling off in a large vinyl swimming pool and round stock tank. There was always the mandatory thirty-minute wait to get into the pool after eating—even though the pool was only about a foot deep! In later years I would learn there was also a difference in how discipline was administered in our households: my cousin claimed she'd never been physically disciplined by her parents. As young children we thought we knew everything about each other, but family dynamics were different in households, and I suppose sharing something of an unpleasant nature would have been much too personal—what would people think?

While spending a summer day on the Wittmayer farm, the three of us often accompanied Mary Jane's father to Newtown. It wasn't really a town; the only buildings were a tiny store, a gas station, and one house! This small dot on the map intersected Highways 10 and 45 and was about five miles from our farm. I suspect Julius may have made the trip to buy more pipe tobacco. We'd usually hop onto the bed of his pickup truck for the short drive; it was perfectly legal to travel that way! On our way home there was always a quick stop to check the rain gauge in one of their fields because it was vital information to find out how much rain had fallen the previous night. I really enjoyed those outings: Julius always treated us to a candy bar or ice cream on our return trip!

Unscheduled midweek trips to town occurred frequently during the busy summer. A broken piece of machinery might require the attention of our smithy, Old Man Schaefer. Midweek trips to Eureka were always a solo trip for Dad, and I suspect he actually welcomed the unexpected interruption from his daily grind of farmwork! It normally took about three or four hours for a repair to be finished and of course the waiting took place in the pool hall! This included a few beers and perhaps several friendly games of snooker with the locals and relatives. Several of Dad's cousins might also be waiting for a repair to be finished. It was another opportunity to socialize, and waiting for the repair usually took the better part of Dad's afternoon.

Meanwhile, back at the ranch—as the afternoon wore on, a noticeable tension began to permeate our household! Mom would be getting cranked up about Dad being gone for a good portion of the workday. I'm guessing she was irritated because Dad was having a good time while she was home working! When Dad finally arrived home there'd be the predictable heated argument between my parents. The questioning would begin: Mom wanted to know what took him so long, how much time had he spent in the pool hall, and who else was in the pool hall waiting for a repair? Did she suspect there was some sort of plot to all gather there? I must say, my sister and I really enjoyed our father's midweek trips to town because he never failed to stop at the dime store to buy us a sack of penny candy. I believe there was a method to Dad's madness; he at least wanted to be in good graces with his children when he arrived home! Throughout my parents' verbal exchange, my sister and I happily enjoyed our welcomed midweek treat.

It was the second summer on the farm that my sister and I discovered an activity we hoped might be profitable for us. Our farm cousins had been telling us about the benefits of gopher hunting, and it sounded like a great idea. This new pastime might keep us busy all summer, but the main objective was the prospect of earning money! Gophers were considered a major pest to agricultural crops in the early fifties, and the state of South Dakota was paying a bounty of five cents for each gopher tail to reduce the population. Summer was prime gopher season, and tails collected would be turned into Barney's Creamery at the end of the summer. We eagerly anticipated a productive summer of gopher hunting, so catalog pages had been carefully earmarked to indicate our intended purchases with all the money we'd be earning!

There were different methods of hunting gophers. We were too young to be toting guns, so trapping seemed to be the next logical solution. There were several traps in the garage, and Dad used them to trap foxes, weasels, and muskrats in the late fall and early winter. He felt lucky to trap a fox, and was paid about twenty-five dollars for the pelt, which was a lot of money in 1951! Mom and Dad quickly nixed the trapping idea, deciding it was much too dangerous; they were concerned we'd pinch off our fingers while setting or releasing traps. It was determined that a much safer solution was to drown gophers out of a hole. Finding the largest pails we could carry, my sister and I began to fill them with water from the cattle tank. Going through the gate and out into the pasture, we struggled with heavy pails of water searching for gopher holes. My sister carried the larger pail while I followed with a smaller bucket of water in one hand and a hammer in the other.

My memory of gopher hunting was being very uncomfortable in the hot sun while walking all over the pasture looking for the "perfect" gopher hole! After locating a gopher's home, water that hadn't sloshed out of the pail was quickly poured into the hole. My job was to wait for the gopher to pop its head out of the hole and quickly hit it with my hammer! Gophers move fast, and much faster when water is coming their way; I just remember being startled as the gopher popped out of the hole. I'd quickly drop my hammer and begin to run!

There were many trips out to the pasture attempting to drown out gophers, but thankfully I don't have recollections of killing a gopher. If I did, no doubt that very graphic image has been erased from my memory! Watching my boy cousins drown out gophers looked effortless: hammers were never dropped, and they managed to accomplish their mission with ease. Cutting off the gopher tail with their jackknives looked easy—from a safe distance! But throughout the summer, gopher tails found their way into our Prince Albert tobacco can, and I suspect Dad had been trapping gophers for us. I'd frequently open the can to count the tails, but we'd have to wait until the end of summer to collect our gopher money at Barney's!

One of my second cousins was the king of the gopher hunters. Larry was only nine years old, but each year he collected more gopher tails than anyone in McPherson County! Every year, his picture appeared on the front page of our local paper, including an article about his expertise in hunting gophers and the number of gopher tails he'd turned in. But Larry had an advantage: he used a gun for hunting! There was speculation by many of us children that he'd cut the tails in half to get more money. Of course this was only a rumor, but it made us feel better to know he might be cheating! I decided gopher hunting was really a boy thing and clearly a gun was far more effective for hunting than a pail of water and a hammer! The reality was that my second cousin made the incredible sum of fifty to seventy-five dollars every summer when he cashed in his gopher tails at Barney's. Not so with my sister and I: at the end of the summer we were lucky to earn three or four dollars for all that water schlepping!

Many farms in our community had unique farmhouses, outbuildings, and interesting yards to play in. One of my favorites was Uncle Ed and Aunt Tillie's farm. Our cousins, Betty and Mavis, were older than my sister and I, but despite the age difference they seemed to enjoy having us little kids around. Aunt Tillie had a lovely flower garden of irises and lilies, and there was also a pretty rose trellis on one side of their house, which was a favorite spot to play. Rummaging through boxes of old clothing we'd dress up for mock weddings beneath the fragrant rose trellis. One boy was chosen as the groom and another the minister. Cousins Royal and Teddy were close to our age; they usually cooperated even though they disliked the whole idea! Preparing for the ceremony was as entertaining as the wedding itself, and we'd pick flowers for the bride's and bridesmaid's bouquets while fashioning old lace curtains to be used for the bride's veil and train. Chairs and benches were set up for cousins who weren't lucky enough to be in the wedding party!

After we all had a chance to be the bride, we'd often switch the play from weddings to funerals! One person was chosen to be the deceased, and they'd be laid out on a bench in front of the mourners. Again one of the boys had to be the minister for the funeral, and he'd begin to pray. It sounds terrible, but to get the emotion and crying started, one of the younger kids might be slapped across the face, giving them a real reason to cry!

An abandoned one-room rural schoolhouse was located on my aunt and uncle's farmyard. Desks, books, large numerals, and an alphabet above the blackboard were still in the building, and there was even a bell on the teacher's desk. Many hours were spent playing school, with a great deal of time and a few disputes deciding who'd get to be the teacher! It was such fun, but play might come to an abrupt end if a mouse scurried across the floor. Girls were quickly on top of a desk or out of the building! Betty and Mavis watched us younger kids when our parents went out for the evening. As soon as our parents left, Betty began to make homemade fudge, which was poured into a buttered pie plate. After we patiently waited for the fudge to cool, it was cut in a pie shape and we were each given a large slice—another food memory of warm fudge melting in my mouth. Uncle Ed, Aunt Tillie, and my cousins moved to Moses Lake, Washington in 1952. I really missed them—and Betty's fudge!

It was the second summer on our farm when Mom was determined to bake an angel food cake from scratch. We always had a surplus of eggs, but our chickens were laying more eggs than usual and prices were extremely low. We were now paid only four cents a dozen; Mom said it wasn't even worth the trouble of crating them! An angel food recipe requires twelve egg whites, so she decided this would be an excellent time to learn how to bake a cake. I have recollections of a cake being baked every day for several weeks, but much to her dismay Mom never mastered a perfect angel food cake. Most were of a pound cake consistency, but my sister and I managed to eat the failures anyway! Mom was really bothered by her unsuccessful attempts at angel food because she excelled at most everything else. I have a vivid memory of her cracking and separating all those egg whites and of us munching on the failures!

Unfortunately the first year of farming wasn't very profitable for my parents, but obviously I was unaware of their financial concerns. I understand they were cautiously optimistic as our second summer crop began to show some promise. With harvest season approaching there were the usual worries of drought or possibly too much rain. There was uncertainty about the optimum time to harvest, which was always a risk for farmers, and as dark storm clouds gathered on the horizon there was also the continual threat of hail. Sadly, our crops again sustained severe damage from hailstorms! Wheat and oat crops that had survived the assault of hail would be harvested with the small combine my parents had purchased. On a more positive note, the header box and binder were no longer needed for harvesting, which meant we wouldn't be shocking!

About twelve men worked for three or four days to bring in our harvest. Much of the threshing crew consisted of relatives, who arrived at our farm before sunrise. My mother had arranged to have several women help with cooking and kitchen duty. Mom helped them when threshing was done on their farms, because that's how things were done—neighbors helping neighbors whenever there was a need. Great organizational skills were required to plan and prepare huge amounts of food for the threshing crew. It was more challenging on our farm because we lacked electricity and adequate refrigeration.

As the sun came up a large breakfast was served before the men began their field work. I don't remember anything about breakfast—this was long before I was awake! I suspect there would have been many pots of coffee, dozens of fried eggs, lots of sausage, and pan-fried toast. Several hours later I was involved with taking a midmorning snack to the workers in the field, which was done to save working time. The snack included kuchen, pickles, cinnamon rolls, more coffee, and water. As the hungry crew arrived at our house for dinner, an outdoor wash station with basins of soapy water and towels was set up.

The largest meal for the threshers was served at noon, and our dining room table was able to accommodate all the workers. Dinner typically included large quantities of either beef, pork, or chicken, with mashed potatoes, gravy, numerous vegetables, cucumber salad, Jell-O with whipped cream, dill pickles, pickled watermelon, and freshly baked bread. Of course, dessert was served after dinner; it was usually a combination of cakes and pies. Three or four hours later a midafternoon snack might include sausage-and-cheese sandwiches, cookies, and brownies, and as in the morning the afternoon refreshment was also taken out to the field. I remember an incredible amount of food being eaten by the work crew!

Throughout the hot, humid workday, we'd replenish numerous glass gallon jugs of well water for the thirsty men. Threshers did very physical work; our new combine helped ease the workload, but it was still very labor intensive. The kitchen help worked from sun up until late into the night. It was very hot in our house: without electricity and the use of fans, it was uncomfortable to have the stove and oven in use the entire day. Harvesting occurred during the hottest part of the summer, which made work conditions more difficult for the kitchen help as well as the threshing crew.

Field work continued until dark. As the tired crew arrived at our house, they were served another meal before returning to their homes. Supper was usually a bit lighter; it might consist of pork sausage, fried potatoes, vegetables, salads, more pickled foods, and bread, and an array of desserts followed. I know what you're thinking—what about this meal would be considered "lighter?" After the kitchen help and threshers left for home, my mother's work continued. She'd begin to prepare more bread dough for the following morning. This was also the time to bake more desserts for the next day. After kitchen duty, stacks of towels were laundered and hung on the wash line. With only four or five hours of sleep, Mom would repeat the whole process!

I really loved the excitement of having all those people around to bring in our harvest. It seemed like a fun social event, but I wasn't aware of how much work was involved. My sister and I were too young to help with food prepping, so our job was to set the dining room table before each meal, churn butter, and help with drying all the dishes. When I recently asked my mother more questions about the busy harvest season, she said there didn't seem to be enough hours in the day to get everything done. Mom was puzzled at how she managed to do all that work without the conveniences she's now become so accustomed to. At the end of our conversation she simply stated, "I really don't want to talk about it anymore…it makes me tired just thinking about it!"

CHAPTER ELEVEN

1953

Much to my delight, we'd again be living with Ma and Pa for the upcoming school year. Clearly my parents realized I was a much happier child living in the Helfenstein household. There was more good news as I prepared to enter the third grade: apparently our prayers had been answered during the summer. Miss B. would not be returning for another year of teaching! In complete contrast, our new teacher was directly out of teachers college, very sweet, and about sixty-five years younger than Miss B.! While sharing recess with the first and second graders, we were now the big kids on the playground, and as an added bonus, we were unrivaled at playing stretch and shooting marbles.

I don't recall much about the school year; presumably I'd finally adapted to living away from home. There were continued difficulties with arithmetic assignments, and the all too familiar phrases "Invariably needs to work harder" and "Inclined to give up too easily" continued to be noted on my report card each grading period. Despite the comments, no one seemed too concerned—not even my very sweet teacher!

1953

Auction sales were frequently held on the corner lot next to the dime store. Outdoor sales occurred in the spring, summer, or early fall when weather was more favorable. Furniture and household items were placed on the vacant dirt lot, and an auctioneer would oversee the event while standing on a flatbed truck. During an evening sale, lights were strung across the lot to illuminate sale items. The auctions appeared to take on a carnival atmosphere with the bright lights and lots of people! The sales lot was filled with furniture, appliances, and household items. Furniture drawers often contained hankies, costume jewelry, and other personal effects to be auctioned off.

It was great fun attending auction sales with my friends because we liked looking at someone else's stuff! Arriving early gave people an opportunity to inspect items and decide whether they'd be doing any bidding. I found the bidding process very amusing, but the only thing I understood during the entire exchange was the word *sold*—everything else sounded like a foreign language! People were always looking for a good bargain, but outdoor auctions were yet another social event to bring the community together.

My great-great-aunt Eva and great-great-uncle Johannes Feder Wolf had a popcorn stand on the lot where auction sales took place. The stand provided them with additional income, but I believe their real intent was to socialize with people. From their tiny silver trailer they sold popcorn, soft drinks, and candy during the midweek sales, as well as those busy Saturday nights. I'd usually stop to visit them, and at times a free bag of popcorn might come my way if I managed to speak a bit of German! They didn't want me to forget my first language, and I suppose it pleased them that I still knew a few words. Johannes was Ma's uncle; he and his wife were frequent visitors at my grandparents' home. I enjoyed spending time with my elderly great-great-aunt and uncle; they were kind, accepting, and very much a positive influence in my life. It was also apparent that they absolutely adored each other! Years later, I realized they weren't old at all—they were only in their late fifties!

Judy, age eight

Throughout the school year Ma continued to be a stabilizing force in my life. Her warm and secure presence was always very comforting. I was unaware of the powerful influence she would have on my life. I'd continue to shadow her while she busily prepared meals and went about her daily household tasks. It pleased me that I was able to be of more help to her. Placing a chair next to Ma while she was sewing, I'd offer my assistance by threading the needle of her treadle sewing machine. My eyes were much better for seeing close-up tasks than hers, so I'd be there just in case a thread broke! A few other chores had been assigned to me, such as setting the supper table and drying dishes. I don't recall breaking a glass or dish but Ma wouldn't have been concerned. There were only a few pieces of good dinnerware in the china hutch; most things in the Helfenstein household were very utilitarian and functional in nature. Obtaining items for purely aesthetic reasons would have been considered unnecessary and too extravagant.

During the early fifties it was customary to acquire sets of glassware and dishes in oatmeal, cereal, and laundry detergent boxes. My parents and grandparents acquired many of their drinking glasses and dishes by purchasing common household products. Companies had found a clever way of marketing a new product to consumers by placing a dish or drinking glass inside the box. It was desirable to collect an entire set of dishes or glasses, but you never knew what was in the box until it was opened, so it was always a surprise! Much sought-after depression glass in today's market was obtained in the same manner during the thirties.

I remember people shopping at businesses providing S&H Green Stamps. Merchants offered green stamps when groceries, gas, and retail purchases were made. Sperry & Hutchison Green Stamps were distributed as a loyalty rewards program from the late 1800's well into the 1960's. I'd volunteer to lick S&H stamps, placing them in books provided by the merchant. After books were filled we'd browse through the green stamp catalog to choose our gift. Stacks of green stamp books were turned in for our selected free item! The redemption center in Aberdeen included small appliances and common household items as well as a few articles of clothing.

Observing my family's frugal lifestyle and food conservation techniques was an invaluable education. Our early ancestors were very familiar with the methods of conservation; they needed to be resourceful out of necessity. Although there was an abundance of food when I was a child, we were taught it was never to be wasted. As with our ancestors, we learned to enjoy basic foods and eat leftovers; by adding a few more eggs or potatoes it would stretch a meal. A number of those simple meals that frequented our dinner and supper table as a child are foods I now refer to as comfort food! All the hardships and depression stories were recounted to us, and there were often pearls of wisdom or words of advice. There'd be frequent reminders to never take more food than you can eat, always put things back where you found them, and try to fix things that were broken! It was also suggested that you should never hire someone to do a job that you can do yourself!

Many women made clothing for themselves and their children, and most garments were recycled. Worn-out adult wool coats and men's suits were often cut down and fashioned into children's outer garments. Articles of clothing no longer serviceable were salvaged: cut into strips, they were often used to make hook rugs and patchwork quilts. Tinfoil, rubber bands, paper products, string, etc., were also saved for additional use. A surplus of white cotton string was found in many households because items purchased in retail stores were often wrapped in brown butcher paper and tied with string. A commercial-sized ball of white cotton string hung above some sales counters to secure packages.

Salvaged string was rolled into balls and saved for future use—recycling was alive and well in our community!

Discovering ways to conserve and learning to be domestic was a big part of my young life, and much of what I learned from my mother and Ma has left a lasting impression. Unfortunately, as often as I watched Ma bake bread, I never acquired that particular skill; perhaps there was an association with the blackened commercial-baking pans she used! I think of her often, especially when I'm baking or cooking one of her ethnic dishes. It's comforting that after all these years I continue to feel a warm closeness to her. Ma would have been astounded at having left such an enduring legacy!

Only one unpleasant memory occurred in Ma's kitchen when I was about eight years old. The incident happened to coincide with a lengthy visit from Great-Grandma Wolf (Ma's mother). Great-Grandma visited each of her children several times a year, and she'd be at the Helfenstein house several weeks at a time. I suppose the words irritable or edgy might best describe Great-Grandma's disposition, and it's possible my continual presence in Ma's kitchen was an annoyance to her. On this particular day as Ma was slicing cheese, in my usual helpful way I ate a small piece of cheese that had broken off onto the cutting board. To my astonishment, Great-Grandma slapped me across the face! I was startled, hurt, and in tears, and Ma immediately took me into her arms to comfort me. She was very angry and scolded her mother in German for slapping me. After that frightening experience I kept my distance whenever Great-Grandma visited!

Regarding Great-Grandma Christina's temperament, it's crucial to be aware of her early beginnings. It's been noted she and my great-grandpa Christian began their relationship in Odessa, Russia. Christina became pregnant and Christian subsequently left Russia to begin his immigration to America! My grandmother (Ma) was born in 1898, and no one is aware of whether Christian knew of the pregnancy before he left Russia. Obviously, history is lacking about the exact circumstances of events. This would not have been a topic of discussion in our family! Undoubtedly, the social stigma of being an unwed mother in that era must have been very difficult for Christina and her family. It's possible her unmarried status prompted her decision to leave Russia in search of the father of her child. But, there is also the probability Christian knew of the pregnancy before he immigrated, and perhaps he needed to earn money in America to arrange for her passage; it's what I choose to believe! We know Christina traveled across the Atlantic, arriving at Ellis Island with her one-year-old daughter in tow. If she arrived in America on her own accord in pursuit of this young man, it wouldn't have surprised me. My great-grandmother was known to be tenacious, headstrong, and very strong-willed; I suspect she would have been determined to locate the father of her child!

Christian D. Wolf was a musician, and the story has it that a number of people in Christina's travels knew of him because of his music. Discovering this young man had settled in the Dakota Territory, Christina located him in Long Lake, South Dakota. They were married shortly after her arrival in 1899. Three more children were added to my great-grandparents' family in the following years. My mother remembers her grandfather as being very good-natured. He joyfully doted on his children and grandchildren, and as his first granddaughter she remembers him always having a stick of candy for her. Music was a big part of their lives: with his accordion and several other musical instruments, he entertained his family and performed for the Long Lake community. My great-grandparents both had a love of music, and sometimes I'd hear Great-Grandma singing church hymns with her good friend as they sat on the Helfenstein front porch. She had a beautiful voice.

Visiting Ellis Island years ago, I was able to verify my great-grandmother's entry into the United States. It was emotionally stirring to be at the physical site to see Christina's signature and my grandmother Eva's name on the 1899 microfiche document! Unfortunately, I wasn't able to search for additional information regarding her port of departure or the name of the ship that brought her to America. We'll never, ever know the real story or mystery surrounding my great-grandparents' relationship. Perhaps it's another reason to document family history, otherwise descendants are left to speculate on the course of events. I thought it was important to share my great-grandmother's early beginnings because we need to remember there are always extenuating circumstances regarding people's actions and behavior. We're definitely products of our environment.

Our Portland relatives stayed with us every summer for their two-week vacation while visiting relatives in Dakota. We were expecting them during the summer of '53 but were uncertain of their exact arrival time. While my parents were doing chores one late summer afternoon, I was startled to hear a plane approaching our farm! As I ran outside, the small plane kept buzzing our farmyard, and in all the excitement I failed to see a tiny parachute that was dropped from the plane. A note attached to the parachute was from our relatives asking us to pick them up at the small airstrip in Eureka. After a lengthy wait at the airstrip, they determined we never saw the note. Boarding their plane, they returned to our farm, and this time they landed in one of our fields! The great plane adventure was about the most exciting event that occurred in the Eureka area that summer!

Patti and Doreen were the Portland cousins who gave us all the beautiful hand-me-down clothes each year. During this visit I was particularly fascinated with their extensive wardrobe, especially the numerous pairs of shoes coordinated with their many outfits! My main focus was on Patti's white leather Capezio shoes. I'd try them on whenever Patti and her family were away from our farm. As our relatives were packing to leave, I intentionally hid one shoe under the sofa! Everyone was searching for her shoe but unable to find it. As their plane soared for the sky, I just happened to discover the missing shoe! I remember feeling absolute remorse about the shoe theft, but at a loss to understand my desperate actions; I only knew that beautiful shoe had to be mine!

Plagued with terrible guilt for the longest time, I somehow convinced myself the shoe theft was a seemingly innocent act. It's really the only naughty thing I remember doing in my childhood—other than roller skating inside the funeral home! It's truly mystifying what the purpose was of the shoe theft, and even more puzzling, what was I planning to do with only "one" shoe that happened to be much too large? That very embarrassing incident was kept to myself. I mean really, what would people think? The shoe caper was finally revealed at a large family gathering about thirty years later. Everyone including Patti thought it was hilarious, and women are now reminded to keep their shoes on at all family events!

1953

As another summer was coming to an end, I was pleased we'd again be living in the Helfenstein house as the new school year began. Moving to the second floor of our grade school caused some angst during the school year. Concerns about the fire escape from the sixth grade classroom were real—it was the fire escape I'd now be using! Other than occasional fire drills and continuing to struggle with math, it seemed to be an uneventful school year. I was happy to discover a few more farm cousins attending school in Eureka, and there were now eight second cousins in my fourth-grade class!

Our farming community was introduced to television when I was about nine years old; it was an eventful experience! Television was in its infancy, and as with most new technology, this device was expensive. Luckily for us, Mary Jane's family happened to be one of the first families in the area to purchase a television. When home on weekends, we'd often get phone calls from the Wittmayer farm. The exact dialogue was, "Come on over, I think we can see something on the television!" We'd quickly finish our chores and hurry to their farm. Seating in their front room faced the small oval screen for ideal viewing. Most of the evening was spent trying to discern the shadowy images moving about the screen. We'd refer to interference on the screen as snow, because it reminded us of a blizzard! At times nothing was visible, but audio to this intriguing device was excellent. That and an occasional image is undoubtedly what kept us coming back for more!

For optimum viewing, antennas could be installed on the roof of a house to pick up the best television signal. Without a roof antenna, a pair of rabbit ear antennas were placed on top of our neighbors' television set, which required someone to repeatedly adjust rabbit ears in a different direction in an attempt to improve the picture! Sometimes a wad of tinfoil was wrapped around each rabbit ear in hopes of securing better reception. Horizontal and vertical buttons needed adjustment when the screen would go crazy. Those two very small flat buttons weren't very accessible because they were located behind the TV. This new technology required ingenuity and lots of patience for very limited viewing. In the early fifties there was only one channel!

Weather continued to be a vital topic of conversation in our farming community. Extreme weather came up quickly on the plains, often bringing torrential rain or hail the size of golf balls or larger! Following a hailstorm, we'd drive from one field to the next hoping our crops had been spared from the devastating hail; we were getting used to this routine. I'd sense my father's overwhelming disappointment; many times our crops were severely damaged in a matter of minutes! Always the eternal optimist, Dad didn't seem troubled by his misfortune for too long, and he'd suggest we begin to gather large hailstones to make homemade ice cream!

Nothing could bring back crops that had been trampled down with hail, so perhaps Dad was determined something "good" might result from all that despair. There's also the possibility he was able to take out his frustrations on the hand crank of the ice cream maker! Mom would begin to make hot fudge and my sister and I would soon be licking the ice cream paddles. While feasting on this frozen treat, our family was able to indulge in second and possibly third helpings—there weren't any snowbanks to keep it frozen! I understand we experienced three years of partial hail damage to our crops, and sadly we were completely hailed out for two years. Regrettably my parents were without hail insurance! As a young child I wasn't aware of my parents' financial concerns, but the continuous struggle to support their family must have been very worrisome for them.

The approaching dark clouds on the western horizon were usually rumbling thunderstorms with dramatic lightning bolts. Sheet lightening often lit up the night sky. It was spectacular to watch but we'd be told to keep a safe distance. There were reminders to stay away from windows and to never use the telephone during a lightning storm. Precautions were always taken during a thunderstorm when working outdoors, and there was an awareness of lightning strikes while carrying metal pails or working with machinery. During hot, dry summers, prairie fires were another concern if haystacks were struck by lightning!

The weather that caused me the most fear was the conditions that might produce a tornado. As a result I learned to watch the horizon for dark clouds forming southwest of our farm. Funnel clouds might appear quickly, and early warning systems weren't in place to prepare for them. Usually there were indications of an approaching tornado: the sky took on a greenish-gray color, an eerie stillness filled the air, and farm animals often became skittish, as if they sensed danger. We learned to watch for those signs, realizing it was time to seek shelter.

When sighting a tornado, it was preferable to reach the infamous root cellar, if there was time to do so. While exploring our farm I'd briefly glanced into that small hole in the ground and announced I'd never go down there! The first time our family descended into that dank underground, it was just as I'd imagined—pitch black and frightening! As cobwebs hit my face, I was convinced a big spider was crawling in my hair. We were below ground and I knew creepy crawling things made their home in this very dark hole. I was thankful for the darkness, because at least I wasn't able to see what our family was sharing this tiny space with!

Years later I would learn my mother suffered from severe claustrophobia, but she never exhibited a fear of being underground. It was a very frightening experience for our family, but obviously the root cellar was the safest place to be. The tornado would move on in ten or fifteen minutes, and after the noise ceased my father climbed the tiny cellar steps to open the door. We'd follow closely behind, adjusting our eyes to the bright blue sky. Our primary concern was whether our house or outbuildings had been destroyed or damaged, but usually we'd just find debris tossed around the farmyard with only minor damage to roofing, buildings, and trees.

Apparently I'd become the self-appointed weather watch. Much to my parents' annoyance, I'd frequently ask, "Do you think there's a tornado in those clouds?" The last year on our farm I'd been ill and wasn't able to watch for bad weather. Confined to bed and unable to walk, I'd been placed on a small cot in the dining room. One early evening as my parents and sister were having supper in the kitchen, they were unaware of a tornado approaching our farm. Glancing out the dining room window, I saw our garage being raised into the air! Paralyzed with fear, I watched the entire building being lifted about fifty feet off the ground—for a brief second, our garage seemed to be suspended in midair! As the building began to spin it exploded with debris, hitting our house—we were in the eye of the tornado! My screams alerted my family that we were in danger. This time we didn't have time to reach the root cellar, so my father hurriedly scooped me off the cot, and with my mother and sister

1953

we managed to reach the basement. Our house was shaking violently as we positioned ourselves in the southwest corner of the basement. Presumably this was the safest place to seek refuge if our house was destroyed. Years later I learned that was a misconception—there really wasn't one particular corner of a basement that was safer than the other! What I mostly recall about this surreal experience, other than absolute terror, was the thunderous sound of the tornado as it passed over our house!

Thankfully, we weren't injured, but this tornado did extensive damage to our farm. Our house sustained only minor damage, but the barn and several outbuildings didn't fare as well. Obviously our garage had taken the direct hit; many contents such as tools, traps, oil drums, and equipment were found several miles away in one of our cornfields. Surprisingly, I don't believe we lost any farm animals. Our dogs Spotty and Netty had apparently found shelter somewhere; they were probably aware of the tornado long before we were! My parents said it was yet another sign for us to think about moving off the farm. I was in agreement: that terrifying event generated nightmares and emotional trauma for several years.

CHAPTER TWELVE

Health Concerns

When I entered the fifth grade, my teacher immediately recognized my difficulties with math. Notably, Mrs. Stahl was the first teacher to make this observation, and she was determined to have me at grade level by the end of the school year. Grateful for her tutoring, I was beginning to receive needed help and encouragement. However, midway through the school year I began to experience health problems. Coincidently my symptoms were similar to the early onset of polio, which gave my parents cause for concern. I was taken to the doctor. Polio was dominating the news front in the midfifties; the disease had reached epidemic stages in the United States. Nils's father had been our family doctor but he'd moved his family to Montana to establish a new practice, so Dr. Macintosh was now the only doctor in Eureka. After an exam and lab work, he determined I'd contracted rheumatic fever. Although it was a very serious illness, at least the fear of polio had been alleviated. We were told it was treatable when diagnosed in the early stages, but I'd need proper long-term care to avoid damage to my heart.

Health Concerns

I was hospitalized for over a month with complete bed rest. Apparently my illness was the result of recurrent bouts of tonsillitis and strep throat; in retrospect, my tonsils should have been removed much earlier, but there wouldn't be a tonsillectomy until I was in better health.

The Eureka hospital had only one private room, located at the end of the main hallway. It was difficult being isolated in this tiny room, and I wasn't allowed out of bed, not even for bathroom use. Remarkably, during the first few weeks of being hospitalized my parakeet was allowed to share my room! Petey (apparently named after my pet chicken) kept me company during my lengthy stay. I'm not sure who fed him every day or covered his cage each night, but Petey provided needed entertainment during my confinement. Scores of library books were read and nurses provided magazines; this was long before televisions were in hospital rooms. My friends visited after school to drop off homework, and they referred to my illness as "romantic fever!"

I had excellent care during my extended hospitalization, and every day a massage followed my sponge bath. My total fascination was with the nurse's aide. This very sweet woman happened to have an extra appendage on the side of her thumb—it was in fact a perfectly formed baby thumb! Initially alarmed that having an extra thumb was even a remote possibility, I began to consider all the different ways of asking her about it. I was absolutely mystified and curious about her miniature thumb, and apparently very bored! Ultimately, after much consideration I decided not to mention anything about her baby thumb, realizing it just might make her feel bad! Years later I discovered the nurse's aide was Mary Jane's aunt, and evidently the baby thumb I was so fixated on had finally been surgically removed!

Blood was drawn every day to determine my set rate. It was not a pleasant experience, however; the worst injection was what the nurse's described as a liver shot. I knew which nurse was likely to administer that painful shot, and I was able to identify the sound of her footsteps with the syringe rattling around in the surgical tray as she walked down that long hallway! Disposable syringes hadn't been invented, and I clearly recall the large, shiny, stainless steel syringe and the length of the hypodermic needle. In my very imaginative mind it resembled a harpoon!

I'm certain my prolonged period of convalescence was the beginning of my awareness of personal health concerns. I'd frequently ask my parents about rheumatic fever. Understandably they soon tired of answering all my questions because they weren't comfortable discussing serious matters. Because of their evasiveness I began to suspect my illness was more dire than what I'd been told, and it suddenly occurred to me that I might be dying a very slow death! After all, I was feeling much better and no longer had pain or discomfort, so why was I still confined to bed? The avoidance of my questions led me to believe I had valid concerns regarding my demise. Visions of being laid out at Straub's funeral home with my friends roller-skating past my casket were very vivid in my mind!

Upon my release from the hospital, Dr. Mac gave my parents and I explicit instructions. Once back home, I'd still be confined to bed and was specifically told there'd be permanent damage to my heart if I put one foot out of bed. I'm grateful my doctor painted such a bleak picture, because it frightened me enough to stay in bed. I was placed in the small downstairs bedroom next to the front room during my recovery, allowing me to be closer to family activities.

The room was bright and sunny with several windows, and a colorful chenille bedspread decorated my double bed where I'd spread out my favorite paper dolls.

Our radio in the front room kept me entertained with several soap operas and music stations. The *Hit Parade* was my favorite program; I quickly memorized the latest popular songs and loved singing along with the recording artists. There were lots of catchy radio ads and jingles; "Halo, everybody Halo," was the name for the brand new shampoo being advertised. Another tune advertised toothpaste: "You'll wonder where the yellow went, when you brush your teeth with Pepsodent!" Burma-Shave, Ovaltine, and Maxwell House Coffee were several other musical ads that caught my attention. I knew of *The Shadow* and *The Inner Sanctum*, but those programs were much too frightening to listen to! The entire spring and most of the summer was spent in this small bedroom.

During this period of convalescing, my mother was doing her best to provide activities for me. Crafts such as paint-by-number kits and painting stenciled flour-sack dish towels were of fleeting interest. Much time was spent paging through new spring catalogs, but as summer was approaching I tired of every activity. I wanted nothing more than to be outdoors! My illness had also altered my parents' busy social life. We had many visitors, but being stuck at home every night was becoming the new normal. Years later, I learned that my prolonged hospitalization and eventual tonsillectomy had been a quite a financial strain for my parents. I discovered the cost of my hospital room had been fifty dollars a day. Comparatively speaking it seems like nothing at all, but this was a considerable expense in 1955! Without health insurance, my parents would be paying off this costly debt for many years.

I was told my lengthy illness spoiled me, at least that's what my sister and Mary Jane said. They were probably right! Obviously I needed lots of personal care. It required everyone's time and energy. The girls were asked to do a lot for me and I'm sure they tired of it. Initially, I enjoyed the extra attention from my parents, but what I really wanted was to be healthy and to play outside with my friends. My thoughts often turned to the amount of school I was missing. Packets of makeup work found their way to our farm. Homework was completed, but my struggles with math continued. I'd been absent for almost half the school year and was unable to get the needed tutoring from my teacher. My fifth-grade year should have been repeated, but at the time there was such a stigma about being held back a grade, which we referred to as "flunking," regardless of the reason!

AS THE SWELTERING SUMMER ARRIVED, IT WAS MORE difficult being confined to bed, but there was one very hot humid day when I finally got out of the house! Rosemarie and Mary Jane asked if I'd like to go down to one of the camps in the trees. It sounded like a great idea. Mom and Dad were both working in the fields—they'd never find out! The girls made a chair by interlocking their arms as they carried me down to the trees. Placing me on the ground, they went off to play somewhere else! Although I was alone, it was so exciting to finally be outdoors! Fortunately I didn't attempt to walk up the hill to the house; instead I sat in the tree camp for the remainder of the afternoon until my parents returned to the farm. It was the only time I escaped!

Health Concerns

My health had improved enough to have my tonsils removed in late June, and several days of hospitalization followed the tonsillectomy. Ether was the conventional anesthesia used. In a groggy state of nauseousness, my first vision was of Dr. Mac standing next to my hospital bed. Holding a surgical tray containing my tonsils and adenoids, he asked if I'd like to take them home in a jar! For a very brief moment I visualized my jar lined up with the collection of other jars in the freezer room at Ma and Pa's house! But the offer was declined, because I just wanted to get rid of those awful tonsils that had made me so ill. I recuperated at Ma and Pa's house. It was a wise decision to be there instead of the farm because I began to hemorrhage and was readmitted to the hospital!

There were three additional days of hospitalization involving uncomfortable ice treatments, but I was finally on the road to recovery. My health had improved, but I was instructed to not overexert myself for one year. Anxious to roller skate, I was told my favorite activity, as well as running, jump rope, and skipping, would have to wait. Despite a slight heart murmur which I eventually outgrew, I'm so fortunate there were no residual effects caused by my illness.

Significant life-changing events occur in our lives. On those days we remember exactly where we were and what we were doing, and the moments seem to be forever etched in our minds. On the morning of July 31st, our family received a phone call informing us that Ma had been hospitalized after having an aneurysm. I clearly remember that warm summer day and seemingly long drive to Eureka. Sadly, by the time we arrived at the hospital, Ma had passed away. She lived for only two hours and left us before we could say our goodbyes to her. Even though I had lost many relatives, her death was significantly different for me. Ma had been such an integral part of my being, I simply couldn't comprehend that she'd never again be in my life! It had only been three weeks since she'd cared for me following my tonsillectomy. I tried to remember if I'd thanked her, and wondered if Ma knew how much I loved her; in fact, had I ever told her?

Ma's passing left a terrible void because she was the person that kept our large family together. I learned she'd been treated for hypertension, but at the time medications for treatment weren't very effective. Apparently her health had been compromised for several years; Ma was only fifty-eight years old! There'd be visitation at the all-too-familiar funeral home. I didn't want to be there, but that wasn't my decision to make. Of course there were the usual comments about how good Ma looked, and I'll never forget watching an uncle stand on a chair to get better pictures of her. He talked of how nice the pictures would be with the new colored film he'd bought. I was so outraged to see him taking pictures of Ma that I felt like smashing his camera! It was the last time I walked through the doors of Straub's funeral home.

Instead of attending Ma's funeral, my sister and I cared for our younger cousins at the Helfenstein house. In this house I'd experienced so much joy, but on that day and throughout the summer I felt an overwhelming sadness. Ma had made an extraordinary impact on my young life: she had lovingly provided a warm and secure presence at a time when I needed it most. It occurred to me that living with our grandparents had created much more work for Ma, and that maybe that's why she became ill. I found it very unsettling.

After Ma's death I came to understand the significance of telling people how much they mean to you. We'd never been taught to show or verbalize our feelings, and it was something I was determined to change in my adult life! I distinctly recall the very first time I told my parents I loved them. It occurred when my parents were wintering in Arizona during the late seventies. We wouldn't be seeing each other for several months, so following a hug I told them I loved them. Hugging had always been uncomfortable for them, but the words "I love you" were way over the top! My parents didn't know how to respond, and it was an extremely awkward moment for everyone. In time, I suppose they both became more accustomed to my boldness and eventually began to reply in kind; it would be the first time my parents said they loved me!

My aunts and uncles were initially just as surprised and uncomfortable when I told them I loved them; it took some time, but they also became accustomed to my demonstrative behavior! Now well into their nineties and over one hundred years of age, it's almost second nature for them to respond, "I love you too!" Regretfully, showing emotion was considered to be a sign of weakness. Of course this wasn't unique to our family because most of my friends' parents had the same common beliefs. I'm pleased to have been instrumental in helping to bring about that change in our family.

After Ma's passing our family moved into my grandparents' home to help care for Pa and my uncles. For the remainder of the summer my father traveled to our farm, working crops and caring for the livestock. By summer's end my parents decided to sell our farm, realizing they could no longer make a living wage as independent farmers. It must have been disappointing for my father, because at the age of thirty-nine he now had the daunting task of searching for a new vocation. Owning our pool hall and farming was the only work Dad had known, and without a high school education his employment options would be limited. When my parents were being educated, very few children in the area attended secondary school. At that time, people in our rural community regarded high school as an unnecessary luxury, and considering a career other than farming was highly unusual.

CHAPTER THIRTEEN

Moving to Oregon

My parents would make the decision to move to Oregon. It was unquestionably a very bold move in 1956! After many years of employment offers by Uncle Richard, my mother finally agreed to work at his steak house. During their annual summer visit he'd watch my parents do their milking chores, frequently stating, "Edna, you could make more money on tips in one night at my restaurant than pulling teats on those milk cows for a whole week." It turns out he was right! We'd be moving the first week in November, and my father would search for employment after we became settled in Portland.

In preparing for the move, an auction sale would take place on our farm. We'd be selling livestock, farm equipment, and household furnishings. I'd always enjoyed the excitement of an auction sale but realized this sale was going to be very personal. The day of the sale my sister and I dismally watched the proceedings from our bedroom window. All our toys were being sold, including the prized dollhouse Mom had made for us. I'd be able to keep my roller skates and one doll. I chose the one with the pretty red hair, whose eyes matched the blue dress Mom had made for her. Many tears were shed that afternoon as we sadly watched our treasures being carted off by hundreds of people.

Our four-door Dodge would tow a small trailer to Oregon. It held only a few household items, such as the small electrical appliances which had been in storage for five years. The largest item was my mother's cedar chest, which was packed with bedding, photos, clothing, and a number of keepsakes. We were traveling light, being told that whatever we needed for our new home could be purchased when we arrived in Portland. Mom didn't seem troubled about parting with many of her things. Always pragmatic in her thinking, she never had a great attachment to or sentiment about stuff. I believe in her mind this move was a complete do-over; she was starting a new life.

I'd learn my mother was instrumental in the decision to move to Portland; farm life had been a real struggle for her. I've also wondered if Ma's death influenced her resolve to search for a new life. My father didn't share her enthusiasm; he expressed concerns about moving so far away from family. A few relatives also shared their opinions: they couldn't understand how or why my parents could take such a risk! One relative seemed to be the most vocal in our immediate family, emphatically stating, "Those two girls will starve to death out west!" But my mother was determined; she obviously needed to be the strong and decisive one in our family. Leaving the region in search of better job opportunities rarely occurred in my parents' generation. Others in our community had endured similar hardships as my parents because they'd also struggled with financial difficulties while remaining on unproductive farms.

My parents took a giant leap of faith. Much like our ancestors many years ago, they had the courage to reinvent themselves. It was their desire to create a better life for themselves and their children. As I said my goodbyes to several cousins, they made comments about me moving "out west," where all the Indians were! Apparently we'd watched way too many cowboy movies at the Lyric Theater—weren't we aware the Sioux Indian Reservation was only a hundred miles west of Eureka?

Early beginnings of another winter season were approaching as we left Eureka. With our trailer in tow, I looked back to see my very sad Pa wave goodbye from the front porch of his home. It had been good to live with Pa and Uncle Curtis since Ma's death, and for the interim my mother had brought some sense of order back into the household. Still, I couldn't shake the feeling that we were abandoning them by moving so far away. I guess Mom thought there were many family members close by to help care for Pa and my uncles. Caught up with the excitement of the move, I hadn't thought of the dramatic changes that were about to take place in my life. Eureka was the only home I'd known. How would I adjust to living in a large city? The long road trip gave me lots of time to think!

During our journey we experienced predictable winter weather. Traveling through Montana involved icy roads and blizzards. Interstate highways weren't yet part of our country's infrastructure, so we'd be traveling to the West Coast on two-lane highways. Our first connection with family was a stop in Moses Lake, Washington to visit my father's oldest brother and his family. It was exciting to see Uncle Ed, Aunt Tillie, and my cousins, Betty and Mavis. It felt as if we were in another world—and by all accounts I suppose we were! Our relatives had just moved into their new large brick home. Contemporary in design with dramatic bold colors and furnishings, it was unlike the farmhouses I was accustomed to. Music filled their home during our stay. My teenage cousins were listening to the new sounds of rock & roll on their portable stereo all day and late into the night! I quickly memorized the lyrics to "Rock Around the Clock," "Green Door," and "Party Doll." The three records (45's) were played continually. Whenever I hear those songs I'm brought back to November, 1956!

My cousin had just begun her first job as an usherette at the movie theater. I watched with curiosity as she changed into her uniform before going off to work. Mavis wore trousers with a matching jacket adorned with burgundy piping and gold buttons. To complete her amazing uniform, a cute little pillbox hat sat on her head at just the right angle! I couldn't believe she was able to watch first-run movies while working. This, I decided, is what I'd do when I grew up—forget sheep shearing! As an usherette Mavis carried a flashlight to seat people before the movie. I wondered what other job could ever be that exciting?

As our brief but memorable visit to Moses Lake ended, we began our journey to Portland. It was early evening as we traveled west along the Historic Columbia River Highway. The final leg of our trip took longer than expected because of the unfamiliar narrow highway, and we were also being introduced to a steady downpour of Oregon rain. The passage we're now familiar with is I-84, but it would be another five years before the new interstate project was completed. Traveling through Troutdale, we continued onto Sandy Boulevard while searching for our relatives' home in the northeast Fremont district. There appeared to be an endless stream of cars, and the bright lights of the city seemed to go on forever! It was quite late when we reached our destination on Northeast Sixty-Fifth street, and our relatives had been anxiously awaiting our arrival.

We lived with our relatives for the next two weeks, and during that time an apartment was located within three blocks of my aunt and uncle's home. My parents were busily purchasing furniture and acquiring necessary household items to furnish our two-bedroom apartment. My aunt and cousins were giving my sister and I tours of the Fremont neighborhood, showing us where we'd be attending school. My sister was enrolled at Washington High School and I'd be attending Harvey Scott Elementary, which was only a block from our apartment on Sixty-Fifth and Prescott. What a contrast it was to my school in Eureka: my new school was on one level, and it had a gymnasium, a huge playground, and a softball field.

It was midmorning when I arrived at Harvey Scott to register for my first day of school. Class was in session, and all eyes appeared to be focused in my direction as I entered the room! My teacher, Miss Madden, introduced me to her sixth-grade class. She asked about my interesting last name—I was puzzled because it was the first time anyone had referred to my last name as being interesting. She wanted to know how my last name was spelled, and after spelling the letters O-P-P there was an immediate outburst of laughter, particularly from the sixth-grade boys! From that moment on I began to spell my name "O double P!" Not only did my classmates find my last name to be unusual, they were also curious about where I came from because of my accent—I wasn't aware I had an accent! Unbeknownst to me my sentences apparently ended on a high note with a sing-song lilt, at least that's how it was explained to me. Suddenly aware of my accent, I became self-conscious whenever I spoke to people. What can I say—I was eleven! I also noticed that my clothes were somewhat different from the girls in my class. Most of my winter clothing was much heavier, particularly my alpaca fur coat! My coat had been purchased the prior year, along with Rosemarie's and Mary Jane's alpaca winter coats. Similar in style, we thought we looked amazing! Although perfect for Midwest subzero temperatures, I soon realized my fur coat was entirely too warm for the moderate climate of the Pacific Northwest, but it would be my winter coat until I outgrew it. Remarkably, despite my unusual last name, Midwest accent, and unconventional clothing, most of the kids were welcoming.

On my first day of school, several girls asked me to join them at their lunch table; Penny, Virginia, and Karen became good friends. A few boys teased me, but I decided that's just what boys did in the sixth grade! I soon discovered teachers in Portland also put math problems on the blackboard! They had the dialogue down: whoever finished their problem first could quickly take their seat—was this humiliating exercise ever going to end? Physical education class was new to me and part of our daily curriculum, but still under doctor's care, I wasn't allowed to participate. For the remainder of the school year I sat on the bleachers while my classmates played dodgeball and volleyball and ran laps around the gym. As spring arrived, I watched with curiosity while my classmates played softball.

Furnishing our apartment was fairly stress free for my parents. It was a time when furniture stores provided an in-house interior decorator to help with the selection of end tables, coffee tables, and lamps when a sofa was purchased.

It was also customary for the store to include several framed pieces of artwork to complete the living room ensemble. Much to my delight, along with our newly acquired furnishings, we now had our very first television! It's amazing how quickly I became addicted to that nineteen-inch black box. Racing home from school every day, I'd watch *The Mickey Mouse Club!* Other favorite programs were *Sky King, Sergeant Preston of the Yukon, The Lone Ranger,* and *The Roy Rogers Show.* Like most children of that era, I watched way too much television. Of course it was entertaining but I'm sure it must have stifled my imagination. It was no longer necessary to visualize characters from my favorite radio shows or imagine what the field and players looked like during a World Series baseball game!

Televisions had only three or four buttons on the front panel below the screen. One button turned the TV on and off, one adjusted volume, and another changed channels. Several add-on features for TVs became available for purchase, such as a multicolored plastic film placed over the screen that now created the illusion of watching color television! Another must-have was an electric color wheel. Directed towards the television, this apparatus rotated primary colors onto the TV screen! Television dramatically altered our cultural behavior during the late fifties, and relaxation time was effectively changed. I think the new technology was instrumental in the need to be continuously entertained and might be accountable for shorter attention spans! Much of our leisure activity, such as board games, puzzles, cards, being outdoors, or simply talking to one another, was overshadowed by this compelling new device.

Some parents mistakenly believed television to be a great babysitter for young children! After moving to Portland there were only three television networks: NBC, CBS, and ABC. In the late fifties channel 12 was added, and those were the only channels throughout the sixties. At times television tubes burned out. After being removed and taken to a grocery store they'd be tested on a machine to determine which tubes needed to be replaced. Changing a channel or adjusting the television volume actually involved a bit of physical activity, because it required someone to get off a chair or sofa! Remote controls weren't introduced until the sixties, with colored television following.

Our apartment was small but comfortable and we were gradually making adjustments to our new surroundings. Mom was working at the family restaurant five nights a week and Dad began to search for employment. There was an immediate realization that he lacked the education and necessary skills to secure a good job; a few temporary jobs came his way, but nothing to his liking. His worst job was hand-stitching mattresses at a mattress company. After working only one day his hands were swollen and bleeding—Dad never returned to the job!

My uncle found Dad a job as a butcher at a nearby grocery store. Obviously he'd butchered cows and pigs on the farm, but much of the beef and pork was ground up. I suppose it became obvious to his employer that Dad wasn't familiar with the various cuts of meat, and after working only a few hours as a "butcher" he was back home. Mom questioned why he was home early, asking if he'd been fired. Dad quickly responded, "No I wasn't fired, they just said they didn't need me anymore!" Despite his disappointment, he was able to find some humor in his very brief employment as a butcher.

Throughout my father's job search and frustration with menial employment, there were frequent arguments between my parents. Our living space was small and I'd hear their heated disputes. The dialogue was always the same: Dad would say it had been a terrible mistake to move to Portland, and he wanted us to move back home to Eureka! Mom's quick response was, "Go ahead and leave, the girls and I are staying here!" I found it worrisome, but after several months he secured full-time employment at Gunderson's shipyards as a shop hand. The job was hard labor but it was a steady income, and at least Dad now felt he was able to provide for his family. I have a distinct recollection of the pungent chemical odor and metal filings on his work clothes when he returned from work each day. Dad worked in that environment for about a year.

My father's luck was about to change. Uncle Richard was searching for a new bartender at the family restaurant, and delighted with the job offer, my father realized it was a great opportunity. Bartending required familiarization with numerous brands of hard alcohol, wine, and beer, as well as the mixology of drinks that were gaining popularity. I'd quiz Dad about ingredients used for martinis, manhattans, gimlets, grasshoppers, etc., with the use of a bartenders guide. There were no concerns: he was a quick study and easily acclimated to his new job. My father had found his niche; he'd come full circle from owning Opp's Recreation Place. There were no longer discussions about moving back to Eureka. My parents were noticeably happier and so was I.

When my parents began working at the family restaurant it was one of only a few steak houses in Portland. The OCK soon became one of the busiest restaurants in the city. It wasn't unusual to have three-hour waits for dinner on weekends, and the long waiting period only increased the bar business! During this time the OCK repeatedly generated more profit from bar sales than food sales. Working together at the restaurant was an ideal arrangement for my parents. Sharing a common interest in the family business, they established lifelong friendships with fellow employees and countless customers frequenting the steak house.

I remember friends making comments regarding my father's expertise and proficiency as a bartender. It seems when the bar was at its busiest, Dad had the ability to tune out all the craziness and loud chatter, and he stayed completely focused while mixing drinks. Humming became a stress reliever, and he quickly developed a reputation as the "humming bartender!" Dad became the bar manager, and he and Mom would both be employed at the family restaurant for over twenty-five years!

My aunt and uncle had started their business venture in 1946. They'd named their restaurant The Old Country Kitchen because at the time it was in the country surrounded by farmland. Initially they served only chicken and rabbit dinners; steak would be added to the menu several years later. Few people are aware it was Aunt Esther's recipe for grilling steak that led to the eventual success of their steak house. The simple method of searing steak on a very hot grill with several pads of butter was acquired when working for a family while attending nursing school in Rochester, Minnesota. I wanted to share that information because women of her generation didn't always receive recognition for their achievements—I was so proud of her.

Within several months of my father's employment, my sister began to work at the restaurant on weekends as a salad girl. My parents and sister left for work on Saturday around two in the afternoon, returning home about twelve hours later. Their Sunday hours were from eleven a.m. until nine or ten p.m. I was twelve years old and certainly old enough to stay by myself, but in retrospect it was a long time to be "home alone!" As they left for work the door was locked and windows were closed, and I was given instructions to never open the door. We were no longer living in Eureka!

To alleviate boredom, the TV was turned on whether I was watching it or not. I dreaded the midnight hour, since that's when television networks stopped broadcasting. It was quite a ceremonious event: the American flag appeared on the screen followed by the national anthem, and at exactly 12:01 a.m. all stations went off the air; the only image on the screen was the TV signal! I'd immediately hear creaking sounds throughout our apartment and police sirens on nearby Prescott Street! I was most frightened by frequent winter windstorms. Peering out of a small opening of the living room curtain, I'd watch nervously as the giant fir trees swayed back and forth in the front yard! Obviously still traumatized by the tornado, my fear was that a tornado might cause a tree to come crashing down on our apartment! I'd be wide awake on those weekend nights until everyone arrived home.

During this home-alone period Mom was once again coming up with activities to keep me busy and entertained. Paint-by-numbers and coloring books helped occupy time. As accustomed as I was to visiting our library in Eureka, it's surprising I hadn't acquired a library card after our move. I'm sure it was just a matter of asking my aunt or cousins where the closest library was, but it never occurred to me. The only books I had access to were our incomplete set of Funk & Wagnalls encyclopedias that were purchased in the early fifties. I suspect the set hadn't been completed because of the expense, but my parents may have also realized they simply didn't have room for the entire set! Our twelve volumes only went through the letter *H*. To be exact, I believe the last book we received ended in the letters *HIE*! It seems hilarious now, but at the time I found it difficult to find research material for school assignments and book reports. Consequently, for the remainder of my sixth grade and all of my seventh grade, research for homework never included subject matter beyond the letters *HIE*!

Lacking a complete set of encyclopedias paled in comparison to another unsettling event. Regrettably my mother hadn't briefed me on the subject of menstruation. Experiencing discomfort and alone in the school bathroom, I was again convinced of my demise! When I hadn't returned to the classroom, my teacher found me in tears. After assuring me this was indeed a normal event, she promptly called my mother. There must have been a verbal exchange with my teacher because Mom seemed annoyed when she arrived at school; most likely she was embarrassed for not having discussed this natural process with me.

Arriving home, Mom quickly opened the linen closet to show me where I could find everything I needed for this monthly occurrence. I couldn't believe what I'd just heard—this would really be happening every month? That was to be her final word about my monthly period or anything related to it! As strained and uncomfortable as that brief dialogue had been for my mother, I knew there'd be no more questions asked—and I definitely had many more questions!

Sometime during the seventh grade my doctor gave me a clean bill of health. I was given permission to participate in physical education and more importantly, roller-skate! It was an amazing feeling to strap on my Chicago skates. The first place I skated was on a narrow sidewalk in front of our apartment building. I recall going back and forth on the short strip of uneven concrete. It wasn't as smooth as skating in front of the funeral home in Eureka, but I was thrilled I hadn't forgotten how to skate! We soon discovered the Oaks Park skating rink. I wasn't able to use my skates on that beautiful floating wood floor, but it was so wonderful to be skating again!

While participating in physical education at Harvey Scott I was introduced to dodgeball, volleyball, and softball. Before playing a game the selection of teams would begin. Of course the captain always chose who was to be on their team, and in 1957 boys were always the captains! Without exception, I'd be the last person chosen! Not concerned about sparing my feelings, their response would be, "Does she really have to be on our team? She isn't very good!" They were right: with the exception of roller skating I wasn't at all athletic. Years later I'd refer to those experiences as character building, but most twelve-year-olds aren't really thinking about character building!

Sometime during our second year of living in Portland, two more people joined our household. Uncle Harvey and his friend Don decided to move to Portland. It was actually a last-minute decision after their brief visit to Spokane, Washington. Weeks earlier a sales representative traveling through the Eureka area had convinced my uncle and Pa about a great opportunity for Harvey in the airline industry. Apparently to attend the school, full payment was required before his arrival in Spokane, which seems as though it might have been highly suspicious! Assured that this was an excellent career choice, Harvey talked his friend Don into joining him. Both young men hopped on a bus for Washington State, but after arriving in Spokane they learned the airline school wasn't what the sales representative had promised.

Harvey said they didn't have enough money to return to South Dakota, and Portland was much closer, so that's how they ended up living with us! There were now six people living in our two-bedroom, one-bath apartment. Both were soon employed at the Nabisco cookie company, where they worked the graveyard shift. I remember my sister and I hurrying out of bed every morning so Harvey and Don could sleep in our bed during the day! Homesick for his family, Don returned to Eureka several months later. Harvey remained in Portland, where he'd continue to live with us until he was married several years later.

Summer was a perfect time to explore the new city we were living in. One of my favorite outings was visiting downtown Portland with Patti, Doreen, and Rosemarie. Everyone always dressed up to go downtown in the fifties; casual wear wasn't considered acceptable attire! Young girls might wear swing dresses with heavily starched crinoline petticoats and white buck shoes. Women typically wore a dress or tailored suit with a hat, matching gloves, and heels. Men always wore a suit, tie, and a classic fedora hat whenever they went downtown—actually, in that era most people dressed up whenever they went anywhere! The mode of transportation was on the Rose City Transit bus line. It picked us up on Sixty-Fifth and Sandy Boulevard, and I was always excited to catch a glimpse of the Willamette River as we crossed the Burnside Bridge.

The skyline of downtown Portland in 1957 seemed really impressive to me. One of the tallest buildings was the eleven-story Meier & Frank department store on SW Morrison Street. I remember a huge ornate clock located at

M & F's main entrance, and the familiar phrase, "Let's meet under the M & F clock" was often used by downtown shoppers. The elaborate wrought iron clock was our meeting place if we became separated from each other. White-gloved elevator operators controlled elevators at M & F until the early sixties. They were greeters but also needed to manually open and close doors and regulate the speed and direction of the elevator. Using castanets, women operators with very melodic voices described each floor: "Second floor, women's lingerie," "Third floor, men's wear," etc., etc. The elaborate Georgia Room was on the top floor of Meier & Frank, and it happened to be one of the upscale restaurants in downtown Portland. It was fun taking the elevator all the way to the top floor just to glance inside the beautiful foyer!

Going into the city always included "doing lunch." Our favorite place to eat was the Chocolate Lounge, which was on the mezzanine in the Lipman-Wolfe & Company department store on SW Fifth and Alder. Egg salad sandwiches and Cokes were our usual choice. Cokes were flavored with either lemon, chocolate, or vanilla syrup, and we always wanted to be seated in one of the booths overlooking the busy shoppers below! I thought it was a wonderful dining experience. I was only twelve years old but I remember feeling very grown up! The Lipman-Wolfe department store has been gone for over forty years, and I still miss it.

My uncle was very generous. For the fun-filled day in downtown Portland he gave his daughters fifty dollars to be used for shopping and lunch; this was a considerable amount of money in the midfifties. My cousins were told to buy bus fare and lunch for my sister and I, and any remaining cash could be used for shopping. Bus fare was a dime, egg salad sandwiches were about twenty-five cents, and Coke another nickel, so subsequently there was lots of money left over to do some serious shopping! It was fun watching my cousins make their clothing selections; it was much more entertaining than paging catalogs! I just seemed to naturally end up in the shoe department of every store we visited. I was still attracted to Capezio shoes, and Meier & Frank, Lipman's, and Charles F. Berg's continued to carry them in their inventories. This stylish Italian leather flat continued to be popular and cost about four dollars, but it was still more money than I had in my little white leather bucket purse!

Throughout an afternoon of shopping I was keenly aware of how much money my cousins were spending. Our family was on a fairly tight budget the first few years after our move to Portland. I knew the monthly rent for our apartment was sixty-five dollars, so fifty dollars for an afternoon of shopping seemed really extravagant to me. But, there was an astute awareness that some of those beautiful clothes might eventually be handed down to me!

The first movie I attended in downtown Portland was at the Paramount on Broadway, now known as the Schnitzer Performing Arts Center. The movie may have been *The King and I*, *Carousel*, or perhaps *Oklahoma*. Of course I loved the movie but I recall being more focused on the interior of the theater; it was breathtaking! During the fifties there were many theaters both on and off Broadway. Along with the Paramount there was the Orpheum, Fox, Broadway, Music Box, Cinema 21, Blue Mouse, Liberty, and Guild.

Bright marquees with colorful neon lights illuminated the exteriors and ticket boxes of the ornate theaters. Strobing Hollywood lights placed in front of theaters often promoted the opening night of a featured film. The elaborate theaters and colorful facades have since been replaced with retail businesses. The only surviving theater and ticket box is the iconic, renamed Paramount, which remains somewhat unchanged following an extensive renovation which took place during the eighties.

In the past sixty years we've attended numerous functions at the former Paramount, but one event created particularly fond memories. Dave and I attended an opera benefit in 1984 coinciding with the theater renovation. Patrons attending the new performing arts center were asked to be dressed in opera costumes for the gala celebratory evening. Weeks prior to the opening we visited the opera wardrobe department to select a costume, which was then tailored to fit. Dave chose an eighteenth-century Russian military uniform, and I selected a floor-length green velvet gown with lace bodice from the production of *Wuthering Heights*. We dined and danced to live music in the magnificent foyer of the renovated Paramount. It was a magical evening in this exquisite theater!

Portland experienced a period from the fifties until well into the seventies when new construction seemed more desirable than the preservation and restoration of historic buildings. Fortunately the Paramount was saved from destruction, but regrettably a number of classic architectural structures were lost, and one of the most notable was the Oriental Theater. The Italian-renaissance-style movie theater was located on SE 8th and Grand Avenue. Constructed in 1927, it had a seating capacity of over two thousand and an orchestra pit. Having been in the theater only once or twice, it certainly left a lasting impression! The exquisite Asian carvings on the exterior and interior of the building were spectacular, and I recall huge dragons on each side of the movie screen—their red eyes lit up! The theater ceiling was in the shape of a dome and I understand the crystal chandelier held over five thousand lights. Sadly, I understand the Wurlitzer pipe organ was one of only a few items salvaged from this distinctive theater before it was demolished in 1970—to create a surface parking lot!

During the fifties and sixties it was customary to drag the brightly illuminated theater district on Broadway in souped-up hot rods and muscle cars. Teenagers of that era were infatuated with cars, and it was considered a rite of passage to make this trek downtown after securing their driver's licenses! Broadway was an excellent place to meet other kids while showing off their wheels. This seemingly innocent activity continued until the city declared it illegal, claiming too many cars were disrupting the traffic flow!

Yaw's Top Notch restaurant was another favorite meeting place for teenagers to gather. The popular landmark in the Hollywood district was established in 1926 on NE 41st street. Yaw's was famous for their great burgers, french fries with gravy, toasted buns, pies, milkshakes, green rivers (lime soft drink), and flavored Cokes. I understand Englebert Franz developed the first hamburger bun at the request of Yaw's restaurant in 1927! The large restaurant had indoor seating as well as a drive-up where carhops (waitresses) on roller skates placed food on our lowered car windows. They needed to be very skilled and agile while carrying heavy trays of food!

Teenagers throughout Portland spent their evenings cruising Yaw's to meet kids. It was another place to be and to be seen, as well as a place to show off their cars! Cruising encompassed a several-block area around the restaurant with a steady stream of cars for hours on end. Police officers directed traffic at crowded intersections every weekend. Their popularity increased with teenagers when they started handing out Tootsie Rolls, and they were soon affectionately known as "the Tootsie Roll cops!" Cars with flashy paint details had all windows rolled down (regardless of weather) with radios tuned to the new sounds of rock and roll: It was an *American Graffiti* scene!

My inaugural visit to Yaw's was with my cousin Patti. She'd been given permission to drive her father's new car and invited me to join her, even though I was six years younger. The car Patti was driving was a 1956 red Cadillac convertible with a white leather interior; they were impressive wheels! Not many teenagers were driving new cars around Yaw's, particularly Cadillacs; they were considered to be the epitome of luxury. After several hours of countless trips around the block of Yaw's, Patti stopped at the busy and very profitable gas station in the neighborhood, requesting two gallons of gas—which amounted to about fifty cents! I recall sitting on my knees with the expectation of looking much taller and older while riding shotgun in this fantastic car, but it made no difference—I was still only twelve years old! It's a special memory, but I wonder if Patti would have invited me to Yaw's if she'd known about her missing Capezio shoe?

In the early summer of '59 my parents bought a new house in southeast Portland. Our home had more living space for the five of us and a large backyard, and it was also much closer to the family restaurant. I was most excited to finally have my own bedroom! The downside of this move was that I'd be changing schools and leaving my friends at Harvey Scott; Penny, Karen, and Virginia couldn't believe we were moving to what they referred to as "the sticks!" My friends had managed to paint a very bleak picture regarding my future, claiming we were moving into a district where all the "greasers" lived! I was mortified—what were my parents thinking? At the time there was a perception that schools in the metro area were somehow inferior to the city schools, at least that was the opinion of kids living in the city!

There were many concerns about moving, but at least I'd be starting school at the beginning of the school year. Still the new kid, but I wouldn't be walking into a classroom that was already in session. Apparently my school started earlier than my parents had expected, and as Harvey came home from work he noticed children waiting for the school bus. Mom rousted me out of bed, informing me that it was my first day of school, I was to quickly dress and eat breakfast, and no there wouldn't be time to wash my hair or take a bath. I begged to start school the following day, and there was intense pleading, followed by a complete meltdown. I ultimately lost the battle with my mother, and to make matters worse my eyes were now red from crying! My mother and I arrived at South Powellhurst Elementary School, and after completing my enrollment and meeting with the principal I was now over an hour late for school. As I entered the classroom all eyes were focused in my direction. My new teacher Mr. Salvo introduced me to the class, asking, "By the way Judy, how do you spell your interesting last name?" It was a déjà vu moment. Without hesitation, I quickly responded, "O double P!"

Without a doubt, after my first day of school I was convinced my friends at Harvey Scott were right. All the kids were definitely greasers; I hated everything about my school! Every day after school there were tears, followed by another couple of weeks of sulking—again, not really unusual behavior for a thirteen-year-old girl. I don't remember how long it took before I realized nothing would change—I'd need to make the best of this bad situation. During this period of adjustment two girls were going out of their way to make me feel welcome, and I would discover they both lived close to our home. We became friends, and because of their kindness I slowly adapted to my new surroundings. Incidentally, after all these years Vickie and Margie are still a part of my life. My friends from Harvey Scott visited me only a few times after our move; perhaps they were intentionally distancing themselves. According to them I was now living in "the sticks!"

Mr. Salvo was my first male teacher. It was his first year of teaching but he was quick to realize my math skills weren't at grade level. I might add those dreaded math problems seemed to magically appear on the blackboard every day; my teacher had the dialogue down: "Whoever finishes their math problem first can quickly take their seat!" Was this dreadful practice ever going to end?

Sometime during the eighth grade I noticed a number of girls being very interested in boys. They were spending a lot of time talking about their latest crushes! It seemed my new friend Margie had taken it upon herself to be the matchmaker for our three eighth-grade classes. I wasn't interested in boys, only puzzled by their strange behavior! Part of our PE curriculum included a dance class, and I clearly remember not wanting to be in the class because it meant I'd have to dance with a boy. I enjoyed the music but disliked dancing with boys, who had warm, sweaty, clammy hands! But in retrospect, when holding hands with someone, how do we know whose hands are warm, sweaty, and clammy?

Sex education? Ours wasn't the first generation to discover that sex education wouldn't be taught in the public school system! I suppose my friend Margie felt it was her responsibility to help fill in the details... if any of us had questions. For most of us children in that era there were indeed many questions, because sex education wasn't taught in most homes either! Was it an assumption that we wouldn't be interested in the subject matter if it wasn't brought up for discussion? Thankfully there were Margies in our lives that gave us just enough information—although her facts weren't always correct!

CHAPTER FOURTEEN

Teenage Years

Reflecting on the age of thirteen, I can explicitly state it's not a time in my life I'd care to repeat. It was a period of feeling awkward and very much lacking in self-esteem. I was critical of my appearance and usually just a heartbeat away from tears! It was an unsettling period, and thankfully relatively brief. There was some comfort in knowing my friends were also going through this painful process of adolescence. As I sought solitude in my room, music became a much-needed distraction. Countless hours were spent listening to music on our local radio station, KISN. Rock and roll was dominating the airwaves, and there were an infinite number of recording artists; it also seemed to be the era of one-hit wonders. My favorite pop idol was Ricky Nelson; his glossy photos from popular teen magazines covered my lavender bedroom walls and ceiling!

Transistor radios were the latest fad for us teenagers. They were the first portable sound systems. Invented in the midfifties, the small handheld radios flooded the market in the sixties as they became more affordable. Portable stereos were the next music technology, and speakers could now be separated to achieve stereophonic sound. My first stereo was purchased after high school, but for the interim our living room hi-fi console would have to suffice. Our console had a radio and turntable that played 33 vinyl albums, and 45 vinyl records. A favorite pastime was visiting the Gateway record store with friends. Most music stores had a number of small, enclosed booths with turntables. The private soundproof booths held several people, allowing us to listen to a record before making a purchase. Single records cost a dollar and each side of the 45 record had one song. In the following years I acquired a small collection of 45s, as well as many vinyl albums.

Decidedly, the most significant event of the summer of '59 was an accidental meeting with Ricky Nelson! The encounter happened while touring the newly remodeled Portland airport with my parents and visiting relatives. I had distanced myself from my family—again, not unusual behavior for a thirteen-year-old! While strolling down the concourse, I literally bumped into my idol! Ricky had performed at the Memorial Coliseum the prior evening, but ticket prices were too expensive for me to attend. I'm estimating, but in 1959 tickets for major music concerts wouldn't have exceeded the amount of three dollars!

Surprisingly, no other fans were around Ricky and the musicians in his band. His guitar was slung over his shoulder. I was speechless, starstruck, and totally focused on his blue eyes! After a very brief, awkward moment he asked if I wanted his autograph. Frantically searching through my purse for a piece of paper and pen brought an outburst of laughter from the musicians! Somehow a pen and an airline brochure magically appeared, followed by his autograph. Blankly staring at the autograph, I saw that he'd written, "To Judy, yours forever, Ricky Nelson." I was stunned: how was it possible he knew my name? When I looked up from gazing at my autograph, Ricky and the members of his band were gone!

After locating my family I described the entire incident, exclaiming in total disbelief that Ricky actually knew my name. It would be my mother who gave me a dose of reality: she reminded me I was wearing my Charles F. Berg's Blouse, which had my name embroidered on the collar! Once back home I called my friends recounting every minute detail of meeting my idol. It was the most memorable occurrence of my thirteenth summer; by the way, I still have Ricky's autograph!

The telephone: it was important to stay connected with my friends, but it was more challenging with two teenagers in our household and only one phone. Thankfully we had a private phone line in our home; some people in the city still had party lines. I was familiar with party lines while living on the farm, but party lines in Portland were shared with total strangers; that just didn't seem right! Basic black rotary phones were issued by the Pacific Northwest Bell Telephone Company. The heavy receivers were cumbersome to hold for lengthy conversations, but we somehow seemed to manage!

The next advancement in phone technology included colorful plastic desk and wall phones. Much lighter in weight, they were more comfortable to hold. Several friends were fortunate to have private phone lines in their bedrooms, and slimline pink and blue princess phones soon became status symbols for teenage girls. A coiled extension cord with about twenty-five feet was a must-have in households with teenagers. It would allow me to carry the receiver into my bedroom for more privacy!

At the time, telephone prefixes were names instead of numbers. A few of the telephone exchange names in the Portland area were: Alpine, Beaumont, Atlantic, Belmont, Butler, Garfield, and Prospect. When giving someone my phone number, I'd actually say, "Alpine 2-5053." In the sixties the phone company replaced the charming names with a full numeric system; it was a huge adjustment! In my lifetime I've experienced vast changes in phone usage, beginning with our oak wall phone on the farm. It's astounding to see the phone advancement of the twenty-first century, but with technology changing at such a rapid pace, there's the realization that our current smart phone may become obsolete in a few years! Although over sixty years have gone by, it's still all about the phone!

With summer approaching, my parents began to plan our annual trip to visit relatives in South Dakota. At the conclusion of every school year, two weeks of our summer were spent in Eureka. For the first few years our family referred to this visit as "going home!" Our early departure for the fourteen-hundred-mile journey always began before sunup. Few speed limits were posted while traveling to the Midwest, and once behind the wheel of his trusty Plymouth Dad would drive like the wind! While traveling through Montana, speed limits weren't posted.

Sometimes we'd be pulled over by a cop for going a bit too fast, but the fine was only five dollars. Dad simply handed the cash to the police officer and we'd be on our way! I understand people kept wads of five dollar bills in their cars' glove boxes, just in case they were pulled over for excessive speeding. After the oil crisis in 1974 speed limits finally became law.

Interstate highways were in the process of being constructed across the country during the late fifties.

Frequent lengthy delays and numerous detours caused by continual roadwork often extended travel time to Eureka. According to Dad it meant he'd need to drive a bit faster to make up for lost time! On rare occasions we'd spend one night in a motor inn. Now known as motels, inns were typically rustic, one-story cabins with a small kitchen, several bedrooms, a bathroom, and a carport. As interstates were completed, new motels such as Best Westerns, Motel 6s and Howard Johnson's appeared; chain restaurants followed, providing additional comfort for cross-country travel. Spending one night in a motor inn or motel was a luxury for our family, so we'd usually drive through the night.

My father always loved his cars. Without a doubt his vehicle of choice was a Plymouth; he didn't think any other car was worth driving! After our move to Portland, a new car was purchased every year or two. Dad liked taking his new car on our annual trips to Dakota. It was a time when car designs changed dramatically from one year to the next, and he wanted to be up on the latest trend. His favorite model during the late fifties through the midsixties was the two-door Plymouth Sports Fury; with sleek, long fins and a flashy two-tone paint detail, it didn't go unnoticed!

One year our new Fury had swivel bucket seats, supposedly making it easier to get in and out of the car. Made for only one year, it was determined this model was quite hazardous; apparently people had been ejected from the bucket seats during accidents! Not totally convinced his favorite car had safety issues, Dad reluctantly traded it in for another Sports Fury. There was remorse about selling his favorite car, because he was convinced it would be really valuable one day.

Traveling in an air-conditioned car would have been wonderful on those lengthy trips, but at the time air-conditioning wasn't standard equipment for cars. While traveling to the Midwest we'd often experience temperatures over 110 degrees. All four windows of Dad's sporty Plymouth were rolled down to get some airflow, even if it was hot air. Adding to the mix of hot air was smoke from Dad's cigars and speeds exceeding ninety miles an hour—it made for interesting travel! On those long road trips to the Midwest we only stopped for gas, a bite to eat, and bathroom stops; Dad was always in a hurry to get back on the road. While traveling the familiar trek to Eureka each summer, we never stopped at points of interest or landmarks along the way. We were within fifty miles of Yellowstone National Park and only a few hours from the Black Hills and Mt. Rushmore, but there was no time for sightseeing. With only two weeks vacation, we had a limited time to visit everyone—there were lots of relatives!

Each year Dad was eager to improve his travel time, and as interstate highways were completed the time was shortened. Our first stop as we arrived in Eureka was always at Elmer's bar on Main Street. Elmer Neuharth was one of Dad's many first cousins, and he'd be curious about how long it took us to make the long drive from Portland. Elmer often questioned Dad's credibility about actual travel time—there might be an expensive long-distance call to Uncle Richard substantiating his claim! Elmer's Pool and Tavern was a popular meeting place for many locals and family in late afternoon. Within several hours, most of our relatives knew we'd arrived "back home" for our annual two-week visit!

Pa had remarried several years after Ma had died, and our family would be staying with he and Lizzie in the Helfenstein house. Pa always seemed so pleased to have us back home. I've had regrets of not spending more time with him during those annual visits because it would have been an opportunity to learn more about him and his early life. There are so many unanswered questions. Sadly, I didn't realize there'd be so few opportunities to connect with him. Our visit to Eureka was always a whirlwind of social activities. We'd be invited to relatives' homes for every dinner, supper, and "lunch" the entire two weeks of our stay. In this small community there continued to be a great emphasis on food!

Sometime during every visit there'd be a nostalgic return to our farm. All that remained was the foundation where the house once stood and several weathered outbuildings. Our house had been moved to a Hutterite community near the town of Selby; it was one of many vacant farmhouses in the county that had been purchased and moved to the religious community. Surprisingly, we were told our house was now located right next to Uncle Ed and Aunt Tillie's former farmhouse! With every visit to our former farm site, my parents reaffirmed how grateful they were to be away from all that hard work. I was in agreement, but also found it sad to see the deserted farmyard and remaining unkept outbuildings. The groves of oak trees that once contained our camps had been destroyed by windstorms, and undoubtedly a number of tornados!

Our farm was just one of hundreds in McPherson County that had been vacated during the fifties and sixties. Many relatives had moved to Eureka after retiring from farming, and others sold their land and left the community in search of employment. Like my parents, people had begun to realize it was no longer economically feasible to farm on a small scale; only larger farming concerns would continue to be successful in the coming years. My hometown had become an aging community; it seemed that with each visit we were spending more time at the cemetery visiting gravesites of our relatives. The population of Eureka was declining as younger relatives were moving to larger cities after completing their education. As our annual vacation came to an end, we'd begin the very familiar journey back to Portland. Mary Jane often returned home with us; she'd usually spend a month with us before flying home.

Traveling to Eureka every year was our family's only vacation, but I'm grateful my parents felt the importance of maintaining a close connection with our extended family. Throughout my adult life I've felt a need to occasionally reconnect with my birthplace and the few relatives that remain in the area, and undeniably there are deep ties to my ancestral community. In the past fifty years our immediate family's four or five visits to my hometown have coincided with several family reunions and local celebrations. Apparently the strong association with my birthplace was evident; our sons observed I began to speak with a German accent when we reached the city limits of Eureka! I've always referred to Portland as my home, but my roots are most definitely in South Dakota.

I entered David Douglas High School in September 1959, and my concerns of living in the sticks and going to school with a bunch of greasers had been long forgotten! At the time, Douglas had the largest enrollment in the state, but despite the number of students I seemed to acclimate easily as an incoming freshman. My high school years were very much a positive experience, but years later I learned it was much the opposite for several friends. Those four years were described as the most challenging times in their lives, because apparently they were dealing with less-than-ideal conditions in their home environments. I wasn't aware of the dysfunction in their homes; we were good friends, but obviously never discussed family problems with each other. The lack of a support system, counseling in school, or an awareness in the community meant people somehow dealt with their own problems. Sharing personal matters with someone outside the family circle wasn't done—what would people think? Much like our parents' generation, we'd all been carefully taught.

I remember my friends and I being preoccupied with being popular and belonging to the right social group when we started high school. In my circle there was much focus on appearance and wanting to look like everyone else—whoever that was! Although over sixty years have come and gone, I don't suppose we were really that different than teenagers of today. It takes a courageous individual to step out and form their own opinions and style, but I wasn't that self-assured and neither were my friends.

There were the usual concerns pertaining to our clothing, as well as anxiety about whether we'd be invited to the big dance—but even more crucially, by the right guy! Back then we always waited for guys to take the initiative to phone or ask us out because it wasn't considered proper behavior to do otherwise. Our roles as young women had been narrowly defined at an early age, and many of us would struggle with those identity issues in later years. The women's liberation movement would shake us to our very core ten years later; in fact it would be a challenging time for both sexes!

For the interim, I suppose the late fifties and early sixties continued to be a time of blissful innocence for most of us. Politics, world affairs, and inequities didn't occupy our thoughts, because we thought racial injustice and discrimination only happened in a few southern states. Being far removed from the racial uprisings in the Deep South, it was something we only noticed on the evening news. There were few people of color and little diversity in our school of twenty-three hundred students, and it never occurred to us that our friends of color weren't treated fairly. Regrettably, racial intolerance and discrimination was taking place in our schools and neighborhoods!

The reality is that much like today, prejudice was all around us, it just wasn't openly acknowledged. Disturbed by the circumstances, I chose an opportunity years ago to ask a good friend if he had experienced prejudice or discriminatory behavior from his classmates and teachers. Jerome said, "You guys were always cool…but we always knew our place!" Sadly, I believe those few words spoke volumes about the times.

In many regards our lives were uncomplicated. Other than church and scouting programs, school activities dominated most of our time. For most families in our community, resources weren't available for kids to attend summer camps to improve their athletic skills. This was a time when boys could play three or four sports during the school year; they just needed to be good enough to make the team! Students weren't required to pay an athletic fee in the public school system, and fortunately school districts still funded music and art programs, which most of us took advantage of.

Improving athletic skills and making the team wasn't a concern for girls when I was in high school; sports weren't available to us. We had an intramural girls tennis team, but at the time it wasn't considered socially acceptable or cool for girls to be athletic or involved in sports. Ours was a supportive role, such as being active in the pep club or cheerleading, and we'd usually attend all the football and basketball games. Game day found athletes proudly wearing their lettermen's sweaters, and girls wore the school colors of red and grey and game ribbons to support our team and encourage school spirit.

Girls were actively involved in student government. We held class offices, but never as president of our class or student body president. We weren't restricted from holding those offices, it just never occurred to us that we could—or should! It is mystifying; certainly we were just as qualified as boys, but instead we chose the more supportive offices of secretary, treasurer, and historian. In retrospect, again very telling of the times, is it possible we were concerned about coming on too strong or worried about damaging the boys' egos? At the time, none of us thought of ourselves as not being equal to boys, it simply didn't occur to us that we should question the logic.

It was obviously a male-dominant culture—but there would be a gradual awakening! In later writings I address the women's movement as it emerged in the late sixties. There would be an increased awareness of chauvinism and the culture of sexism as women began to enter the workforce. Inequities were finally being addressed and women of my generation became inspired by the crusade!

I was interested in acquiring a summer job while in high school, but our two-week vacation to Eureka prevented me from seeking employment. There was always the option of picking berries or green beans to earn a bit of spending money, but that was usually a last resort! At age thirteen, I thought field work with a few of my friends might be fun;

at least the prospect of earning money sounded appealing. Berry picking lasted only a few days. I must not have picked strawberries fast enough because I made very little money. The only thing I remember about that brief experience was being miserable working in the hot sun and having very sticky hands! If interested in field work, people didn't have to travel far. At the time most of the Gresham area was an active farming community. Farmers encouraged young people to harvest their crops, and kids were bussed from numerous pick-up locations to work in their fields.

Seasonal agricultural jobs helped cover the cost of school clothing and provided spending money for the upcoming school year. As Portland grew into the suburbs, land became more valuable in the outlying farming communities, and the Gresham area wasn't an exception. Scarcity of land in the early sixties happened to coincide with child-labor laws which were being readdressed, and there were concerns that young children were being subjected to harsh working conditions. The local agricultural economy began a sharp decline as farmers experienced a shortage of workers. As a result most farms in the Gresham area began to disappear, prompting the development and rapid urban growth of east county. Within a few years the existing farmland in Gresham had been transformed into residential housing as well as a robust commercial area.

Summer jobs for teenagers were plentiful. Boys earned additional income by doing yard work, construction, or working as gas jockeys at service stations. Minimum wage was $1.25 an hour and most earnings were spent on cars and insurance. Older cars could be purchased for less than a hundred dollars; however, paint, bodywork, and upkeep for older cars was costly. On the upside, gas prices were less than thirty cents a gallon! Personalized details with creative designs and names made vehicles very unique. Cars might be raked or the whole chassis might be lowered, leaving little clearance between the car and road. Gleaming chrome adorned those old cars. Lastly a pair of felt dice might be hung from the rearview mirror!

Cars were particularly important to teenage boys, because it was a status symbol to have what was referred to as "a sweet ride!" One of my friends drove a white forties vintage coupe with a rumble seat. Jack had actually removed the front bench seat of his car, replacing it with two toilets! I think it was probably illegal to do that, even in 1961! Unique upholstery with creative adornments of rabbit fur might line a glove box or portions of the interior of vintage cars. Restoring and detailing classic cars was a passion and creative outlet for many high school boys.

A number of friends babysat full-time during the summer, but babysitting didn't interest me. Watching children would've been fine, but it wasn't uncommon to find a sink full of dirty dishes, vacuuming, or piles of laundry waiting for me! It was an expectation that babysitters do household chores as well as watch children for the meager wage of twenty-five cents an hour. I thought if child labor laws were being addressed for fieldworkers, perhaps the law should also apply to babysitters! Babysitting wages increased to fifty cents an hour after midnight, but I thought wages should have been higher when the children were awake.

Mom paid me two dollars each week to do the family's ironing. It usually involved several hours of ironing because blended fabrics weren't available; most clothing was cotton and wrinkled easily. Extra money was earned to style and comb my aunt Esther's wigs each week—she was quite generous! Wigs were a fashion statement for middle-aged women during the sixties; they were worn so hair didn't have to be styled every day. It was an interesting trend: length of hair, color, and styles drastically changed from one day to the next! I was also hired to do charting for the family restaurant: every month I recorded numbers of dinners and different types of steaks being sold.

I'm certain my aunt and uncle created those jobs for me, since they regretted not being able to hire me as an employee at the restaurant. I had hoped to work on weekends as a salad girl, but was only able to substitute on holidays or busy weekends. My uncle's brother and partner in the business claimed there was entirely too much nepotism at the restaurant! Obviously disappointed, I was the first family member not to be employed at the OCK. My uncle felt so bad about the turn of events, he gifted me a gold charm bracelet!

Before summer's end there was usually a visit to the Pendleton Woolen Mills in Washougal, Washington. We'd select fabric for Mom to sew our wool pencil skirts that matched hand-me-down sweaters from Patti and Doreen. We were pleased to acquire several reversible pleated Pendleton skirts that my aunt had made for our cousins, since they were very popular. Before school started I'd visit Charles F. Berg's on Fifth and Broadway to purchase the infamous blouse with my name embroidered on the Peter Pan collar! Fashion trends would come and go, but this white rayon name blouse with black embroidery continued to be very popular with teenage girls throughout the Portland area; it was a fundamental part of my wardrobe!

I suppose our teen years pretty much resembled scenes from *Happy Days* and *American Graffiti*! Music was a big part of our lives, and it dominated most of our social activities. We discovered large parking lots on Council Crest and Rocky Butte to be excellent places for night street dances! Parking our cars in a circular fashion with headlights on, car radios were tuned to our favorite station. It was our version of outdoor stereophonic sound! It was great fun dancing under the stars on a warm summer night—that is, until the police came by to break up our gathering! There wasn't anything illegal going on; their reasoning was that there were way too many teenagers gathered in one area!

Dating, music, and working all summer to achieve a perfect tan took up much of my time. Several friends had already acquired their driver's licenses, so we'd spend long summer afternoons at Rooster Rock or Blue Lake, both favorite swimming areas. With swimsuits, towels, and snacks for a full day in the sun, we'd locate a dock or beach area providing the best sun rays. Coppertone sun lotion was expensive, so instead we mixed cocoa butter, baby oil, and a few drops of iodine to achieve that desired bronzed appearance! It was important to show off our summer tan on our first day back to school—this was long before we knew that excessive sun exposure was harmful to our health.

Double dating was popular when I began to date at age fifteen. It wasn't the norm to date as a couple; we thought it was more fun to hang out with another couple. There was always the latest crush, and "going steady" was probably another symbol of our social status. Remembering my first love as a teenager, I found it to be an emotionally confusing time. Experiencing the extremes of joy and heartbreak as a teenager was unfamiliar territory for me; it was overwhelming and disorienting. Was this new heightened emotion I was experiencing love or infatuation? It was puzzling as a teenager, but I would realize adults also found it bewildering to identify the difference.

Whatever the age, I believe that first romantic relationship and love interest as a teenager serves a healthy educational purpose in developmental growth. Being with someone you're comfortable with, sharing interests, having the ability to be your own person, voicing different opinions and knowing it's okay are beneficial in future relationship building. There's something genuinely pure and special about our first teenage love that few of us ever forget. I suppose it's forever etched in our memory.

Drive-in movies happened to be a favorite activity for most of my friends on a warm summer night; it was an inexpensive date for four people because we brought our Cokes and popcorn from home. Our local drive-in theater was the 104th Street Drive-In on Powell Blvd. A clip-on speaker with volume control was attached to the window of our car. "Buck night" was sometimes advertised at the 104th, so we'd pack kids into our car, taking advantage of the one-dollar-per-car admission! Cars didn't have seatbelts in the early sixties, so bench seats allowed us to easily fit ten kids into our car. On regularly priced nights, a few daring individuals might even climb inside the trunks of cars to avoid paying the fifty-cent admission!

My father was really excited when my sister and I began to drive. I know most parents find it unnerving when their kids reach that pivotal milestone, but not my father: he'd now be able to justify buying a second car. Having secured my driver's permit at age fifteen, Dad surprised my sister and I with a red '52 Plymouth convertible! Mom was responsible for teaching me how to drive. Apparently she seemed more relaxed in the passenger seat than Dad!

There were a few obstacles to overcome with our car: the bench seat wasn't adjustable, and to reach the clutch, brake, and accelerator, I sat on pillows. As with most older cars, ours had a standard transmission, but the gearshift was on the steering column and I had trouble getting the car into reverse! After getting my license I'd often stop at McDonald's, and there were times my guy friends had to back up my car when I was ready to leave!

IT WAS IMPORTANT FOR TEENAGERS TO SECURE THEIR driver's licenses on their sixteenth birthdays. Arriving at the DMV on my birthday, my concern was being able to find reverse while parallel parking during the exam, and fortunately that went well. Feeling confident, I was told to drive on a small portion of the newly completed Banfield Freeway, and happily that also went well. Exiting the freeway and returning to the DMV, I was told I'd failed! Apparently I ran a red light at a particularly tricky intersection in the Hollywood district. I wouldn't have my license for my birthday, but passed the exam two weeks later. Fifty-eight years have come and gone, but whenever I reach that confusing intersection in the Hollywood district there's a flashback to my sixteenth birthday!

We had our red convertible for over a year, but without our knowledge Dad decided to trade it in. He was always checking want ads and looking for great car deals, and I guess he felt it was time to make a change. Unbelievably, while trading in our car, Dad purchased two cars—my mother couldn't believe it either! My sister would now be driving a '58 Plymouth Sports Fury. Her car had quite an impressive sound to it: you could tell it just wanted and needed to go faster! With a very straight face, Dad maintained he was unaware of the powerful police engine under the hood! With his affinity for cars, I doubt this was a big surprise. Predictably, there was an exchange between my parents regarding this car, but Dad was insistent we keep the car, claiming he'd gotten a "really" good deal on it!

The car my father bought for me was a four-door fifties vintage Dodge (still a Chrysler product), with fender skirts (wheel covers) and a huge black continental kit on the trunk. The year of this car is totally irrelevant; it was beyond a doubt the ugliest car I'd ever seen! My car was two-tone pink and black: black top, Pepto-Bismol pink body, and black fender skirts. Did I mention it was a four-door? The upholstery was none other than pink and black PLAID! I simply wasn't able to hide my disappointment. It would be so embarrassing to be seen driving this car, I mean really, what would people think? Dad's exact response was, he "taught" it was really cute and after all, it was pink! With Dad's difficulty pronouncing his *th*'s, he then stated he didn't "tink" there was another car like it. I was in total agreement!

After my initial disappointment, I was quickly reminded that my parents had paid for the car and insurance; additionally Dad always took care of the maintenance and never failed to fill up our cars with gas! It was very generous of him to buy each of his girls a car—the only thing required of me was to "enjoy my ride!" I definitely missed our red convertible, but this singularly unique pink and black car was to be all mine until I left home!

Throughout high school, clothing regulations were strictly enforced by Mrs. W., our dean of girls. Pencil skirts with matching sweaters or blouses were worn to school every day, and it was also essential to have stylish black leather flats. Bare legs weren't shown, so we wore nylon hose; because pantyhose hadn't yet been invented, our nylons were held up with a garter belt or girdle! In case you're unfamiliar with that archaic item, a girdle is an elasticized corset extending from waist to thigh—and yes, it was uncomfortable! Unfortunately, we weren't allowed to wear pants during school hours because it wasn't considered proper attire!

The most common clothing infraction was wearing our skirts too short. In fact, the dean patrolled the hallways looking for likely suspects! When stopped by Mrs. W. we were told to kneel on the linoleum floor. If our skirt didn't touch the floor it was considered to be too short and we'd be instructed to go home and change into something more appropriate! I was sent home only once for the skirt infraction in the four years at Douglas!

President Kennedy's program for physical fitness in 1960 had gotten the attention of our PE teachers, and particularly most of us high school girls! There were required fitness tests, including sit-ups, chin-ups, and running, obviously excellent conditioning for students but also very foreign for us nonathletic girls! Physical education was mandatory for students but very few girls enjoyed the class. I remember we didn't like sweating, messing up our hair or make-up, and taking group showers! We also disliked the regulation-blue PE shorts and white blouses we were required to wear.

I suspect our dean of girls might have been partially responsible for us not liking PE class because she regularly reminded us, "Girls should never sweat...horses sweat, men perspire, but women should only glow!" How misguided was that? Again, another sign of the times. I'm pleased barriers and norms have been broken. It's exciting to see young girls participating in athletic endeavors and competitive team sports. Reaping the rewards of improved fitness and being physically strong are so beneficial in building one's self esteem and developing leadership skills.

For ages teenagers have striven to achieve individual expression with clothing or unique hairstyles, and our generation wasn't an exception. Casual wear for girls in the midsixties was cutoff jeans as well as one of our dads' button-down white dress shirts! Tails of the oversized shirt hung out and sleeves were rolled up to our elbows, and white Keds or flip-flops completed our attire. Big, bouffant hairstyles such as page boys, bubble cuts, and flips were the "in" look. Before bedtime I'd roll my hair in large rollers; apparently I became accustomed to sleeping with sharp bristle curlers on my head!

It would be several more years before conventional hair dryers, hot rollers, or curling irons were available to us. To achieve the bubble style, my hair was ratted (back combed) with a toothbrush, then combed over ever so slightly. We wanted to be certain that our hairstyles were held in place during the strongest of windstorms, so lots of hairspray was used! Large cans of hairspray were carried in our oversized black leather purses for occasional touch-ups during the school day!

Variation in hairstyles, unique clothing, and fads continued, but far more significant changes were taking place as women began to enter the workforce during the sixties. Whether supplementing family incomes or searching for more independence, many of my friends' mothers were beginning to acquire part-time or full-time jobs. My mother was employed full-time at the family restaurant but it wasn't the norm. Many middle-aged women of that generation, including my Aunt Esther, had worked full-time in shipyards and factories during the Second World War as "Rosie the Riveters."

Men had enlisted or were being drafted into military service, which led to a shortage of workers. Women were encouraged to move into the active labor force, taking jobs previously held by men. While producing munitions and supplies for the war effort, they'd proven to the nation and themselves to be capable of doing the same work as men. Over fifteen years had passed since the war; after raising children, more women of my mother's generation were anxious to reenter the workforce. As a result, there were a few adjustments taking place in households; it was no longer a given that a woman's place was in the home! The sixties would turn out to be a decade of change for both women and men!

As women found employment outside their homes, less time was spent in the kitchen. It was challenging to find ready-to-eat or takeout dinners for their families during that era: prepared foods weren't available in grocery stores and microwave ovens didn't exist. It was timely that the first ready-to-eat frozen dinners introduced in the early sixties were TV dinners by Swanson; I remember the selections were meatloaf, fried chicken, and turkey. Each entree included vegetables, potatoes, and dessert served on a sectioned aluminum tray. Despite the meals being high in sodium, high in fat, and high in price, undoubtedly they must have been a welcomed addition in many homes. I recall eating them only once or twice because of the novelty, but realized the new TV dinners didn't at all compare to my mother's wonderful cooking!

After frozen TV dinners were introduced, the invention of TV trays followed. Four folding metal trays on a roller rack soon occupied a corner in living rooms across the country; they were a must have. I suppose owning a set of innovative TV trays made it perfectly acceptable to watch television while eating dinner!

For people of middle income, eating in a restaurant was usually reserved for special occasions, and doing otherwise in our community was considered an unnecessary luxury. Chain restaurants were nonexistent; at that time most eateries in the Portland area were family owned and had been in business for several generations. Henry Thiele's, Huber's, The Pantry, Caro Amico, The Kitchen Kettle, Ye Old Towne Crier, Ford's, Monte Carlo, and The Old Country Kitchen were some of the long-established restaurants. Upscale restaurants included The Hillvilla, The River Queen, The Anchorage, Paluso's, Jerry's Gables, The Georgian Room, Bart's Wharf, The Ringside and Eddie May's Prime Rib. Typically, they were restaurants we visited after our high school winter formal or prom.

Large chain supermarkets and big box stores we're now familiar with hadn't yet appeared. Instead, small family grocery stores were found in most neighborhoods throughout the city. Service-related stores such as hardware stores, shoe-repair shops, barbershops, beauty shops (hair salons), appliance-repair stores, bakeries, and drug stores were also conveniently located in many neighborhoods. There was a sense of community when frequenting those independent stores, because merchants usually knew our names. Soda fountains with counter seating could still be found in a few neighborhood drug stores. Menus consisted of sandwiches, burgers, fries, milkshakes, malts, banana splits, sodas, and sundaes.

Stores were usually within walking distance from peoples' homes, which is perhaps the reason there were more shoe-repair stores—people seemed to do more walking! Replacing heels and soles of shoes for extended wear was something I was accustomed to while living with Ma and Pa, and I was surprised they were doing the same in Portland. Appliance-repair stores were also alive and well during that era: instead of purchasing new toasters, coffee makers, electric razors, etc., small appliances were usually taken to a repair shop.

The year after we moved to Portland the concept of one-stop shopping had been introduced by Fred Meyer, and he'd recently opened a new store in our Rose City neighborhood. Our family shopped at the store because Fred Meyer was an acquaintance of my aunt and uncle: he and his wife Eve were frequent customers at their restaurant. At the time I thought the Fred Meyer store was huge; there were at least three checkout counters! Shopping for all one's needs under one roof was considered to be very innovative. The Rose City store had unique rooftop parking and an escalator; it was the first escalator I'd seen!

I'm certain this busy Fred Meyer store had a significant adverse effect on a number of independent stores in our neighborhood. In time, one-stop shopping effectively changed the commercial landscape throughout our city. In the last fifteen years it's been exciting to see a revival of small, independent businesses in many Portland neighborhoods. As some people are choosing more urban lifestyles, old and tired neighborhoods seem to be more vibrant. I'm pleased inner-city Portland neighborhoods are coming back to life—they're beginning to look much like they did over sixty years ago!

Meeting friends and socializing dominated much of my time as a teenager. We hung out at favorite eateries enjoying fries and Cokes for a few hours without having to spend a lot of money. We frequented Yaw's, The Speck, TickTock, Flanigan's, Rutherfords XXX, The New Cathay, and Vans. Of course we were disappointed that carhops were no longer delivering our food on roller skates! Most teen hangouts had indoor seating, but we also liked to eat in our cars. There weren't drive-thru windows; I believe that concept arrived when fast-food restaurants appeared. Several favorite restaurants still had mini-jukeboxes at each booth. The New Cathay Chinese restaurant on 82nd Avenue was a particular favorite of ours because they had a full-size jukebox and a dance floor—we fed that jukebox lots of nickels! I never gave it much thought at the time, but just how unlikely is it to find a dance floor in a Chinese restaurant?

I remember drive-in food to be tasty and nutritious; mass-produced food wasn't delivered to restaurants by Sysco trucks. Restaurants purchased produce from local farmers in east county, beef and poultry were provided by independent butchers, and our local dairies, Alpenrose and Darigold, delivered dairy products. Pastries and desserts were usually made in-house or came from a local neighborhood bakery. While charting for the OCK, I was aware of the huge amount of beef being served at my uncle's steak house. Each year Uncle Richard traveled to the Midwest to select and purchase only corn-fed beef because he was always very particular about the quality of food being served in his restaurant.

The vast number of fast-food establishments we're so familiar with today didn't exist in that era. Fast food arrived in 1959 when the first McDonald's appeared in Portland on

91st and Southeast Powell. Several years later the unique drive-in opened a second location in our neighborhood on Southeast 122nd and Glisan St. The golden arches had a simple, inexpensive menu: burgers cost fifteen cents, fries eleven cents, and shakes were only nineteen cents! Several friends obtained their first jobs at McDonald's, but at the time only boys were hired! I never developed a taste for their food. I'd only purchase fries and a Coke, because after all there wasn't a better hamburger than the Old Country Kitchen's!

Our family didn't eat out often, but when relatives visited from the Midwest they'd usually be taken to the family restaurant sometime during their stay. On several special occasions my aunt and uncle invited us to join them at Eddie May's Prime Rib on Sandy Boulevard, which was one of their favorite restaurants. The chef served our prime rib table-side in a large, dome-covered copper serving cart. After making a prime cut selection, our dinner was served with potatoes, Yorkshire pudding, au jus, and creamy horseradish. I remember the ambience of miniature table lamps on starched white linens, red-flocked wallpaper, and dimly lit crystal chandeliers in the dining room—another special memory!

We sometimes ate at Caro Amico, an Italian restaurant on SW Barbur Blvd. It was one of the rare occasions when our family crossed the Willamette River to the west side of the city! The owner of Caro Amico was a frequent customer of the OCK and an acquaintance of my parents. Kenny enjoyed my dad's martinis and a steak dinner most every Sunday night after closing his restaurant. He claimed the steaks were the best in the city, and my father felt it was important to reciprocate by visiting Kenny's restaurant.

Caro Amico is still owned and managed by the third generation. They continue to serve their signature square pizza, which was my very first pizza. It's pleasing to find the exterior and interior somewhat unchanged after sixty years. The current owners have successfully retained the retro look of the sixties and the food is still amazing. A World War II photo of Kenny still hangs in the stairwell—it takes me back in time!

Most teenagers had a curfew imposed upon them. Mine was midnight on Friday and Saturday nights, and fortunately my friends had the same curfew. Most always I'd be able to negotiate an extension for special events, such as the prom or winter formal. I suppose it would have been easy to take advantage of my parents' late-night schedule at the restaurant, but it wasn't my nature to do that. I was trusted, or most likely threatened, to be home on time! There was a brief period during my sophomore year when my mother determined I could go out only one weekend night! There was never a decision; I chose Friday night because sock hops followed football and basketball games. My mother's explanation about going out only one night? She said she didn't want me to be too popular—being "too popular" apparently meant something entirely different to her!

THE INFAMOUS SOCK HOPS WERE DANCES HELD AFTER every home football and basketball game. I don't recall missing a dance in the four years at Douglas. Sock hops were originally held in our school gymnasium, and shoes were removed to avoid scratching the new wooden basketball court. I'm guessing there was a method to their thinking, because after a few hours of dancing our socks might have actually helped polish the floor! Several years later sock hops were held in our school cafetorium. This large space had a linoleum floor, so we were now allowed to wear shoes, but dances were still called sock hops.

History was made at a sock hop in 1961; a group of classmates calling themselves The Kingsmen introduced us to their new song. They became an international success, and we've been dancing to "Louie, Louie" ever since! Music, music, music—the cafetorium (a combined cafeteria and auditorium) had a well-stocked jukebox with the latest 45 records. It was another jukebox we fed with nickels during our snack period each morning and again during lunch. Music and dancing continued to be a big part of our high school social life!

My circle of friends were really good kids, only a few were a bit more rebellious. At the time smoking cigarettes and having an occasional beer were considered to be quite daring! Beer was never a problem in our household because of the culture I grew up in. As a teenager my parents allowed me to have a small glass of beer if I wanted—at home! Consequently, I never felt the desire to sneak around with my friends. A number of my friends' parents kept alcohol under lock and key at their houses, making it more tempting. Friends sometimes invited me to drink beer with them on Rocky Butte but it never interested me, so I'd make up excuses to not join them. My cousin had lost her life eight years earlier because the driver of the car was intoxicated: memory of the tragedy and the graphic image of Maxine had been etched in my mind.

Several friends had begun to smoke, often hiding cigarettes from their parents. I suspect their parents' concerns were of it turning into a costly habit, because this was long before the effects of nicotine were determined to be harmful and addictive. Finding clever ways to market their product, tobacco companies sometimes sent sample cigarette packs to people's homes. Late one night I decided to light up a "free" cigarette just to see what I might be missing. Thankfully it tasted awful, and I wondered how anyone could enjoy this terrible pastime!

A lot of advertising was being done by the tobacco industry. Television was a relatively new marketing tool and cigarette commercials captured a huge audience. Large billboards were still allowed throughout the city, illustrating the familiar Marlboro Man and Camel cigarettes, presumably designed to appeal to young, impressionable teens. Magazines, as well as the influential movie industry, also portrayed smoking as being cool and sophisticated for both men and women. The result was that a large segment of the population had begun to smoke. I learned the armed forces introduced servicemen and women to cigarettes during World War II and the Korean conflict; apparently they were included in C rations! Consequently, within several decades people were beginning to experience significant health effects from making unknowingly bad choices.

After attending several drama productions my first year at Douglas, I decided to take drama as an elective in my sophomore year. It was definitely a bold move and totally outside my comfort zone! Initially I was terrified of performing in front of my small drama class, but months later I auditioned for *The Teahouse of the August Moon*. My first stage appearance was the role of a geisha girl. I was captivated! It was fun to engage and interact with the cast, from costumes to makeup, and lastly being on stage. I found it appealing to play different character roles while performing in one-act plays during my sophomore year. As a student of the drama department it was possible for me to write and direct plays, but more specifically, drama was instrumental in improving my self-esteem.

After several performances I was anxious to take additional classes. My drama coach Mrs. R. (as we fondly referred to her) gave me needed encouragement and confidence to stretch myself while auditioning for larger roles. Gaining experience as an advanced drama student in my junior year, I was taking on leading roles for productions at Douglas, as well as performing in one-act plays at the University of Portland. All facets connected with the drama department became my passion; it consumed much of my time and energy.

Each year, Mrs. R. selected one student that she felt should consider a career in theater: it seems I was tagged to be that student in my senior year—she repeatedly stated I was to take my craft seriously! Being actively involved in the drama department for several years had been a wonderful experience, and it had made a positive impact on my young life. Prospective career opportunities were on my mind but I hadn't seriously considered theater to be one of them. After expressing my thoughts to my drama coach she was noticeably disappointed in my decision.

Coincidently, Dave and I had just started dating. Mrs. R. wasn't pleased, stating he'd be taking up too much of my time; she was concerned he'd be a distraction from the drama department. I was told to choose either the drama department or my boyfriend. I couldn't believe what I'd heard. She was giving me an ultimatum—of course I chose Dave! I'd only be directing plays and working behind the scenes for the remainder of my senior year, and there were no longer *A*s in her class! Mrs. R. had been my favorite teacher, but sadly our relationship would never be the same.

Mrs. R. often shared regrets of giving up her career in theater. Instead she became a drama coach, then married and had children. Undeniably an amazing drama coach, she enjoyed motherhood and appeared to have a satisfying career, but clearly her first love was the stage. There was such determination that one of her students might fulfill her lifelong dream of becoming a successful actor, and I believe she felt compelled to live vicariously through her students.

Much to her delight and guidance, she did produce a number of actors graduating from our high school during her tenure. Sam Elliott, Lindsay Wagner, Barbara Niven, Michelle Clunie, and Bruce Abbott all achieved success in the movie industry and in television; she was incredibly proud of their accomplishments. I have few regrets of not acting and performing in my senior year, but I do have the distinction of being Sam Elliott's first leading lady. In my junior year, Sam and I were both cast in and starred in the production of *Death Takes a Holiday*.

College and career choices were in my thoughts at the end of my junior year, and it was time to make some serious decisions regarding my future. Looking for answers, I met with my school counselor for much-needed career guidance, but the results weren't what I was hoping for. What I was looking for was advice and dialogue with my parents, but I'd be winging it! At the age of seventeen I was still searching for structure from my parents. I'm sure they must have had concerns about my future, but that would have involved a serious conversation.

Throughout my education I was hopeful they'd take an interest in my classes and general education. It may seem amusing, but during my sophomore year I remember a self-imposed two-week grounding period because I got a C in a math class! The motive was to have my friends believe my parents were just as concerned about my grades as their parents were.

I recall statements such as, "It's all right to be average" or, "I don't want you to be too smart!" I'm certain those comments weren't made to keep me from being a better student or from achieving certain goals. Indeed, there's nothing wrong with being average, but those comments don't necessarily motivate children to achieve their full potential. Kids tend to live up to their expectations. The statement about not being too smart may have stemmed from a basic distrust of highly educated people in the Eureka community. People might be referred to as being "overeducated" and "too smart for their own good!" Those remarks were often made in humor, but I think they exhibited the cultural environment I grew up in. The comments were usually made by people who were sensitive about their own lack of formal education.

Talking about obtaining a specific achievement or setting ambitious goals for oneself might also be considered bragging or "blowing your own horn"—what would people think? I believe it was Garrison Keillor who made an amusing statement on NPR. He jokingly made reference to children's expectations being lower in the Midwest, and it was explained that if parents don't expect too much, children don't have far to reach their goals! Considering my upbringing, there's possibly a bit of truth in that humorous remark.

In the midst of making decisions about my future, there was beginning to be more uncertainty about the world we lived in. Children of my generation had grown up during the era of the Cold War, and we'd become accustomed to all the duck-and-cover films shown to us since grade school. However, the possibility of a nuclear attack became a distinct reality during the US confrontation with Russia during the Cuban Missile Crisis. Our country was in crisis for two weeks in October of 1962; it was a frightening and pivotal event in our young lives.

Fortunately the crisis with Russia was averted, but years later we discovered how perilously close our country had come to a nuclear attack. We'd later learn full disclosure to the general public of the situation may have created a state of panic throughout the country. For the first time in our young adult lives there was the realization that we lived in a world of uncertainty. Our future was tenuous and it felt as though our carefree days of innocence were over.

Throughout high school, English, history, and the arts were classes that most appealed to me. I only took the required science and math classes needed for college entrance. After the meeting with my counselor I realized counsel regarding career choices wasn't their strong suit; their priority was to seek scholarships for honor students who'd achieved higher academic success. I'd learn it was much the same for many students who were searching for advice regarding trade schools or other vocations. I didn't fall into that category. Social interaction had always been a higher priority, and consequently my grades were mostly *B*s.

CHAPTER FIFTEEN

College and Career

If obtaining a college degree I'd most likely become a teacher or a registered nurse, since those two careers seemed the only viable directions for women with four-year degrees. In that era it was highly unusual for women to pursue degrees in law or medicine. There were exceptions, but it would have been a challenge to break into those male-dominated professions. Attempting to seek a degree in accounting, finance, or marketing would also have been an uphill battle for women in male-occupied vocations. If following a business path, women were typically employed in supportive roles, specifically as typists, file clerks, receptionists, or secretaries. The banking industry and savings and loans employed women, but rarely in managerial positions.

Several friends made the decision to attend business college after graduation. Courses were provided with advanced training in office management, shorthand, typing, and keyboarding. Being able to type with great speed and proficiency with electric typewriters was essential to secure a job in the business sector. Women might also consider a career path in service-related fields such as working in the retail trade or becoming beauticians. Another option was employment in the travel industry. Were there inequities? Absolutely, but at the time no one questioned the logic. Times were very different, and I don't recall anyone thinking it was unfair or biased.

I did have an interest in becoming an airline stewardess (flight attendant); it was actually considered to be a glamorous career in that era! Now a gender-specific term, women were referred to as stewardesses because at the time men weren't employed in that capacity. After submitting my application to several airlines, I learned applicants needed to be 5'4" to reach the overheads; I was 5'2"! Initially disappointed, I'm now pleased that my applications were rejected because apparently certain rules were enforced by many airlines in the sixties. I understand women needed to maintain a certain weight, their teeth had to be straightened, and eyeglasses weren't allowed. Stewardesses were required to resign if they married and there was a mandatory retirement at age thirty-two! All those sexist rules disappeared when Title VII of the 1964 Civil Rights Act declared that policies based on age, race, gender, weight, pregnancy, and marital status were discriminatory.

Late in my junior year I was dating the guy Mrs. R. felt was responsible for diverting my attention from her drama department. I'd known Dave since our freshman year but we never shared classes. Unlike myself he was taking lots of math and science courses, so our paths rarely crossed! My friend Margie, still very much the matchmaker, was responsible for arranging our first date. Both of us were between steady dates, so the timing was perfect for us to attend the spring dance. I found it refreshing to go out with someone who appeared more self-assured and mature than most of the guys I'd dated. I admired Dave's honesty and integrity, and he always seemed to make sound decisions. Fellow students respected his decisive leadership in student government, as well as being a valued member of the DDHS football team.

Prom, 1962

By the beginning of our senior year, Dave and I were going steady and I was wearing his pin. Going steady and being pinned was an important event in high school and college. As members of our respective social service clubs, we proudly wore our pins to identify our affiliations. This was a time when high school boys and girls in the Portland area were actively involved in social service clubs, which were precursors to college sororities and fraternities. Social service clubs had been formed years earlier to provide a service to their schools and communities; inevitably, there seemed to be more emphasis on the social aspect of clubs!

Receiving a bid to the "right" club in our sophomore year was of great significance for students, and we anxiously waited for that important bid to show up in the mail! It was exciting to receive the bid I'd hoped for, but I also remember how distressing it was for friends who didn't get their first choice or were denied a bid! I understand social service clubs are no longer sanctioned in Portland high schools because they were found to be exclusionary and detrimental to students' self-esteem. I'm not at all surprised at their findings; fortunately students now have more relevant topics of interest to explore in their high school curriculums, which results in a much healthier environment.

In the following year, despite several brief breakups, Dave and I felt confident about our relationship. But in retrospect, we were very young and still discovering so much about ourselves—and who we were about to become! Just how unlikely is it to meet your life partner at such a young age? Statistically, high school relationships are destined for failure. The only explanation I can offer is that we both evolved in the same direction as we matured. We were also fortunate to share similar values and comparable socioeconomic backgrounds. It's been said that the difference between a successful relationship and a failing one is whether couples grow together. Most importantly, throughout the years we've been best friends and have maintained a mutual respect for one another. Ultimately, I suppose finding your life partner also involves excellent timing and an incredible amount of luck!

As our senior year began, classmates were focused on applying to colleges and considering career choices. If attending college, my options were limited to the Portland area, since I understood that it wouldn't be economically feasible for me to live on campus. It wasn't the ideal college experience I'd envisioned, but dorm and living expenses would be avoided if attending college in Portland while residing at home. All of us thought college tuition was really expensive; it's all relative, but tuition for Oregon state colleges in 1963 was only one hundred and ten dollars a term! Many friends were struggling with the same heady decisions regarding their futures, and I've often wondered why we felt such urgency to make lifelong commitments?

Following our parents' footsteps, there was an awareness that stability, job security, and developing the proper work ethic were highly valued. We were definitely products of the depression era. It was highly unusual to make career changes; once on a set track, it would most likely be our designated path. If indecisive about college or a chosen career, no one even considered taking a gap year to find themselves; that was an unfamiliar term! Our high school years had felt like a safe cocoon for most of us—we must have thought it was time to quickly grow up and become responsible adults!

Feeling compelled to make a commitment but lacking enthusiasm, I decided to attend Portland State University. However, after attending only two terms, it became evident that the urban college setting wasn't going to be a good fit. Unfortunately, none of my friends were enrolled at PSU, and undeniably I also found it difficult to focus on my new surroundings while Dave was attending the University of Oregon in Eugene. Having been very socially active in high school, I remember it being a lonely existence; I felt completely lost! Clearly, more time was needed to make the adjustment, but I was unhappy; frankly, at the time PSU reminded me of a big high school with ashtrays!

In the short time I attended Portland State, a November day in 1963 would dramatically change our country. President Kennedy had been assassinated in Dallas, Texas. It was a defining moment in our young lives! A student interrupted my psychology class to inform us of the shooting. Classes were immediately dismissed and time seemed to stand still for all of us when we heard the news. I joined hundreds of students gathered in the student union as we watched the unfolding tragic events on a small black-and-white television.

Within several days, live coverage of the accused assassins murder began to fuel conspiracy theories, and what followed was growing skepticism and distrust of our government. The assassination seemed to be a turning point in history. Profound changes were about to take place, and we'd learn it would have a direct impact on many lives. During this national crisis our nation was also in the midst of an escalating war in Southeast Asia. Increased military involvement in Vietnam was on the daily news front, as were the alarming Civil Rights disturbances in the South.

In the next few years, Medgar Evers, Malcolm X, Martin Luther King, and Robert Kennedy would also be assassinated; most of the sixties were filled with turmoil and

College and Career

unrest! It's been said that for us postwar Baby Boomers, the sixties became the "best of times" and also the "worst of times." Almost sixty years have passed, and I believe we're still searching for the truth. I remember it being a very bleak period in our nation's history.

As our country was experiencing some very turbulent times, it was coincidentally an unsettling period in my own life. Finding it difficult to stay focused after leaving PSU, I began to diligently explore career options. I don't recall what inspired me to become a dental assistant, but after talking to my personal dentist he informed me of the opening of a new dental practice. While interviewing for the job, Dr. Fry indicated on-the-job training was his preference. If I was interested he offered to pay my tuition for a two-year program at the University of Oregon dental school. Pleased with the educational opportunity, I accepted the position as his assistant. I began taking night classes at the dental school, and upon completion of my courses I'd become certified as a dental radiologist, lab technician, and chairside assistant.

One-girl dental offices were quite common when I began working for Dr. Fry. My duties were chairside assisting, lab work, as well as taking and developing X-rays. Additional responsibilities included accounting and billing and being the office receptionist. A great deal of phone time was required to schedule appointments. Answering machines weren't available, so it was necessary to repeatedly call patients until I reached them. X-rays were processed in a dark room, and film attached to a metal clip was dropped into a developing solution. The entire procedure took me about fifteen minutes! Lab work involved pouring dental molds for crowns, inlays, and dentures. While aspirating during procedures, fluids traveled to a large container concealed in a cabinet. It was my job to empty the fluid-filled jar every few days to disinfect the jar and line—I remember it to be the worst part of my job!

Advancements in dental equipment and procedures that seem very routine in the twenty-first century weren't yet available to us. Without the use of disposable syringes, it was necessary to autoclave stainless steel syringes, and all surgical instruments needed to be autoclaved after use. The term multitasking was an unfamiliar term, but my new job was definitely that—on steroids! I'd often be mixing amalgam or aspirating while answering the phone in one of the two operatories. Other duties included cleaning the bathroom, vacuuming, dusting, and washing office windows inside and out! Household tasks were completed each week when the doctor took an afternoon off. Fortunately I'd always been very detail oriented; with all my responsibilities I somehow managed to keep this busy practice running efficiently.

Dr. Fry practiced general dentistry, which included extensive oral surgery and endodontia work for treatment of root canals. Full extractions for dentures were common in our clinic, as well as treatment and surgery for periodontal disease, such as gingiva recession. It was unusual to refer patients to specialists; at that time there were few oral surgeons, endodontists, periodontists, or pedodontists in private practice. With a sizable lab, Dr. Fry did much of his own lab work. It seems unimaginable, but at times he opened his office in the middle of the night to treat complete strangers; he had great empathy for people requiring emergency dental care. Upon my arrival to the clinic, both operatories needed to be cleaned and surgical instruments autoclaved before our busy day began!

Neither of us wore latex gloves, surgical masks, or eye protection while doing routine dental procedures—they weren't considered essential! Our uniforms were a splattered mess at the end of a workday! Yikes, I shudder to think of what we were potentially exposed to, but this was the sixties, long before we knew anything about the AIDS virus. Years later, dental personnel would be encased in protective equipment after it was determined the AIDS virus could be contracted through bodily fluids. Dental offices now employ three or four people to do the work I've described. Despite the organized chaos in this busy practice, I was learning a great deal, being challenged, and discovering dental school to be a perfect fit! I was delighted with my new job and was pleased to have made an excellent career choice.

Dave was returning to Portland about every other weekend during his freshman year at Oregon and occasionally I'd travel by bus to spend the weekend in Eugene. In retrospect, it certainly wasn't an ideal college experience for him. I suppose we both missed out on social activities and the building of other friendships. At the time we weren't interested in dating anyone else but if our relationship was meant to endure, a brief separation during college shouldn't have been so threatening to us. Of course, I can say all this in hindsight; after all we were only nineteen years old!

There was a strong incentive to be in good academic standing while attending college in 1965. The selective service was keeping close tabs on all young men over the age of eighteen, because that's when the first combat troops were being sent to Vietnam. As the war continued to escalate, more ground troops were being deployed to 'Nam. After Dave experienced academic difficulties with two classes in his sophomore year, it put him in a very tenuous situation with the draft board! In the interim he retook the two night classes at PSU, allowing him to return to the U of O. Unfortunately, Dave's draft number came up before his reenrollment! The draft notice arrived during his first visit to Eureka while vacationing with my family and I. After a lengthy bus trip back to Portland, he felt fortunate to obtain one of the last slots in the Oregon Air National Guard.

Phil Saxton was instrumental in securing the National Guard position for Dave. He'd been a lifelong friend of Dave's parents and served as a colonel at the Portland Air National Guard Base. Phil had known Crawford and Lucille since the third grade. Years later, at Lucille's funeral, Phil revealed it was Dave's mother who had tearfully begged him to intervene on his behalf, saying he simply couldn't refuse her plea. At the time we knew Phil was responsible for getting Dave into the Guard but were unaware Lucille had initiated the request.

We were confident Dave was going to be stateside during the Vietnam war since the National Guard or reserves weren't called into combat duty during that period. At the time their primary responsibility was to guard the nation in the event of an attack or respond to national emergencies. He'd go through basic training at Lackland Air Force Base in Texas, followed by additional training in Wichita Falls, Texas. The entire length of Dave's basic training and subsequent technical school was about six months. Additionally, there were monthly guard meetings at the Portland air base, as well as two weeks of summer camp at various locations throughout the country during his six-year obligation with the Air National Guard.

Dave and I announced our engagement on Christmas Eve, 1965, just before he left for basic training. Following our marriage we'd move to Eugene where he'd continue his studies at the University, and I'd search for employment in the dental industry. While Dave finished active duty in Texas, I was nearing completion of my certification and busily making plans for our September wedding. I felt grateful to be living at home while working at the clinic because it had allowed me to save a substantial portion of my salary. It was our intent to purchase a new car when Dave returned home the following June. After his return we began our car search, and I'm fairly certain we were thought of as newbies as we entered the car dealership! After negotiating the purchase price of our car, the salesman was noticeably shocked as we handed him a cashier's check totaling twenty-six hundred dollars—it was full payment for our new 1966 Pontiac LeMans! The salesman questioned us, assuming we didn't understand that most new cars were purchased with monthly payments, but we knew what we were doing!

Admittedly, we were quite proud of ourselves and determined to begin our marriage with no outstanding debt. Our new Pontiac was a burgundy-colored sporty two-door with a black interior, bucket seats, and a four-speed on the floor. It was a fun car to drive but more importantly, it was the first thing we owned together! I'm not sure when my infamous pink-and-black car disappeared, I just wish there was a photo of this one-of-a-kind car!

CHAPTER SIXTEEN

Marriage

After a flurry of wedding preparations, showers, and parties, Dave and I were married in a candlelight ceremony at the Laurelhurst Presbyterian Church on September 10th, 1966. Like most mothers of the bride, my mother was actively involved in helping to plan our wedding. It's not unusual to have a few glitches on a wedding day, but minutes before the ceremony the minister abruptly announced that candles wouldn't be allowed for our candlelight ceremony! Mom was not happy with his last-minute decision—she had a very "short" conversation with him! The upshot is that the candelabras on the alter were absolutely aglow for our ceremony!

Months before our wedding, Mom had voiced another concern: she'd been working with Dad to pronounce the word *mother* correctly. His lifelong difficulty pronouncing *th*'s had never been a problem before, but Mom was very insistent he not say, "Her mudder and I" when the minister asked, "Who gives this woman to be married?" Determined to correct his speech, she'd frequently tell Dad, "I just know you can pronounce the word *mother*!" She must have been worried about what people would think, but in fact, most of our extended family knew she'd been coaching him for months. My father did not disappoint; however, there was a spellbinding moment when guests on the bride's side of the sanctuary collectively held their breath as Dad painstakingly responded, "Her MOTHER and I"! I was so proud of my father!

Dave & Judy, September 10, 1966

About three hundred people were in attendance for our wedding, and Pa and Lizzie traveled from Eureka for the wedding festivities. Several family members and a number of close friends served as attendants. There seemed to be more protocol and formality at weddings during that era. I recall a number of people commented that it was the first wedding they'd attended where the wedding party and guests looked like they were actually having fun! I also remember our wedding colors of pink and burgundy were considered to be rather bold. I thought it was important to match the burgundy carpet aisle in the church!

Our reception was held in the church basement with a traditional receiving line followed by the serving of cake, coffee, punch, mints, and nuts. Of course, everything about the reception was also color coordinated. Despite the first heavy rain of the late summer, we thought our wedding was absolutely perfect! There was a post-function for close friends and family—my parents hosted a "real" party at their home following the church reception. Dad had just completed a covered patio in time for the rainy reception. In typical fashion, my parents threw a fantastic party!

Following the reception our wedding night was spent at the Benson Hotel in downtown Portland. Our honeymoon destinations were San Francisco and Carmel. We were excited to take a road trip in our new car. As we traveled the 101 coastal highway into Northern California, we decided to tour several wineries. Wine tasting was a very new concept; of course we were novices, but it seemed like a very grown-up thing to do! After several days of touring San Francisco, we reached picturesque Carmel; it was a perfect honeymoon! On our return, we stopped in Reno, Nevada where we attended several shows, played blackjack, and tried our luck at slot machines before arriving in Eugene.

Our first home was Bendix Manor, a new apartment complex on 19th and Patterson. Returning from our honeymoon, we discovered our parents had already paid us a visit: they'd traveled from Portland to "shivaree" our apartment! Imagine our surprise as we attempted to enter our bathroom—it was filled with crumpled newspapers from floor to ceiling! As newspapers were removed, we discovered plastic wrap on the toilet seat and found our bed had been short-sheeted with a layer of oatmeal flakes between the sheets!

Our parents had successfully convinced the apartment manager to unlock our apartment on the pretense of delivering wedding gifts. Undoubtedly, this was my parents' idea, because shivarees had been an important part of their culture while living in Eureka. In the early nineteenth century shivarees were a traditional practice in the Midwest, apparently a custom from our European ancestors. Newlyweds were often disrupted on their wedding nights, and intruders might bang on pots and pans, shoot guns, and even kidnap the couple! I've read that in some parts of the Midwest the mayhem and hazing involved newlyweds being dunked in the cattle tank and paraded around town! All things considered, I guess Dave and I were lucky! My parents were always looking for ways to have a good time, and I'm certain the four of them had a wonderful time creating all that chaos!

Dave was beginning his third year at the university in pursuit of his accounting degree and I was seeking employment to support us and help pay for his education. Many of our friends and new acquaintances were doing the same—women were getting their PHTs (putting husbands through). It may now seem like an antiquated way of thinking, but it was a familiar term and a common practice during that era. While settling into our new surroundings in Eugene we developed friendships with a number of married students from regions throughout the US, as well several couples from Europe.

My job search was more difficult than anticipated. I was surprised there were few jobs in the dental field and also found wages to be lower in the Eugene area. But, I suppose it was most disheartening to learn that my credentials from dental school didn't seem to make a significant salary difference in this college town! After a month of job searching, I felt fortunate to secure employment as one of three assistants in a very busy dental practice on the edge of campus. As the sole practitioner, this man was also active in local and state politics, and he wasted no time telling me how well-connected he was with the "right" people.

Within several hours of my first day at work, I realized that my employer was deeply troubled. He was terribly condescending and seemed to take great pleasure in ridiculing the staff. At one point he snuck up behind me and popped a balloon next to my ear, just to see what my response would be! He forcefully grabbed my arm when I mistakenly placed a bank deposit in his right coat pocket, instead of the left. What followed was a lecture explaining to me the difference between left and right!

After that harrowing incident, I was actually brave enough to question him regarding several office procedures. The most disturbing was informing me to not sterilize his surgical instruments; I was instructed to simply rinse forceps and scalpels with alcohol! My reply was that all surgical instruments needed to be sterilized and I would instead be using the autoclave. I don't think he was accustomed to having someone question his routine office procedures. Additionally, he told me that in his three-girl office, one of us would be required to be his "arm candy" for lunch at an upscale restaurant every Friday!

Thankfully, I wouldn't have to worry about having lunch with this lunatic! On my third day at work he was working on a cuspidor with a plumber's wrench in one of the operatories while I was using the phone at the front desk. The dentist called my name, and as I looked up, he threw the wrench at my forehead! He started laughing and claimed he was aiming for my stomach because he thought I might be pregnant!

Injured and upset, I managed to call Dave asking him to pick me up. While the two other employees bandaged my head, they were quick to respond that he was only kidding around; clearly they were worried about their jobs if they showed too much concern.

Dave was stunned and in disbelief when he arrived at the office. I just remember wanting the two of us to quickly get away from this deranged man—I was terrified for both of us! While seeking medical care, the urgent-care doctor asked what happened as he treated my injury. After I described the disturbing incident, he replied, "I happen to personally know this man and I know he would never do anything like that!"

When people noticed my bandaged forehead, word of my injury and very brief employment was discovered by several friends in our apartment complex. Ironically, one of our friends was a fraternity brother of the dentist's son, and apparently word reached campus about his father's actions. Within forty-eight hours this crazy man was knocking on our apartment door. The purpose of his visit was to intimidate us: he claimed I'd made up the entire incident and accused me of telling lies about him! We were told if we mentioned anything more about the matter he would use his power and influence to keep Dave from getting his degree at the University. I was then told he'd make certain no other dentists in the Eugene area would ever hire me. At the conclusion of his alarming visit, he said I'd be lucky to find any other employment in the city. If it was his intent to frighten us, he'd accomplished his mission!

Dave and I were young and naive but convinced this terrifying man would act on his promise. The dentist was a very prominent man in the Eugene area and well-known throughout the state of Oregon. I was terribly discouraged, but understood it would be necessary to put my dental career on hold. I'd be looking for another job! After three or four weeks of searching, I managed to find a job in bookkeeping at the Eugene main branch of First Interstate Bank. Thoughts of running into this disturbed man played heavily on my mind, even though I worked in an area of the bank where I didn't have exposure to customers. After several months I was offered a position on teller row. It was a higher wage but made me more visible to the public. While working in bookkeeping, I was aware this man had numerous bank accounts for his dental practice—it was only a matter of time before he'd show up.

Reluctantly I took the job on the row. It was unnerving but I decided to keep a watchful eye for the dentist if he came into the bank. Several months later I was offered a placement in special deposits, where I'd be making change orders and taking deposits from commercial customers.

My new job gave me access to the bank vault—that's where I hid the day I noticed the dentist walking through the lobby! Paralyzed with fear I managed to close my window, staying in the vault until my coworker told me he'd left the building. If he'd seen me, I felt certain he would've insisted on my termination, and was convinced the bank officers would comply with his demands.

This traumatizing experience had shaken me to the core. It was the first time in my life I'd encountered a ruthless, mean-spirited person! The entire incident seemed like a terrible nightmare, and for the longest time I had concerns of this man somehow reappearing in my life. My fears were answered several years later when Dave and I vacationed at a resort on the Oregon Coast. I was struck with terror when I saw him walk through the lobby of our hotel! My anxiety resurfaced as I experienced a panic attack—we quickly checked out of the hotel.

So many years have passed, but while recounting this unsettling event in my writings, it continues to cause me a certain degree of anxiousness. I had hoped to one day resume my work in dentistry, but that terrifying event had thoroughly traumatized me. Obviously I should have sought counseling after that unsettling experience; post-traumatic stress is very real. But my generation had been taught to deal with our own problems and to "get over it!" I briefly considered resuming my dental career after our children were in school. Regretfully, still unnerved by the event, I simply couldn't bring myself to seek employment in another dental office. I was unable to confront my fears, and sadly the outcome of this traumatic incident would end my dental career.

All things considered, I was fortunate to have secured employment at First Interstate Bank. I found the banking world to be interesting and challenging. My salary paid for Dave's tuition, books, and most of our living expenses. Along with Dave's part-time position at the U of O business office, our jobs kept us afloat and out of debt. We never found it necessary to apply for student loans. My final promotion at First Interstate was in the installment loan department, where there was limited exposure to customers. My chances of running into this terrifying man were minimal—I was fairly confident he wouldn't be applying for a loan!

Clearly, during my very brief employment with the Eugene dentist, I'd experienced verbal, sexual, emotional, and physical abuse. But after I began working at the bank there was an acute awareness that sexual harassment was considered normal behavior! Most of my coworkers were women of my age who were also putting their husbands through college. Being employed in a predominantly male environment, we were apparently regarded as fair game to our supervisors and bank officers. Most of us young women were subjected to blatant sexual innuendos, off-color jokes, and inappropriate comments on a daily basis. It was all about grown men behaving badly and getting away with it. When we complained about their behavior, they suggested it was all in fun, asking why we weren't able to take a joke! If things got too uncomfortable we were told, "You always have the option to quit. This is a college town, there are lots of girls just waiting to take your place!"

Miniskirts were a fashion statement for most of us young women in 1967. While ascending escalators in the bank lobby, bank officers had the audacious behavior to roll their desk chairs close to the escalators. Leaning over in their chairs, they attempted to gaze under our skirts! We were forced to endure their sophomoric behavior; they of course thought their actions were harmless and amusing.

I'd had a positive work experience while working for Dr. Fry; he was very respectful when I was in his employment. But while attending dental school several of my classmates had shared disturbing incidents of improper behavior regarding dentists they'd worked for. The unprofessional behavior I experienced from my employers at First Interstate Bank apparently wasn't all that unusual. As more women began to seek careers in the sixties, sexual intimidation was presumably occurring in many male-occupied workplaces.

The National Organization for Women (NOW), a civil rights group, was founded in 1966 to promote equal rights for women, and the women's liberation movement soon followed. Much welcomed and very timely, both organizations were gaining significant momentum by the late sixties—women began to heed the messaging. After struggling for equality and experiencing workplace improprieties, women were beginning to feel empowered for the first time in their lives.

The feminist movement would also bring birth control to the forefront; easier access to oral contraception now gave women effective control over their fertility. It would be a decade of innumerable changes, and the outcome would often have unsettling effects on relations between men and women of my generation. There were new, unfamiliar rules on the horizon; some men viewed the changes as a threat to their masculinity. I was fortunate to be married to a man who was progressive in his thinking and supportive of the crusade; Dave didn't seem daunted by the infinite changes taking place.

Laws were finally enacted in the late seventies to protect women from sexual harassment in the workplace. But sadly, the Me Too movement of 2018 has made it disturbingly clear that inappropriate conduct still continues to exist in some workplaces. Having dealt with similar experiences over fifty-five years ago, I'd hoped women were no longer being subjected to working in an offensive environment. It seems the age-old problem has plagued women since they left the kitchen and entered the workplace!

Returning to Portland for Dave's monthly National Guard duty at the Portland air base was at times an inconvenience while we lived in Eugene, but we were also very aware of our good fortune. As young men were being drafted into the military, their educations and lives were being disrupted by the continued involvement in Vietnam. Initially, being married qualified as a deferment from military service, and as a result mass flower weddings were taking place in the countryside of Eugene to keep the draft board at bay! The selective service was keeping close tabs on all young men; deferments were changing almost monthly. Before long, being married no longer qualified as a deferment, and having a child now exempted men from the military draft—predictably, a baby boom followed! However, within a short period of time the child deferment also disappeared.

From the onset, military involvement in Vietnam was unpopular with a large segment of our country. Anti-war sentiment began with ongoing violent uprisings occurring in large cities and on many college campuses. The University of Oregon campus happened to be one of the many hot spots for student demonstrations against military action in 'Nam. Daily arrests were made for the burning of draft cards, and on one occasion a group of protesters bombed the ROTC building!

Throughout the unrest and frequent disturbances on campus, we never took an active stand against the war or became involved with protests. When the demonstrations started on campus, Dave and I felt it was mostly the hippie movement leading the charge, and we thought protesters were possibly being too radical. Having both grown up in conservative households, we were still of the mindset to not question authority. We believed our elected officials must certainly know what was best for our country, but as the war dragged on we began to change our opinions!

As the Vietnam War continued to escalate, all young men over the age of eighteen were now fair game for the draft board. I suppose our lives seemed somewhat charmed compared to a number of friends and relatives. People were finding it necessary to make difficult decisions regarding military, marriage, and having children when they weren't prepared to be parents. It was a recipe for disaster, and it's not at all surprising that many couples began to experience marital and financial difficulties. It was an unsettling time in our history, and Americans were becoming war-weary due to the increased casualties of military personnel and escalating costs.

Continual anti-war sentiment across the country would ultimately end our Vietnam involvement in 1973; our troops were finally brought home. Several close friends and family served in 'Nam, and sadly many lives were changed after returning from their one-year tour. Physical disabilities and/or post-traumatic stress disorders were prevalent with a large number of returning soldiers. In the following years, countless members of the military, including several friends and relatives, were diagnosed with illnesses related to exposure to the toxic chemical Agent Orange while serving in Vietnam.

The draft came to an end in 1973 as the US armed forces moved to an all-volunteer military. If the draft had continued, I don't believe our country would have tolerated the senseless, lengthy wars in Iraq and Afghanistan. As a result, these two conflicts haven't directly effected as many young people as our involvement in Vietnam. I admire the men and women who voluntarily serve our country and understand the vital importance of maintaining a strong military. It may be wishful thinking to expect that mankind is capable of resolving global controversies through diplomacy and negotiations, but it has to be our first attempt at maintaining peace. Throughout history we've seen how the destructive result of war can affect the human spirit.

Early in our marriage, I suppose my political opinions may have leaned a bit more to the left than Dave's. As a result of the war in 'Nam, I probably became more skeptical and disillusioned with government policy, realizing it was perfectly acceptable to question the judgement of our government. I think it was the radicalization of the Republican Party's social policies that may have pushed Dave more to the left with his political ideology. Since that time, I'd say we have similar opinions regarding politics and for the most part, tend to share like views. Having a significant difference in our politics wouldn't have been of such importance to me fifty years ago, but in today's political climate, I simply can't imagine being married to someone whose views were so opposed to mine!

It's been noted that most couples experience periods of instability during their marriages. Certainly we've had disagreements about a number of issues over the years, but I don't recall a time our marriage was ever at risk. We've always tried to respect each other's views and opinions, even when we disagreed about important matters. Early in our marriage we had the foresight to anticipate problems that might cause a strain in our relationship. As I've stated, it was our objective to not acquire debt as college students; it was part of our plan and the big picture! We were both fiscally responsible, aware that financial difficulties could possibly create a stressful effect on our marriage. Another part of the big picture was for Dave to obtain his accounting degree to secure our future. Acquiring his degree and passing the CPA exam would hopefully increase his career prospects.

Fortunately, in the late sixties, accounting firms were offering substantial employment opportunities for men. At that time it was considered more important for men to complete their college educations, as men had far more earning potential than women. Without question, it seems very biased in the twenty-first century, but as I've repeatedly mentioned, times were really very different!

CHAPTER SEVENTEEN

Children

With Dave's accounting degree in sight, we were anxious to start our family. My doctor had implied it may take several years to get pregnant; well, the doctor was proven wrong! Dave had already begun the interviewing process with accounting firms, but the reality of our baby on its way did bring on a bit more urgency on his part to secure a job! It turns out his concerns weren't at all warranted, because he received four or five job offers from the big eight accounting firms. Dave accepted a position with Peat Marwick Mitchell in the Portland office; we were elated!

Our move to Portland in December '68 occurred during one of the worst winter storms in recent history. Navigating I-5 north on snow and ice, we managed to move our belongings to Beaverton. Our new home was a two-bedroom duplex on Southwest 6th and Menlo Drive. Dave was on the audit side of the firm, and he immediately began to travel out of state for Peat. During those extended audits, I was busily preparing the nursery and anticipating the arrival of our baby. It was good to be back in Portland reconnecting with family and old friends, and meeting new people in the Peat family. A number of friends in our social circle are people we met at the firm, and we've maintained a close connection after all these years.

After continual snowstorms throughout the winter, the following summer turned out to be one of the hottest on record. My due date for delivery was June 20th, but the date came and went! With continual ninety-five-degree weather and a lack of air-conditioning, many late afternoons were spent in a small kiddie pool, attempting to stay cool and calm. After a lengthy labor, Maurice Grant (soon to be known as MG) arrived on June 26, 1969 at 9:44 p.m. We were now a family—what an absolute joy and delight our new baby boy was to us! Admittedly, I was a novice at caring for our new son, but miraculously I managed; after all, our baby was new to this as well! My intention was to be a stay-at-home mom after having children because it was important for me to be fully engaged as a mother while anticipating our child's firsts; I feel very fortunate to have been given that opportunity.

MG six months

In 1971 we purchased our first house, located on SE 142nd street. Our new home provided us with a larger living space and a spacious backyard for MG. The move allowed us to be in closer proximity to both grandparents, and they were very supportive and helpful while doting on their only grandson. We were grateful for their offers to babysit and their involvement with MG's activities. My father was so delighted to finally have a boy in the family that he bought a Shetland pony for his grandson! A shelter was built for "Cricket" in their oversized backyard, and his diet was supplemented with dated vegetables from the Old Country Kitchen. My parents often hitched Cricket to a surrey; they enjoyed traveling the short distance to our home with a trail of neighborhood children following them!

Our family was completed with the birth of Rian Christian on July 26, 1973, at 11:09 a.m. Rian was in a hurry; he arrived two weeks before his due date. He was very thoughtful to his mommy because my labor was only two hours long! We soon realized Rian was always going to be in a hurry with everything he attempted to do! We were so pleased to have a second son and a brother for MG. I clearly recall how protective he was of his new little brother; he called him his "baby butter!"

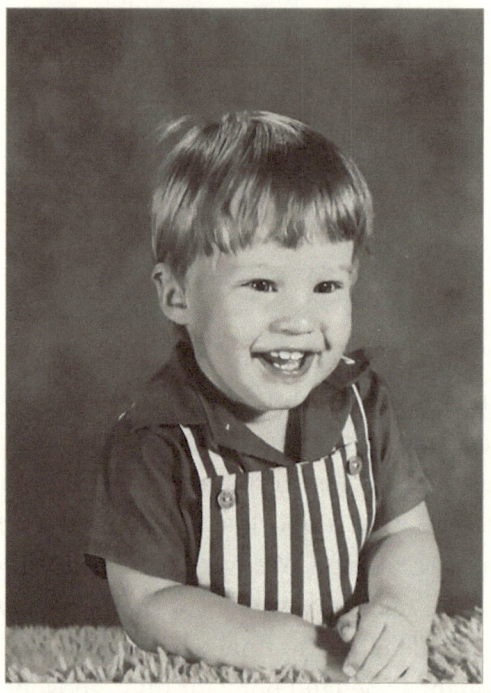

Rian, age one

We found the four-year age difference between our sons to be perfect for us. Managing a household while raising two very active little boys kept me busy. Motherhood was my calling—I loved caring for our family! I began to volunteer as a room mother at MG's school and occupied myself with our children's numerous activities. Satisfying my creative outlets, I decorated our home, took up tole painting, macrame, enjoyed gardening, canning, cooking, and doing all things domestic! There never seemed to be enough hours in the day, but there was still time to take an occasional yoga class.

Our children were introduced to my native South Dakota at the ages of six and two. I was pleased to have them meet their extended family and particularly anxious to introduce them to the rural community where I'd grown up. Our sons would have two other visits to my hometown, the last occurring in 1987 and coinciding with the Eureka Centennial. During this visit, at the ages of thirteen and seventeen, they both had a better understanding regarding the size of our family. It's difficult to comprehend, but approximately ten thousand people were in attendance for the three-day celebration! MG and Rian were astounded to discover how many relatives they had! While walking through large crowds of people on Main Street, they asked, "Are we really related to all these people?" They were stunned to learn many relatives weren't able to attend the celebration! I'm so pleased to have given them an introduction to their familial background.

> "Thou dost not really know thyself unless thou hast come to learn something about the generation of thy forebears."
>
> —Gustav Freytag, German historian.

Children

Rian & MG, ages four and eight

Our new home in northwest Portland was completed in 1977 when our sons were eight and four years of age. The new neighborhood of Torreyview was filled with young families—it was a wonderful place to raise our children. I became an active volunteer for their elementary school as a tutor, room mother, and PTA member, and would serve a one-year term as the West Tualatin View volunteer coordinator. Once our sons reached middle school, they weren't as enthused to have their mother volunteer—a very normal reaction! This now gave me the opportunity to seek volunteer positions outside of the Beaverton School District. Timing was perfect to join the Junior League of Portland and the Urban Tour Group. Being involved in both organizations was socially engaging and very much a positive experience. As an active League member I held a one-year office for our annual Holiday Showcase fundraiser and continued to participate with league activities for a number of years.

What Will People Think?

Accepting a part-time position as an independent contractor, I began to work for Nike, Columbia Sportswear, Nordstrom, and Meier & Frank. Joining a small group of women in the Portland area, I worked behind the scenes during fashion shows assisting models during the eighties and nineties. Most shows and benefits were held in large venues or hotels in the Portland, Seattle, and Salem areas. Our jobs were demanding and chaotic; it was also exhilarating to see the latest fashion trends while interacting with designers who'd brought their trunk shows to the Northwest. The excitement of the glamorous fashion industry and working with professional models was a whole new world for us stay-at-home moms, and as an added incentive we were given generous in-store discounts by our employers!

Involvement with the fashion industry and being a tour guide in Old Town was a perfect combination for many years. As a history enthusiast, I was excited to learn more about the historical richness of our city, and took a particular interest in the architecture of numerous ornate cast-iron buildings in Old Town. While touring with schoolchildren, my thespian skills often came into play while sharing fascinating anecdotes of Portland's early beginnings. Within several years changes were occurring in the Old Town district of our city, and as tour guides we began to notice increased aggressive behavior from street people. Finding it worrisome to conduct tours with young children, I reluctantly made the decision to leave Urban Tour Group.

The women's movement was making great strides by the early eighties. Although much welcomed and timely, the result of the movement was beginning to have a significant effect on many of us stay-at-home moms. It had always been my intention to be home with our children, but women were now being told they could and should be doing so much more with their lives—at least Betty Friedan, Gloria Steinem, and the media seemed to be doing their best to enlighten us! Perhaps the barrage of messaging was strong enough to make us question our judgement. I now find it laughable, but at the time many of us it felt there was no longer a great deal of importance in being a homemaker. I suppose some women of my generation felt pressured into "having it all." As a result, women were beginning to enter new vocations in search of more fulfilling lives. There were successes, but personal lives and careers were at times compromised.

In the following decade there appeared to be a gradual awakening; the idea of being a perfect wife, supermom, and chauffeur, and juggling domestic duties while managing a full-time career, seemed almost unachievable. Women realized it was nearly impossible to achieve this nirvana, understanding it was demanding to give one hundred percent of themselves to every aspect of their busy lives. Eventually, I believe women of my generation became more comfortable with that reality.

Fast-forwarding to the twenty-first century, I know women are continuing to deal with identical issues, but I've seen vast differences in how household chores and child-rearing responsibilities are being shared by working parents. Functioning together as a couple makes parenting, careers, and home life more achievable. I'd like to think we've come full circle; most importantly people should be valued for whatever pathway they choose. Whether choosing a full-time career or becoming a domestic engineer, I reached the conclusion that certain sacrifices are always necessary if you're going to succeed.

Reflecting on the outcome of the movement, I'm pleased that women are now able to attain career paths of their own choosing. I find it gratifying to know my granddaughters will have vast opportunities to explore career choices. A whole new world has been opened up for them, and defining career preferences by gender is ancient history. Fortunately, demands for equal pay for women continue to gain momentum. We're almost there, but I find it astonishing that after all this time we're still trying to totally resolve that issue! The suffrage movement began 150 years ago, and throughout the years women have fought for equality on many fronts. Thankfully barriers continue to be shattered.

As a result of the women's movement there were moments of soul-searching and self-doubt. Thankfully my husband was understanding and supportive, always encouraging me to follow my heart. When our sons were in grade school and middle school, part-time employment seemed to be an ideal solution because it would allow me to be home from work at the end of their school day. I made a hasty decision to become a travel agent, but my brief career as a cruise specialist was short-lived. After several months I found my new career to be very stressful; it wasn't at all a good fit. Instead, I decided to resume my career in banking, taking a part-time position in customer service at the Lovejoy branch of US Bank. Innumerable changes had occurred in the past fifteen years since I'd left the banking industry. Women were now in supervisory and management positions; I was also delighted to discover the workplace environment had vastly improved for women!

Children

I would leave US Bank after about twelve years to begin a new career in the retail industry. As a part-time customer service representative for Restoration Hardware, I was excited to help open their first store in the Northwest. Having discovered my niche in sales, I found the retail industry to be well suited for me. I'd be with Restoration Hardware for about ten years before retiring. Both careers in banking and retail were enjoyable and challenging, and they were the right choices for me at the time. But without question, my short vocation in the dental industry would prove to be the most fulfilling and gratifying.

It seems the age-old adage I repeatedly heard from my mother was true: time really does have a way of making everything fall into place! Essentially, I came to understand what was most important to me. It wasn't all that complex: my objective was to provide a loving, nurturing home for my husband and children. Choosing the path of motherhood and being a domestic engineer was unquestionably the right choice for me, because even with its challenges it proved to be immensely rewarding. I now realize my greatest lifetime achievements are my two amazing sons.

CHAPTER EIGHTEEN

Reflections

Sadly, I would lose my wonderful mother three years before completing my memoirs. In typical fashion, Mom was in a hurry after her illness was diagnosed. She told me it was her time, then quickly announced everyone was waiting for her! Living a rich, full life of almost ninety-four years of age, Mom was continuing to teach me. She taught me about acceptance and courage. During her short illness, she showed such dignity and grace; my mother seemed very much at peace. In her last month of life I read portions of my memoirs to her. Listening attentively, she asked how I was able to remember such details. I'd like to think she'd be pleased with the final outcome.

In my mother's final weeks we shared a closeness I had always longed for. We held each other and cried, talking of life, family, and death. There was such a surprising softness and vulnerability about her. For the first time it felt so easy to talk with her, but I also found it disheartening—she'd now be leaving me. Her persona had always been one of no nonsense. She had a strong exterior, and perhaps it had been a defensive wall to protect herself. My mother passed away exactly one month after her diagnosis. I miss her every day and consider it a gift to have had that treasured time with her.

Mom & Dad's 50th Anniversary

MY LIFE HAS BEEN AN AMAZING JOURNEY. I HAD THE good fortune of living a rich and extraordinary childhood while growing up on the plains of South Dakota; it was an era when our lives were seemingly uncomplicated and less hurried. In my childhood I remember anxiously waiting for the next holiday or birthday, always wishing life would move faster! Time seemed to stand still when I was a young child, but we didn't have a television, smart phone, computer, or social media to fill up our days. What a sharp contrast from our lives in the twenty-first century!

Our world has been greatly enriched with the advancement of technology; how could we ever manage without our devices? My generation has often struggled to meet those challenges, but we can be assured that innovation will continue at an accelerated pace. In retrospect, I'm now very grateful to have experienced a much slower pace of life as a child! I've voiced concerns of addiction to social media and our devices as well as multitasking becoming the new norm. As a society we seem to be rushing around attempting to fill up our days with more. You've heard it before, but I'm here to remind you, "less can actually be more!"

It's been said the most significant key to happiness is finding the right partner in life, and there is no doubt I've prevailed. To have found my best friend and partner in marriage at such a young age is truly remarkable—a lifetime of blessings and good fortune have come our way. Our lives have been enriched with the love of our children and grandchildren, good health, friendships, and strong family ties. Together we've experienced vast changes in our lifetimes. We've been fortunate to enjoy our retirement years with considerable international and domestic travel. Our horizons have been broadened by experiencing foreign cultures. A heightened sense of curiosity and wonder has been opened up about the world around us, and we're eager for more!

Reflections

Dave & Judy

As parents, we know our finest accomplishment was raising our two sons. They've been the light of our lives and have brought us such immeasurable joy throughout the years. It was our mission to love and nurture our children, giving them guidance so they'd have wings to fly. I know we achieved our objective. Our sons have far exceeded our expectations, and we're incredibly proud of the men they've become. We find it most gratifying to know they've both found extraordinary life partners to share their lives with, and together they've become loving and nurturing parents to their children. The circle of life continues!

Rian & Heidi, Carol & MG
Soriah, Ryder, Kiona

We've been given the precious gift of three amazing grandchildren. It's been a blessing to watch our grandson reach adulthood, and we couldn't be prouder of his accomplishments. Ryder has a beautiful soul. We share a very special bond with him and feel confident he'll achieve his life goals and aspirations. How do I begin to describe our two amazing granddaughters? Kiona and Soriah are absolute delights—they continue to fill our days with pride, smiles, and laughter! I've felt a very special attachment to them since they were infants; it was such a privilege to have had one "Nana" day each week with both girls until they began school. While caring for them I was always acutely aware of Ma's positive influence when I was their age. Both of our beautiful girls have very unique talents, and we're certain our granddaughters will grow up to become extraordinary women!

Reflections

As I began my memoirs, there was a heightened sense of excitement. With every story it felt as if I was revisiting my childhood, from the unforgettable people who touched my life, to the countless food memories! It was my intention to give our children and grandchildren a glimpse of what made me the person I became. Life experiences shape our lives and our stories define us, and knowledge of our lineage gives us a better understanding of who we are. However, revealing our true selves can also be alarming; it can also expose the truth about ourselves!

I had curiosity about my ancestors' lives as a young child, always wanting to learn more of their history. It appears they may have intentionally kept many stories to themselves; truth be told, perhaps they were just struggling to survive! As descendants, it's important to be mindful that our ancestors persevered while experiencing countless obstacles. Endless opportunities were created for us because of their selfless sacrifices; an enduring legacy has been left for generations that follow.

Throughout the years family and friends have questioned whether my memoirs would ever be finished. Yes, I've been at this writing project for a very long time, but somewhere I've read it's not the speed, but the journey! The final outcome has been immensely rewarding and cathartic, but as I near completion I've been surprised by an unexpected reaction. There's always a beginning and an end to everything—but letting go and releasing this labor of love has been more difficult than I ever imagined. Perhaps, like my ancestors, I have an element of apprehension in revealing my life story. After all, what will people think?

Made in United States
Troutdale, OR
02/05/2024

17224225R00184